American Cooking: The Northwest

Foods of the World

American Cooking: The Northwest

by

Dale Brown

and the Editors of

TIME-LIFE BOOKS

studio photography

by Richard Meek

TIME-LIFE BOOKS, NEW YORK

THE AUTHOR: Dale Brown *(far left)* is a staff writer for TIME-LIFE BOOKS. With his wife and daughters, he has ranged widely through the Northwest sampling the foods of this diverse region. Brown is the author of two other FOODS OF THE WORLD volumes: *The Cooking of Scandinavia* and *American Cooking.* He also wrote *The World of Velázquez,* a volume in the TIME-LIFE LIBRARY OF ART.

THE STUDIO PHOTOGRAPHER: Richard Meek *(left)* made both the studio and field photographs for *The Cooking of Scandinavia* and *The Cooking of the Caribbean Islands.* He comes to this volume with a vested interest in the Northwest: one of his ancestors, William Meek, planted some of the first apple orchards of the Pacific Northwest. Other field photographers for this book were Fred Schnell of Chicago, Robert Kelley of Seattle and Joseph Rychetnik of Anchorage.

THE CONSULTANT: James A. Beard *(far left),* one of the leading authorities on American cooking, grew up in Portland, Oregon. Drawing upon his firsthand knowledge of the foods of the Northwest, he provided many of the recipes for this book from his personal files. Among his many books is *Delights and Prejudices,* which contains recollections of the cooking in his parents' home.

THE CONSULTING EDITOR: The late Michael Field *(left),* who supervised the writing of the recipes, was one of America's best-known culinary experts. His books include *Michael Field's Cooking School, Michael Field's Culinary Classics and Improvisations* and *All Manner of Food.*

THE COVER: Fresh from a clear lake, rainbow trout wait to be dipped in flour, fried in bacon fat and served with lemon. Though they occur from Mexico to the Aleutians, rainbows are found in greatest concentrations in the Northwest, particularly the Rocky Mountain area.

TIME-LIFE BOOKS

EDITOR: Jerry Korn
Executive Editor: A. B. C. Whipple
Planning Director: Oliver E. Allen
Text Director: Martin Mann
Art Director: Sheldon Cotler
Chief of Research: Beatrice T. Dobie
Director of Photography: Melvin L. Scott
Associate Planning Director: Byron Dobell
Assistant Text Directors: Ogden Tanner, Diana Hirsh
Assistant Art Director: Arnold C. Holeywell
Assistant Chief of Research: Martha T. Goolrick

PUBLISHER: Joan D. Manley
General Manager: John D. McSweeney
Business Manager: John Steven Maxwell
Sales Director: Carl G. Jaeger
Promotion Director: Paul R. Stewart
Public Relations Director: Nicholas Benton

FOODS OF THE WORLD

SERIES EDITOR: Richard L. Williams
EDITORIAL STAFF FOR AMERICAN COOKING: THE NORTHWEST:
Associate Editor: William Frankel
Picture Editor: Grace Brynolson
Designer: Albert Sherman
Staff Writers: Helen I. Barer, Gerry Schremp
Chief Researcher: Sarah B. Brash
Researchers: Doris Coffin, Brenda Huff, Julia K. Johnson,
Patricia Mohs, Timberlake Wertenbaker
Test Kitchen Chef: John W. Clancy
Test Kitchen Staff: Fifi Bergman, Tina Cassel, Sally Darr, Leola Spencer
Design Assistants: Elise Hilpert, Anne B. Landry

EDITORIAL PRODUCTION
Production Editor: Douglas B. Graham
Quality Director: Robert L. Young
Assistant: James J. Cox
Copy Staff: Rosalind Stubenberg, Eleanore W. Karsten, Florence Keith
Picture Department: Dolores A. Littles, Joan Lynch
Studio: Gloria duBouchet

The text for this book was written by Dale Brown, recipe instructions by Michael Field, Gerry Schremp and Helen I. Barer, and other material by the staff. Assistance was given by these individuals and departments of Time Inc.: Editorial Production, Norman Airey, Margaret T. Fischer; Library, Peter Draz; Picture Collection, Doris O'Neil; Photographic Laboratory, George Karas; TIME-LIFE News Service, Murray J. Gart; Correspondents Don Davies (Madison), Jane Estes (Seattle), George McCormick (Minneapolis), Joseph Rychetnik (Anchorage).

Contents

The Recipe Booklet that accompanies this volume has been designed for use in the kitchen. It contains more than 140 recipes, including all of those printed here. It also has a wipe-clean cover and a spiral binding so that it can either stand up or lie flat when open.

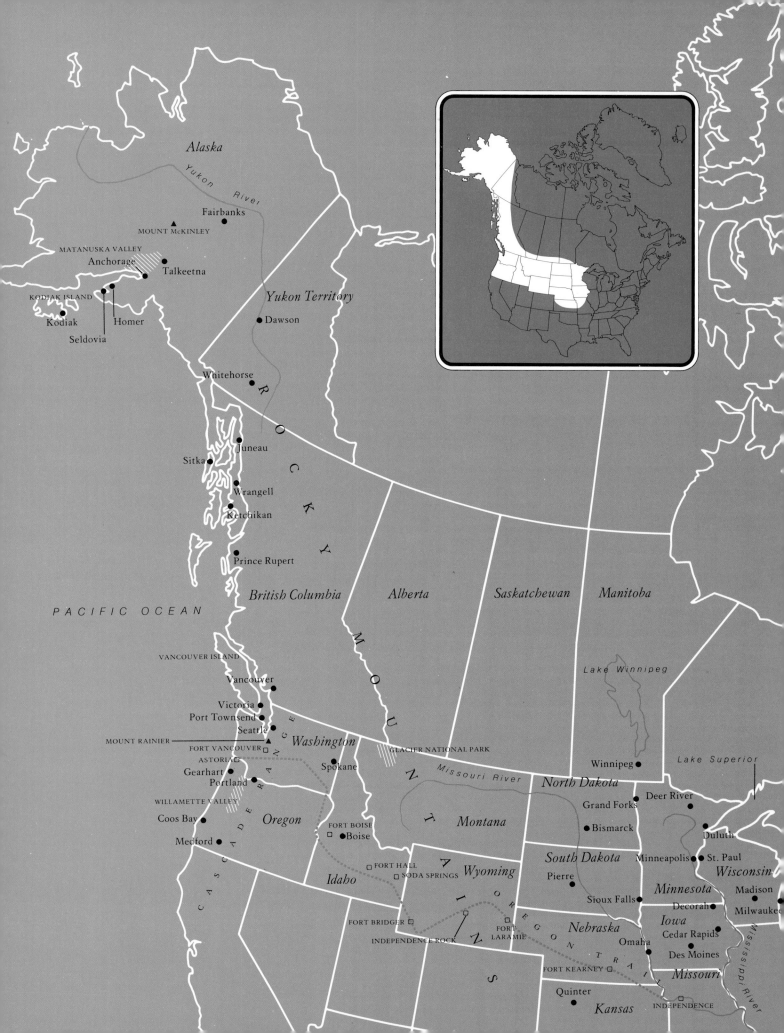

I

The Trail of the Pioneers

This region of North America actually encompasses a whole succession of Northwest frontiers, old and new, ranging all the way from Wisconsin to Alaska. Each older frontier, in turn, relinquished its claim to the title as pioneers probed farther and farther beyond settled places, following routes like the Oregon Trail across mountains and plains in a restless search for a better life.

The region encompassed by this book is enormous and varied. It is edged on the east by Iowa, Minnesota and Wisconsin. Its western boundary runs from Oregon through Washington and British Columbia to Alaska. And in between lie the mountain states of Idaho, Wyoming and Montana, the plains states of Nebraska and North and South Dakota, and Manitoba, Alberta, Saskatchewan and the Yukon Territory in Canada. How can the food of so sprawling and diverse a territory be the subject of a single volume?

The answer lies in the region's newness. Less than 150 years ago most of Northwestern North America was wilderness; much of it still is. The frontier past seems very much alive here; many are the residents whose grandparents or great-grandparents were pioneers, and the legacy of the pioneers ties the region together. Though the face of Northwestern North America has been greatly altered over the past century, with prairies, plains and valleys turned into ranches, farms and orchards, the feel and the psychology of the frontier still prevail in these quiet places.

Breakfast, for example, continues to be a big meal in many households, as if a long day on the trail stretched ahead. It may consist of a heaping platter of fried eggs and ham and hashed brown potatoes, splintery crisp around the edges, or stacks of pancakes in one of their many variations—buttermilk, buckwheat, whole wheat—topped off with plenty of toast, jam and strong black coffee. Along with the forthright patterns of meals many of the old attitudes toward food survive. Gimcracks are abhorred; a dish must speak plainly and its appeal must be honest—but

7

then, there never was much of a reason to play tricks with absolutely fresh ingredients. Many people of this region know and cherish the flavor of game, of fish taken from mountain streams, of mushrooms gathered in the forest, of wild berries picked from a bush. And since food of this kind produces good cheer as well as health, they see it as something to share. The stranger is as welcome at their tables today as he would have been a century ago at the tables of their pioneer forebears.

Let us go back to the beginning when almost all of the country west of what is now Wisconsin was still wild. The explorers Lewis and Clark were among the first to penetrate that country, and they returned east in 1806, after a two-and-a-half-year journey, with wondrous tales of all that they had seen beyond the Mississippi. They told of two mighty rivers, the Missouri and the Columbia, the one muddy, the other glass-clear; of mountains that pierced the clouds; of deserts that shimmered in the sun; of vast tracts of fertile land; and of fish and game in abundance.

Promising though this sounded, over a quarter of a century elapsed before more than a few stouthearted trappers, miners, missionaries and surveyors dared take the same venture. Then, in 1843, the first sizable group of emigrants set out in covered wagons from Independence, Missouri, for the "Oregon country"—a somewhat ill-defined region that comprised the present states of Oregon, Washington and Idaho. The westward rush was on. These emigrants were the great trailblazers of their time, and their trek fired the imaginations of those who stayed behind. In their letters, diaries and recollections they left detailed records of the hardships they faced, the deprivations they suffered, and what they ate to survive.

For these men and women, the decision to go west meant not only forsaking kinfolk and friends whom they might never see again, but abandoning comfortable households and farms and gardens they had carefully cultivated. To some of their contemporaries this seemed madness. "The poor devils who start for Oregon generally spend all they have to scrape together a wagon, some cattle, and a small outfit of provisions," read a letter in the *Missouri Republican* of June 11, 1844. "They will spend the summer in the severest toil getting there. . . . In truth, no man of information, in his right mind, would think of leaving such a country as this, to wander over a thousand miles of desert and five hundred of mountain to reach such as that."

But few turned back, and some apparently had a certain lightheartedness as well as a sense of adventure. "We have been 18 days on the plains, amid the greatest show in the world," wrote a correspondent to the *New York Tribune* in 1852. "The [wagon] train is estimated to be 700 miles long, composed of all kinds of people from all parts of the United States, and some of the rest of mankind, with lots of horses, mules, oxen, cows, steers and some of the feathered creation, moving along about 15 or 20 miles per day; all sorts of vehicles from a coach down to a wheel barrow; ladies on horseback, dressed out in full-blown Bloomers; gents on mules, with Kossuth hats and plumes, galloping over the prairies, making quite an equestrian troupe and a show ahead of anything Barnum ever got up."

However great the emigrants' optimism, there were hard realities they

Opposite: Roast young buffalo is carved in a frontier setting, to be served with oven-browned potatoes and mashed turnips. A 19th Century dinner gong stands alongside the carving board. Rich and tender, buffalo meat resembles choice roast beef in flavor but costs as much as $3.75 a pound.

Budding epicure James Beard with his parents

A Gourmet's Beginnings

During the preparation of this book its chief consultant, James Beard, discussed his own happy youth in the Northwest:

I grew up in Portland, Oregon. My father was of American pioneer stock—he came west from Iowa in a covered wagon when he was five—my mother was English, and our cook, Let, was Chinese. All three influences went into the developing of my palate.

As a boy, father had learned to hunt, fish, and gather wild foods. It was fantastic how he could find things others overlooked, such as that elusive mushroom, the morel, and "swale" huckleberries as big as cherries.

Sunday breakfast was when father shone as a cook. He might fry a mess of trout he had just caught, or sauté chicken and serve it with a bacon-and-cream sauce and toasted crumpets. In winter the meal would feature sausage or country ham, supplied by a local farmer who also made jerky for us —sun-cured beef, an old pioneer standby that father adored.

Mother's tastes in food were more cosmopolitan, in part because of her success as owner of the Gladstone, a Portland hotel

could not ignore. One of the myths of American history depicts the West as a region wide open to any comer. The fact was that only those with the means to outfit themselves and the skills to start a farm in a virgin land could hope for success. A stout wagon and at least three yoke of oxen were needed to transport the 2,500-pound load of supplies and provisions that every four adults required for the six-month journey.

If their cooking at home had been plain, in an era of salt pork and cornbread, it was still plainer on the trail. Nourishment was not the only criterion in selecting provisions: they had to be the kind that lasted, yet were compact and light to carry. Joel Palmer, who went from Indiana to Oregon in 1845 and wrote a widely read account of the journey, advised would-be followers in his footsteps that for each adult "there should be two hundred pounds of flour, thirty pounds of pilot bread, seventy-five pounds of bacon, twenty-five pounds of sugar, half a bushel of dried beans, one bushel of dried fruit, two pounds of saleratus [baking soda], ten pounds of salt, half a bushel of corn meal." He also urged the purchase of half a bushel of parched ground corn and a keg of vinegar. On this Spartan list variations were possible but frills were few. One Dillis B. Ward took along a three-gallon keg of "the best proof brandy," and a certain Basil Longworth made room in his load for five pounds of pepper, three pounds of allspice, a pound of ginger, six pounds of mustard and 26 pounds of cheese. Others took dried fish, and a few later travelers, in what sounds like sheer luxury today, packed canned oysters.

Cooking equipment was restricted to essentials. Palmer's recommended list included a sheet-iron stove, a skillet, a Dutch oven, a tin coffeepot, tin plates, cups and saucers, two churns (one for sweet milk, the other for sour), and a large water keg. One family went to the trouble of having cups made that fitted inside each other; presumably because of the space thus gained, the mother was allowed to take along her glass saltcellar. In her diary she proudly noted that it was "the only glass dish on the whole train throughout the journey."

Considering all the limitations, it is to the enduring credit of the pioneer women that they managed to feed their families three meals a day. Cooking conditions were, to say the least, primitive. Makeshift kitchens had the sky as a roof and the earth as a floor. The water was often brackish or alkaline or, worse, contained "wriggle-tails" (mosquito larvae). Wood was scarce, and the women made their fires with hay, weeds, sagebrush and buffalo chips (dung), gathered in sacks. Each fuel imparted its own special flavor to the food, and the wind often blew ashes into the skillet; one cook complained bitterly that sagebrush, which burned with a fury, showered so many cinders on her flapjacks that they turned black. And because the heat from such fuels was so unreliable, no woman could ever be certain whether the soda-rising bread she baked in her Dutch oven would come out scorched on the bottom or uncooked in the middle.

Meals, perforce, were simple. Breakfast usually consisted of bread with fried bacon or buffalo meat, washed down with hot coffee or tea. The midday meal was generally a meat sandwich and coffee, and supper was a repeat of breakfast. On occasion, the morning or evening meal might be varied a little with sour pickles, or beans baked in a pit of ashes and coals,

10

or as a special treat, a dried-apple pie with a crust that had been rolled out on the leather seat of the wagon. For the families that brought cows, there was milk, cream and even butter. These rare dairy products provided almost indescribable pleasure. Ezra Meeker, who traveled to Oregon in 1852, told of hoarding butter in the center of his flour. "Albeit the butter to a considerable extent melted and mingled with the flour, yet we were not much disconcerted, as the 'short-cake' that followed made us almost glad that the mishap had occurred." The jostling of the wagon churned the contents of the milk can to butter, and at the end of the day the butter would be scooped out and the buttermilk drunk. "What luxury!" Meeker wrote of the buttermilk. "Yes, that's the word—a real luxury."

Meeker made no mention of "the humpbacked beef of the prairies," the buffalo, but for many of his fellow travelers this proved the most memorable food of all. The lumbering beasts moved in great dark herds across the plains, and hunters were quick to ride out among them. To the emigrants the buffalo was a welcome source of fresh meat, but they found that to the Plains Indians it was everything—food, raiment, shelter and a great deal more. No part was wasted. The hides were cured—often with the brains rubbed in as a softener—and turned into clothing, tepee coverings, shields, bridles, lariats. Split tendons and sinews served as thread. The hair was braided into ropes. The paunches became stewpots and buckets, the bladders pontoons. The horns were steamed and shaped into spoons, ladles and other small utensils. The leg bones made good scrapers, and the ribs made sleds for the Indian children. The tough membrane enclosing the heart was carefully removed for use as a baby's bottle, and the scrotum, dried and filled with pebbles, served as a rattle.

Still, it was as food that the buffalo excelled. The Plains Indians were by no means gluttons, yet they thought nothing of downing pounds of the fresh meat at one sitting. Among the European employees of the Hudson's Bay Company eight pounds of it came to be considered a normal daily ration, and it was said that in good times, when buffalo were plentiful, a man could swallow that much at a meal, sleep for a few hours, then consume the same amount all over again.

Buffalo killed during the summer months were in prime condition, with a three-inch roll of fat around their ribs, and great quantities of the meat were preserved by the Indians for winter use. They sliced the meat along the grain in thin strips and let the strips dry in the sun or, when the weather was damp, in the smoke of fires built inside their tepees. An entire cow could be reduced to 45 pounds of jerky, as the dried meat was called. The Indians usually processed jerky into pemmican, pounding it as fine as sawdust and preserving it in tightly sewed skin bags. Ordinarily fat was added to the pemmican, and occasionally crushed wild fruit and berries were tossed in as well. Pemmican was rich food; a pound might contain up to 3,500 calories. (By way of comparison, a pound of lean beef contains about 750 calories, a pound of butter about 3,200.)

Following the Indians' example, the emigrants dried much of the buffalo they obtained. A day or two might be spent at the task, giving everyone a welcome breather from the endless traveling. If a prolonged stop could not be made, the strips of flesh were draped from the crossbars

well known for its dining rooms. By the time I was born she had sold the hotel, but she remained an exacting mistress of her own kitchen and the shrewdest of shoppers. Sometimes I went with her to buy some delectable comb honey—clover or buckwheat or wild huckleberry—to be served with superbly light biscuits; or we would pick up a fine natural Oregon Cheddar, to be served hot and bubbling on toast and topped by bacon "well-curled" in the English manner. A special trip to Portland's Chinatown was deemed well worth it when mandarin oranges came in from China by boat. But we had only to step out of our house to pick Gravenstein apples and Royal Anne cherries and greengage plums from our own trees.

The bounty and variety at our table were almost endless. I well remember the braised wild duck with chestnuts and Madeira that Let did so beautifully, and his Oriental specialties, among them a curry with kumquats, and the Christmas Eve midnight buffet featuring a steaming stew of tiny Olympia oysters.

In summer, we moved ourselves —and our appetites—to the seaside at Gearhart, northwest of Portland, where the finest of fish and seafood was ours for the asking. Summertime was one long round of clamming, berrying, fishing, picnicking, cooking succulent dishes over a driftwood fire on the beach. One I can still taste is a clam chowder in which we used razor clams, potatoes and onions, but then also added Tabasco—and cognac. Effete Easterners never dreamed of a chowder so good.

JAMES A. BEARD

Continued on page 17

Dressed for the ride, Mrs. Floyd Miller pursues a pioneer occupation —harvesting wild plums. A century ago many women used such wild fruit in a pie filling or a jam.

Across the Great Plains and Back into Another Time

Anyone with a hankering to know what it was like to journey west in a covered wagon can join one of several overland expeditions that are run every summer by a Quinter, Kansas, organization known as Wagons Ho. The brain child of Ruth and Frank Hefner, two history-minded wheat farmers, Wagons Ho provides the covered wagons, mules, horses and staff for 11 tours a season. The wagons embark from Quinter and over a three-to-six-day period partially trace the route of the old Smoky Hill Trail, a Kansas section of one of the old wagon-train routes to the Rockies. Guests sleep in the wagons or out under the stars, and many of the foods served are in the pioneer tradition. Most important of all, the pace of travel is authentically old-fashioned—the wagons roll across the prairie at three to five miles an hour.

A train of 22 Wagons Ho wagons, each large enough to accommodate six adults, rumbles across western Kansas. Guests may ride horses if they wish, but most of the "pioneers" prefer to ride in their wagons. Travel on the prairies builds mighty appetites, and all of the food served during the trip is hearty. A typical main dish is the ham-and-apple stew shown below, with its rich dumpling batter.

At the end of the day the wagon train pulls into a circle *(below)*, and supper is eaten by twilight. It consists typically of such simple food as boiled sweet corn *(opposite)*, meat loaf and a dried-apple pie, shown at left on a bed of Kansas sunflowers. For many pioneers, a pie baked with dried apples was a treat, but others found it could get tiresome. "I loathe, abhor, detest, despise/Abominate dried apple pies," began a poem of the wagon-train days; it ended, "Tread on my corns and tell me lies/But don't pass me dried apple pies."

of the wagons or hung on ropes to dry. When supplies ran low, the emigrants sometimes got jerky from friendly Indians—though Mrs. Narcissa Whitman, one of the first American women to make the overland journey to the far Northwest, complained that "I can scarcely eat it, it appears so filthy, but it will keep us alive and we ought to be thankful for it."

As the half-year trek wore on, weariness set in. Much of the country through which the wagons passed was treeless, with alkaline soil that cracked the hoofs of the oxen and cattle and left the animals lame; what was worse, many animals sickened and died after eating the alkaline grass growing along the trail. One man noted that "where 200,000 cattle have passed this season, there are, for 400 miles, from one to four carcasses to the mile. . . ."

The weather was itself a blight. The sun beat down and baked everything dry. "You in the States know nothing about dust," one emigrant wrote home. "It will fly so that you can hardly see the horns of your tongue yoke of oxen. It often seems that the cattle must die for the want of breath, and then in our wagons, such a spectacle—beds, clothes, victuals and the children all completely covered." And one day's dust could turn to the next day's "mizzling rain and sozzling mud." Often the rain made cooking impossible, and days might pass before raw bacon and crackers could be replaced by warm food. The women did their best to outwit the elements. One gallant if unlettered traveler recorded in his journal: "May 28 . . . after a verry tidious & toilsome dys drive I arived at my mess wet as water could make me . . . and here let me say there was one young Lady which showed herself worthy of the bravest undaunted poieneer of the west for after having kneaded her dough she watched and nursed the fire and held an umblella over the fire and her skillit with the greatest composure and baked bread enough to give us a verry plentifull supper. . . ."

By the time the wagon trains reached Fort Laramie, about 475 miles from Independence, most families were low on supplies—and on the funds to replenish them. The prices asked by Laramie traders were exorbitant; sugar went for 25 cents a pound, bread for 50 cents a loaf, brandy for 18 dollars a gallon. Now, more than ever, anything edible that the environment might offer was seized upon, and some diarists described the strange wild fruits they had eaten—almost always, with a certain wistfulness, comparing them to the cultivated fruits that were now so far behind them. "The native plum grows on a dwarf bush, perhaps 10 to 18 inches high, and has the flavor of a peach." "This evening found a plenty of berries called hawthorn on the stream where we have encamped. They are as large as a cherry and taste much like a mealy sweet apple."

When the travelers got to South Pass, the 7,500-foot-high notch through the Rockies, they were lucky if they still had some bread, bacon and coffee, and nearing the Oregon country many people found themselves totally without rations. A mother of five used the last of her flour for a supper of flapjacks—then settled back to pray that Providence would deliver her family from starvation. (The next morning her prayers were answered; a few fish were caught with a pin for a hook and grasshoppers for bait.) Two men who stayed behind in camp while their com-

Opposite: A substantial stew simmered in a cast-iron kettle bespeaks a cooking tradition that goes back to pioneer days. This one, based on braised oxtails *(Recipe Index),* contains onions and carrots and is simmered in a red wine.

panions went in search of game were reduced to eating dog meat, which they got from the Indians. Another man who became separated from his party survived on frogs and rose hips. And a sick little girl was saved by stews made from the meat of rabbits that her pet cat caught each morning.

The monotonous and increasingly meager diet of the travelers eventually took its toll in the form of a variety of ailments from colds and fevers to scurvy, dysentery and cholera. There was hardly a wagon train that did not leave some of its members behind in lonely roadside graves. But once the emigrants came down the mountains' western slopes and crossed the Snake River Valley to the Columbia, joy reigned.

Mrs. Whitman was dumbfounded by the choices confronting her at Fort Vancouver, at the site of present-day Vancouver, Washington. In her diary she lovingly enumerated all that she had eaten: "For breakfast we have coffee or coaco, Salt Salmon & roast duck . . . and potatoes. When we have eaten our supply of them our plates are changed & we make a finish on bread & butter. For dinner we have a greater variety. First we are *always* treated to a dish of soup, which is very good. Every kind of vegetable in use is taken & choped fine & put into water with a little rice and boiled. . . . The tammatoes are a promanant article. Usually some fowl . . . is cut fine & added . . . then comes a variety of meats, to prove our tastes. . . . Roast duck is an every day dish, boiled pork, tripe & sometimes trotters, fresh Salmon or Sturgeon, yea to numerous to mention. When these are set aside a rice pudding or an apple pie is next introduced. After this melons next make their appearance, some times grapes & last of all cheese, bread or biscuit & butter is produced to complet the whole. But there is one article on the table . . . of which I never partake, That is wine."

Now the settlers moved on to their final destination—most of them to the valley of the Willamette River. There, as in a dream, they found "groves of oak timber . . . grass from a foot to two feet high, the whole country carpeted in spring and summer with flowers most fragrant, an abundant supply of pure water from a thousand streams; with fish and game in abundance, a soil most fertile—surely no country was more beautiful, more healthy or richer in promise of future possibilities. . . ."

The settlers spread out into the valley, felled the trees and from the sturdy trunks built their dwellings. One by one the countryside surrendered its treasures to their tables. Wood duck and grouse, roasted with an onion to check the "wild" flavor, made excellent eating, as did deer and even bear—providing the animal was a young one. From the streams came trout, salmon and smelt. A favorite dish was salmon boiled in the same pot with potatoes, and served with them under a blanket of crisp bits of crackling. After gardens had been planted and livestock bred, the cooking reverted somewhat to patterns traditional back East. Baked beans, rich with salt pork and molasses, chicken pot pie with a biscuit or mashed-potato topping, or a plump hen stewed with chunks of salt pork to extend the flavor—these dishes smacked of home.

Decades passed before other waves of settlers filled the vast flatlands between the Mississippi and the Rockies. Men called this region the Great American Desert, and the name conveys something of the awe and fear with which they regarded it. Here was a land utterly different from the rich Atlantic Seaboard and the fertile Willamette Valley: a land of few trees, of low rainfall, of a soil so dense and root-matted that the old iron plows of Eastern farmers could not break it. One of the first Americans to explore the region, Major Stephen H. Long of the United States Army, delivered himself of a sober judgment that was to stand long unchallenged. "In regard to this extensive section of country . . . ," Long wrote, "we do not hesitate in giving the opinion that it is almost wholly unfit for cultivation, and of course uninhabitable by a people depending upon agriculture for their subsistence." Clearly, men needed strong inducements to tackle the hard job of settling the Great Plains.

But there was one such inducement—the passage of the Homestead Act of 1862. The law entitled an American, or a foreigner who intended to become one, to lay claim to 160 acres of the hitherto ignored region. Gradually, a freshet of homesteaders turned into a torrent of emigration that reached flood tide during the '70s and '80s. In the words of historian Ray Billington: "They filled Kansas and Nebraska, engulfed the level grasslands of Dakota, occupied the rolling foothills of Wyoming and Montana. . . . A larger domain was settled in the last three decades of the century than in all America's past. . . ."

Families arrived by riverboat and by railroad—and some still came by covered wagon. "We watched the schooners come up from the south," wrote a South Dakota man of his boyhood in 1880, "zigzagging up the tortuous trail like ships beating up against the wind. Slowly they drew nearer—sometimes one, sometimes five or six in a fleet. . . . Usually the

A Wisconsin family of the 1890s show off the proofs of their success —plump vegetables from their garden, their original log cabin, enlarged but now outgrown, and a new frame house. The photograph first appeared in *Handbook for Homeseekers,* a book printed in Wisconsin and distributed in the East to lure pioneers westward.

woman was sitting at the front driving the team, and beside her or peeking out the front opening were a flock of dirty, tousled, tow-headed children. Often she held a small baby in her arms. Behind followed a small herd of cattle or horses driven by the man and boys on foot, for the rate of travel was a walk." The wagons would draw to a stop, greetings would be exchanged, then each prairie schooner would sail on, "very much like a real ship plowing its way over a trackless sea and then disappearing below the horizon."

Once on the plains, the pioneers set out to master their new, strange land. The sod had to be broken—or busted, as the language of the day had it—and they had new steel plows with which to do it. The roots of the prairie grass, which lay in thick, resistant tangles, snapped and crackled as they were cut, "the sod rolling smooth and flat from the plow, a gull or two following for the worms, and blackbirds chattering around."

Equally pressing was the problem of shelter. In a treeless land timber was scarce, and most people turned to the earth to answer their need. Some made themselves dugouts, others cut the sod into blocks and piled them like bricks, to build houses of what was locally called "Nebraska marble." The interiors were dark, and the roofs little more than soil held together by roots; in dry weather, dust and dirt sifted down on the occupants, and in a storm they were showered with mud and rain.

Problems of food and water also beset them. Before a well could be dug, the only source of drinking water might be a stream, creek or river a dozen or more miles away. And until crops could be planted and harvested and a few animals spared for butchering, foods were mainly

In another early Wisconsin photograph, two farm hands rest from their labors in a field of sorghum, source of one of the pioneers' basic sweeteners. Sorghum stalks were crushed and the sap was boiled in huge vats, producing a clear golden molasses widely used in candies, cakes, cookies and pies.

gathered and hunted, just as they had been by the Oregon emigrants. The early waves of settlers drew upon still-bountiful supplies of game, including deer, elk, antelope and buffalo, rabbits, prairie chickens, wild turkeys, ducks and geese. Homesteaders on the eastern prairies found wild fruits, berries and nuts plentiful. Pecans, walnuts, hickory nuts and hazelnuts were gathered and stored, and plums, strawberries, grapes, currants and elderberries were eaten out of hand, made into sauces, dried or otherwise preserved.

One of the first crops to be planted was corn. In their haste, some settlers did not even plow their new fields the first year; they simply gashed the sod with an ax and dropped the seeds directly into the gash. As the most productive of grains, one that flourished handsomely on the prairies and plains, corn became the chief food of the homesteaders, eaten morning, noon and night; in hard times it was often their only food. Wheat remained a rarity until hardy new strains were introduced, and the small stock of white flour a housewife might have was saved for piecrusts or biscuits, which were eaten with the zest normally reserved for cake.

Almost as important as planting corn was starting a garden, and when the gardens yielded their harvests, almost everything that could be preserved for winter use was set aside and processed. Green beans, pumpkins, juicy stalks of rhubarb were spread out in the sun or hung before the fire to dry. Brining was another preserving method. Whole ripe tomatoes were put down in brine and scooped out when needed. Root vegetables were kept under straw and layers of dirt in cool earth cellars or pits.

To the stores of fruits and vegetables were added smoked and dried

meats. Stewed with a little wild onion, jerked buffalo or venison could be delicious, and both were excellent in meat pies or as the major component of a boiled dinner. Emigrants from Pennsylvania chopped buffalo or other dried meat and used it in lieu of pork in their scrapple. Cooking posed many problems on the plains, not least of which was the fire. Before coal became available, the only fuels in unwooded regions were buffalo or cow chips—and grass. Wild prairie hay was twisted into cords and burned in specially designed stoves, but reportedly two men and a boy were needed to keep such a fire burning. The heat was intense, if brief, and noxious fumes gave many a cook a violent headache. Corncobs and stalks were also used, and in years when the price of corn fell, whole ears were fed into the flames.

The ingredients at the disposal of the prairie cook were limited. She made vinegar by combining a quart of molasses with a pint of yeast dissolved in three gallons of rain water. The best vinegar, however, came from wine or cider that had been allowed to sour—and the worst must have been the one concocted from molasses, water and acetic acid.

Challenged by shortages, the housewife became adept at finding substitutes. In place of sugar, which was always scarce, she could use molasses, wild honey, or the juice of watermelons reduced to a syrup. Of these it was molasses that she used most frequently, dribbling ribbons of it into her puddings, custards, pies, preserves, relishes and pickled cabbage. In place of coffee—also a scarce item—parched barley, rye, wheat or peas, scorched bread crusts, pumpkin or squash, toasted dandelion roots and even oven-browned slivers of potato all made do at one time or another

A work-worn Nebraska couple, with their team and horse-drawn plow, stand for a period-piece portrait in a field of sprouting corn. The house behind them, built of sod blocks and roofed over with more sod, probably endured only five or six years of burning sun and pelting rains. Yet houses such as these sheltered nine out of every 10 newcomers to Nebraska during the third quarter of the 19th Century.

in the coffeepot. "Take a gallon of bran," reads one old recipe, "two tablespoons of molasses, scald and parch in the oven until it is somewhat brown and charred. Bran treated this way and cooked the same as coffee provides a very tasty drink."

For the many New Englanders who settled in the West, pie was still a dish to be eaten three times a day, and again the housewife had to improvise fillings that would pass muster. When she ran out of dried apples, she crumbled soda crackers into a bowl, stirred the broken bits with honey, milk, cinnamon, nutmeg and some citric acid, and poured the mixture into her pie shell. At another time she might soak potatoes in vinegar and use them as mock apples, deceiving no one. To make mincemeat, she ground up green tomatoes, and succeeded so well with the imitation that her husband was often fooled. Pumpkin steeped in vinegar, with wild grapes instead of raisins, was another mincemeat substitute. Sheep sorrel, a weed, sweetened with molasses, made a tart pie; another—still loved—had vinegar for flavoring and was topped by a fluffy "merang."

With the taming of the wilderness, the era of plainness and privation came to an end. The fertile soil turned by the plow provided a bounty the likes of which few men had ever seen. Kitchens, smokehouses and cellars —to say nothing of bellies—began to bulge with the results. Hams hung fat and brown from rafters, and sausages curved around broomsticks in sagging loops. Fresh-churned butter gleamed in crocks set on the earth floor of the creamery, and buttermilk brimmed in huge barrels. Jars of canned beans, peas and beets, fruits and juices, jellies and jams weighed down shelves. By the late 19th Century, what could not be raised, caught or borrowed could be bought in a country store, and ex-New Englanders could indulge their occasional homesickness with a keg of oysters shipped from the Atlantic Coast. More and more, however, the cooking came to reflect the region and its special foods. The wild berries that had seemed so strange, even the mushrooms ignored at home, became table favorites.

But one sad note emerged in time: the buffalo had vanished. Charles Russell, the great painter of the wild West, once told an audience that had assembled to honor him, "I have been called a pioneer. In my book a pioneer is a man who comes to virgin country, traps off all the fur, kills off all the wild meat, cuts down all the trees, grazes off all the grass, plows the roots up, and strings ten million miles of bob wire. A pioneer destroys things and calls it civilization. I wish to God that this country was just like it was when I first saw it and that none of you folks were here at all." With that, Charlie Russell strode off the podium. He was being unfair, and he probably knew it. Not the people he lectured, but the merchants of hides, bones and tongues—and government officials who set out to "pacify" the Indians by destroying their chief source of food—were those most responsible for the slaughter of the buffalo. Still, Russell's words have an element of stinging truth, and wherever I traveled in Northwestern North America, I remembered them. The land that was wild is conquered now, and we are the beneficiaries. I like the sight of a herd of cattle, a field of tasseled corn and a sea of yellow wheat. But I am more moved by the cloud-shadowed open spaces, and I had an experience in South Dakota that would have pleased Charlie Russell.

About 30 miles from Pierre, the state capital, there is a 50,000-acre ranch, some 18 miles long and 10 miles wide, and on it graze 1,500 buffalo. They stand about in groups of twos and threes like monuments to themselves—earth-brown shaggy beasts with ponderous heads and tipped-back horns. It is hard at first to believe that they are real, but I have walked among them. Although I had read about their ferocity, I found them gentle. They looked at me with wet dark-brown eyes, and then backed away, some making piglike oinking sounds.

These buffalo belong to the family of Roy Houck, a rancher of independence—and now of means—who has instilled in his two sons and two daughters the view that the earth is only on loan to the living and must be respected if the generations to come are to enjoy it as well. "I've always felt that we're obligated to leave the land in better condition than we got it," Roy has said, and his ranch, which he bought in 1959, shows that he, for one, has met the obligation. A dozen years ago the site seemed to hold little promise; it had been overgrazed and overplowed. But now the hills are covered with grass again, and the scars left by erosion are being erased. Roy and his sons wrought the change. They helped the grass come back by rotating their herds from pasture to pasture, and to conserve rainfall they built 230 ponds ranging in size from one to 10 acres. An animal never needs to walk more than half a mile for water.

Some cattle are raised here, but the chief "crop" is buffalo. The Houcks started their buffalo herd with a dozen animals from Montana, supplemented by breeding stock from Custer State Park and elsewhere. They soon confirmed that buffalo, after centuries of evolution, are eminently suited to life on the plains. "Buffalo don't take as much feed to put on weight as cattle do," says Roy. "Three can live on range that would support only two cows." Moreover, buffalo are guided by the kind of instincts most ranchers wish cattle could have. During a snowstorm, buffalo head into the wind; cattle move with the wind until they are stopped by a fence, where they often freeze to death. When buffalo are unable to find shelter, they run to keep warm; and where snow and ice cover the ground, they root through to get at the grass.

Apart from these natural attributes, buffalo have other virtues that make raising them worthwhile. A three-year-old bull standing six feet tall at the hump and weighing 1,500 pounds will dress out at about 750 pounds, and the meat can match the best beef in quality. All the stories about the toughness of buffalo meat probably sprang from the experiences of pioneers with old animals. A booming market for buffalo meat exists in many parts of the West, and the Houcks have plans to enlarge their herd by another 1,500 head.

I was eager to try this most indigenous of American foods, and delighted when Roy's son Jerry asked me to join him for a buffalo steak after we toured the ranch. Before entering the house, we paused at a big corral to examine a group of 100 yearlings that had only recently been separated from their mothers and seemed sullen in their confinement. Jerry struck the gate with a stick to set the buffalo in motion, and a stampede was on. For the first time in my life, I heard the noise that I had read about so often in wild West stories. I had expected the hoofs to beat like thunder

on the ground; instead, they sounded like a heavy pelting rain, retreating and coming again.

We walked toward the house, and the land spun out around us in a great undulating circle. The noon sun was dazzling, the sky soaring. We seemed to take some of the space inside with us. Jerry's wife Lila, their four-year-old daughter and a hired man were waiting for us. We sat down at the table in a clean, glowing room, and helped ourselves to buffalo steak. I cut into mine and forked up a piece. The meat was indeed tender, and just a bit sweet. It had none of the gamy flavor I had expected; it tasted like very good, very rich beef. There was hardly any fat and no gristle at all, and I could understand how the oldtimers had been able to eat so many pounds of buffalo at a sitting without discomfort.

But then I became distracted by the hired man, who chewed his steak with grinding noises of his teeth. He was old, and he wore faded blue overalls, patched at the knee. In the white light streaming in through the window, he looked like a pioneer with a story to tell. I was about to talk to him when Lila asked me to try some of the ranch's *Braunschweiger,* made from the liver, tongue and heart of the buffalo. I took a slice and savored it, and told the Houcks how much I liked it. When I turned again to the hired man, he was gone. He had finished his dessert of apple pie, shoved back his plate, and vanished wordlessly, like the ghost of another, earlier time. "You should hear what he has to say to us about the old days!" Lila said. "But he's shy with strangers."

The trim kitchen of the Cornelius C. Beekman house, built in 1880 and now maintained as a museum in Jacksonville, Oregon, shows the degree of comfort achieved by pioneer families after years of toil. On the table are old Oregon favorites: blackberry pie, ground-cherry preserves, peach and pear conserves, and spiced crab apples.

An Up-to-Date Ranch Where 1,500 Buffalo Roam

Raising buffalo is a big business for Jerry Houck, manager and part owner of the 50,000-acre Standing Butte Ranch near Pierre, South Dakota. Using breeding stock like the animals below, Houck and his father have increased their herd from 12 head in 1959 to about 1,500 head today. In the picture opposite, Houck stands in a corral with yearlings recently separated from their mothers. After receiving an ear tag that identifies its herd, sex and age, *(right)*, each yearling will be turned out to the range; two to three years will pass before the males are ready for slaughter. Young bulls have the best meat, but they can be ornery creatures at roundup time. When men, horses and trucks fail to do the job, aerial buzzing by Jerry's Piper Cub pushes the herd along.

Buffalo Roast

To serve 14 to 16

MARINADE
2 cups hard cider
2 cups fresh sweet cider
½ cup red wine vinegar
2 medium-sized onions, peeled and coarsely chopped
1 medium-sized carrot, scraped and coarsely chopped
3 sprigs fresh parsley
¼ teaspoon crumbled dried thyme
1 medium-sized bay leaf, crumbled
6 whole juniper berries
10 whole black peppercorns

A 7-pound eye rib buffalo roast, or substitute venison, reindeer or any other game meat

In a 2- to 3-quart enameled or stainless-steel saucepan combine the hard cider, sweet cider, vinegar, onions, carrot, parsley, thyme, bay leaf, juniper berries and peppercorns. Bring the marinade to a boil over high heat, reduce the heat to low, and simmer partially covered for 30 minutes. Pour the marinade into a deep crock or a stainless-steel or enameled casserole large enough to contain the meat.

Cool the marinade to room temperature, then add the meat and turn it over to coat it evenly on all sides. The marinade should come at least halfway up the sides of the meat; add as much water as necessary. Cover with a lid or with foil and marinate the meat at room temperature for at least 24 hours, turning it over every few hours.

Preheat the oven to 500°. Remove the meat from the marinade, pat it completely dry with paper towels, and place it on a rack in a large shallow roasting pan. For the most predictable results, insert the tip of a meat thermometer at least 2 inches into the thickest part of the roast. Strain the marinade through a fine sieve set over a bowl, reserve the liquid, and discard the vegetables and seasonings.

Roast the meat in the middle of the oven for 20 minutes. Reduce the heat to 350°, and baste the meat with ½ cup of the marinade. Continue to roast, basting with a similar amount of the marinade every 15 minutes, until the meat is cooked to your taste. A meat thermometer will register 130° to 140° when the meat is rare, 150° to 160° when medium, and 160° to 170° when it is well done. If you are not using a thermometer, start timing the roast after you reduce the heat to 350°. For this size roast, you can estimate approximately 16 minutes to the pound for rare meat, 18 minutes to the pound for medium rare, 20 minutes to the pound for medium, and 26 minutes to the pound for well done. Transfer to a heated platter and let it rest for 15 minutes for easier carving.

This roast is best accompanied by peeled potatoes cooked in the roasting pan with the meat.

Mashed Turnips

To serve 8 to 10

3 pounds yellow turnips, peeled and cut into ½-inch cubes (about 7 cups)
1½ teaspoons salt
4 tablespoons unsalted butter, softened
¼ teaspoon freshly ground black pepper
½ teaspoon sugar
½ teaspoon ground nutmeg, preferably freshly grated

Place the turnips in a 6- to 8-quart pot and pour in enough water to cover them by about 1 inch. Add 1 teaspoon of the salt and bring to a boil over high heat. Lower the heat, partially cover the pan, and simmer for 20 minutes, or until the turnips show no resistance when pierced with the tip of a small, sharp knife. Drain in a colander, discarding the water, and return the turnips to the pot in which they were cooked. Slide the pan back and forth over low heat for 2 to 3 minutes, until they are dry. Then, in a heated mixing bowl, purée the turnips either by mashing them with a potato masher or by forcing them through a potato ricer or through a coarse sieve with the back of a spoon. Beat the butter into the purée a tablespoon at a time, then beat in the remaining salt and the pepper, sugar and ¼ teaspoon of the nutmeg. Taste for seasoning and serve at once in a heated vegetable dish, sprinkled with the remaining nutmeg.

Sour-Cherry Pie

With a pastry brush, spread the tablespoon of softened butter over the bottom and sides of a 9-inch pie tin. Make pastry for a double-crust pie, divide it in half, and chill for at least one hour.

On a lightly floured surface, roll half of the dough into a rough circle about ⅛ inch thick and 12 to 13 inches in diameter. Drape the dough over the rolling pin, lift it up, and unroll it slackly over the pie tin. Gently press the dough into the bottom and sides of the tin. With a pair of scissors, cut off the excess dough from the edges, leaving a 1-inch overhang all around the outside rim. Refrigerate while you prepare the filling.

Combine the sour cherries, tapioca, sugar, lemon juice and almond extract in a large bowl, and toss together gently but thoroughly. Let the mixture rest uncovered and at room temperature for about 10 minutes. Then spoon the contents of the bowl into the unbaked pie shell and, with a rubber spatula, spread out the cherries as evenly as possible. Dot the top of the filling with the butter bits.

Preheat the oven to 450°. For the upper crust, roll the remaining half of the dough into a circle about ⅛ inch thick and 12 to 13 inches in diameter. With a pastry brush dipped in cold water, lightly moisten the outside edge of the pastry shell. Drape the dough over the rolling pin, lift it up and unroll it over the pie. Trim off the excess pastry from around the rim with scissors, then crimp the top and bottom pastry together firmly with your fingertips or press them with the tines of a fork. Cut a 1-inch hole in the center of the top of the pie. Bake in the center of the oven for 10 minutes, then lower the heat to 350° and bake another 40 to 45 minutes, or until the top is golden brown.

To make one 9-inch double-crust pie

1 tablespoon unsalted butter, softened, plus 2 tablespoons unsalted butter, cut into ¼-inch bits
Short-crust pastry for a double-crust pie *(Recipe Index)*
6 cups pitted sour cherries (from about 3¾ pounds)
¼ cup quick-cooking tapioca
1 cup sugar
1½ tablespoons strained fresh lemon juice
¼ teaspoon almond extract

A sour-cherry pie like this one would have pleased many a pioneer, homesick for cultivated fruit in a wild land. Cherry trees were among the first trees planted by settlers on their homesteads.

Among the culinary treasures of the pioneers was a great galaxy of pickles and preserves. The containers shown here include some of their favorites, such as raspberry vinegar, which was often mixed with water and sugar and drunk as a refresher on a hot day.

To make 3 cups

3 pounds (about 9 medium-sized)
ripe tomatoes
2½ cups sugar
¼ cup strained fresh lemon juice
1 cup lemon peel (from about 8
lemons), cut with a small knife
or rotary peeler, discarding any
bitter white pith, then cut into
strips about 1 inch long and ⅛
inch wide
½ cup crystallized ginger, finely
chopped

To make 1 pint

1 pound fresh cranberries
½ cup finely chopped onions
½ cup water
½ cup white distilled vinegar
1 cup sugar
¾ teaspoon ground cloves
¾ teaspoon ground cinnamon
¾ teaspoon ground allspice
¾ teaspoon salt
¾ teaspoon celery seed
½ teaspoon freshly ground black
pepper

To make 3 quarts

1 pound white cabbage, cored and
finely chopped
8 cups fresh corn kernels, cut from
about 12 large ears of corn
¾ cup finely chopped onions
1 cup finely chopped green bell
peppers
1 cup finely chopped red bell
peppers
1 cup sugar
1 tablespoon salt
4 teaspoons celery seed
2½ cups cider vinegar

Tomato Marmalade

Drop the tomatoes into a pan of boiling water and let them boil briskly
for about 10 seconds. Drain, run cold water over them and, with a small,
sharp knife, peel off the skins. Cut out and discard the stems, then chop
the tomatoes coarsely. There should be about 5 cups.

In a large glass, ceramic or stainless-steel bowl, combine the tomatoes
and sugar, and toss with a wooden spoon to distribute the sugar evenly.
Let the mixture rest uncovered at room temperature for about 1 hour.

In a 2- to 3-quart enameled or stainless-steel saucepan, combine the
tomato mixture, lemon juice, lemon peel and crystallized ginger, and bring
to a boil over high heat, stirring constantly. Then lower the heat and simmer the mixture for 1 hour, or until it is thick enough to hold its shape almost solidly in a spoon. Stir frequently while the marmalade thickens to
prevent it from sticking to the pan.

With a slotted spoon, skim off and discard any foam that may appear
on the surface of the marmalade and ladle the marmalade into hot sterilized jars or jelly glasses, following the directions for canning and sealing
in the Recipe Booklet.

Cranberry Ketchup

Wash the cranberries under cold running water. Combine them with the
chopped onion and the water in a 2- to 3-quart enameled or stainless-
steel saucepan and bring to a boil over high heat. Reduce the heat to low,
cover the pan tightly, and simmer for 10 to 12 minutes, or until the mixture can be easily mashed against the side of the pan with a spoon.

Purée the cranberry mixture—with its cooking liquid—through the
fine blade of a food mill or rub it through a fine sieve with the back of a
spoon, pressing down hard on the berries before discarding the skins.

Pour the purée back into the saucepan and stir in the vinegar, sugar,
cloves, cinnamon, allspice, salt, celery seed and pepper. Bring to a boil
over high heat and cook uncovered for 15 minutes, or until most of the liquid in the pan has evaporated and the ketchup is thick enough to hold its
shape almost solidly in a spoon. Stir from time to time to prevent the
ketchup from sticking to the pan. With a slotted spoon, skim off and discard any foam that may appear on the surface of the ketchup and taste for
seasoning. Ladle the hot ketchup into hot sterilized jars, following the
directions for canning and sealing in the Recipe Booklet.

Traditionally, cranberry ketchup is served as an accompaniment to wild
game, other meats or poultry.

Corn Relish

In a 6- to 8-quart enameled or stainless-steel casserole, combine the cabbage, corn, onions, peppers, sugar, salt and celery seed. Pour in the vinegar
and, with a wooden spoon, stir the ingredients together. Bring to a boil
over high heat, stirring the mixture frequently, then reduce the heat to
low and simmer uncovered for 20 minutes. Taste for seasoning, then immediately ladle the relish into hot sterilized jars, following the directions
for canning and sealing in the Recipe Booklet.

Raspberry Vinegar

To make 2 quarts

3 pounds fresh raspberries
6 cups malt vinegar
6 cups sugar

Starting three days ahead, place the raspberries in a sieve and wash them quickly under cold running water. Drain thoroughly and transfer them to a glass or ceramic bowl. Pour in the malt vinegar and stir with a wooden spoon until the berries are thoroughly mixed. Cover with plastic wrap or aluminum foil and steep undisturbed in a cool place—but not in the refrigerator—for three days.

Pour the contents of the bowl into a sieve lined with a double thickness of cheesecloth and let the liquid drain through. With the back of a wooden spoon, press down hard on the berries to extract as much of their juice as possible before discarding them. Pour the drained liquid into a 3-quart enameled or stainless-steel saucepan, stir in the sugar, and bring to a boil, stirring constantly until the sugar has dissolved. Let the vinegar boil vigorously for 3 minutes, then slowly pour through a funnel set into the mouth of pint- or quart-sized bottles and cool to room temperature before corking tightly.

Or, if you are not planning to use the raspberry vinegar within the following month, ladle the hot vinegar into hot sterilized jars and seal them at once, following the directions for canning and sealing given in the Recipe Booklet.

Traditionally raspberry vinegar is used in place of other vinegars as a dressing for fruit salad. It is also used to make a refreshing summer drink by combining the vinegar and cold water (in the proportion of ⅓ cup raspberry vinegar to ⅔ cup water), then pouring this mixture into tall ice-filled glasses.

Oxtail Stew

To serve 4 to 6

3 pounds oxtails, cut into 2½-inch pieces
1 teaspoon salt
¼ teaspoon freshly ground black pepper
½ cup all-purpose flour
¼ cup vegetable oil
8 tablespoons unsalted butter, cut into bits
1 cup finely chopped onions
¼ cup scraped, finely chopped carrots
1 teaspoon finely chopped garlic
½ cup dry red wine
1½ cups chicken stock, fresh or canned
2 tablespoons tomato paste
¼ teaspoon ground thyme
1 small bay leaf

Preheat the oven to 325°. Season the oxtails with the salt and pepper, then roll the pieces in the flour one at a time and shake briskly to rid them of excess flour.

In a heavy 10- to 12-inch skillet, heat the oil and butter bits over high heat until the butter is melted and the mixture is very hot but not smoking. Brown the oxtails, 6 or 8 pieces at a time, turning them with tongs and regulating the heat so that they color richly and evenly without burning. As they brown, transfer them to a heavy 3- to 4-quart enameled or stainless-steel casserole.

When all the oxtails have been browned, pour off and discard all but 2 or 3 tablespoons of fat from the skillet. Add the onions, carrot and garlic and, stirring constantly, fry over moderate heat for 6 to 8 minutes, or until the vegetables are lightly colored. Pour in the wine and let it boil for a minute or two, then add the chicken stock, tomato paste, thyme and bay leaf. Bring the mixture back to a boil, then pour it over the oxtails.

Bring the casserole to a boil over high heat, stirring constantly, then cover it tightly and place it in the middle of the oven, regulating the heat if necessary to keep the casserole at a slow simmer. Cook the oxtail stew for about 3 hours, until tender.

With a large spoon, skim off and discard as much fat as possible from the sauce. Taste for seasoning, and serve the oxtail stew directly from the casserole or from a large heated tureen.

II

Alaska, the Outermost Frontier

Tangy sourdough bread and rolls, Alaskan style, are made from a "starter" —a ferment of flour, water and yeast, stored in a crock and continually renewed. Traditionally, the longer a starter is kept, the better it becomes; some Alaskan sourdough starters are now a half century or more old.

One day in 1890 Americans learned from the Superintendent of the Census that their frontier had come to an end. The nation's "unsettled area," he announced, "has been so broken into by isolated bodies of settlement that there can hardly be said to be a frontier line." An outermost edge of civilization, with wilderness beyond it, no longer existed; the last horizon had been reached. But the frontier has lived on in the minds of many who want to believe that there will always be one more wild place to go. I am such a person, and I went to Alaska because it is a land that is still more wilderness than civilization, a land where the rambunctious pioneer spirit survives and the cooking has the wild and zestful ring of our American past.

Game, fish and berries still abound, and Alaskan cookbooks (there are surprisingly many for a state with only about 300,000 people) include appetite-rousing recipes for venison stew, caribou Swiss steak, breast of ptarmigan in sour cream, salmonberry-and-rhubarb jelly, red-and-blue-huckleberry pie and sweet kelp relish. Where but in Alaska would a cookbook tell how to braise bear chops, pot-roast beaver, make a cake with sea-gull eggs, and concoct an "ice cream" from snow? (The last, a dessert that pioneer women used to stir up in the winter for the pleasure of their children, calls for a cup of evaporated milk, three quarters of a cup of sugar, a teaspoon of vanilla and enough fresh-fallen snow to produce a mix with the consistency of ice cream.)

It is fitting, too, that Alaska is today the home of sourdough, one of the most American of foods, yet one that few present-day Americans have ever eaten. Northwestern North America literally grew up on this basic leaven from which housewives made their breads, biscuits and pancakes. No pioneer family took the trail or established a homestead without its sourdough starter, kept in a crock or keg and zealously guarded. With the advent of commercially packaged yeast, sourdough began to disappear in the States, but gold seekers took it north with them in the 1890s. They ate so much of it while working their claims that the term sourdough also came to stand either for a prospector or any oldtimer, and today it is the name for any true-blue Alaskan. I had tasted sourdough bread, but only in its elegant San Francisco incarnation, which is really a variety of French bread, and I went north determined to have it at its homeliest—as the West once knew it.

But I went north for another reason, too: to see an unspoiled country, to get a sense of how some of the regions encompassed by this book may have looked and felt a hundred years ago. And I was not to be disappointed, for all the modernity of Alaska's cities or the airborne ease with which Alaskans move about their state.

Even getting there was a beautiful experience. My wife Liet, my two young daughters and I took the Alaskan ferry *Taku* from Prince Rupert, in British Columbia. The ship follows the Inside Passage, where the Pacific flows as calmly as a green river between the mountainous coast and the rugged offshore islands. Glaciers glide out from steel-gray peaks, and waterfalls trail down forested slopes like white ropes. The cool air has an invigorating bite, and with its clean, pervasive smell of spruce blows away the agues of 20th Century living. As the ferry worked its way northward, it was as though we were escaping time altogether and entering a region where past, present and future blend in an eternity that keeps the land forever young.

The *Taku* was two days enroute, passing snug cities with romantic names—Ketchikan, Wrangell, Juneau. And then, suddenly, we were at Skagway, the gateway to the Yukon and the mother lode of memories of the Gold Rush of 1898. Here, withered to a population of 750, was the town once swollen with 15,000 prospectors on their way to the Yukon. The squatters' tents are long since gone, but the wooden sidewalks and many of the old frame buildings remain, among them our two-story hotel. The Golden North has a staircase that seems as steep as a mountainside, and sharply sloping floors that sent me tottering a couple of times. But we loved the place. The headboards of our beds were well over six feet high, paneled and veneered and elaborately carved—like much of the massive, expensive (and awful) furniture that was made in the East and shipped around Cape Horn to Alaska.

Through most of the next day we traveled north over the mountains on the narrow-gauge railroad that runs from Skagway to Whitehorse, in Canada's Yukon Territory. The countryside was vast, filled with rocks and boulders and stunted evergreens. Every mile brought reminders of the Gold Rush. There was the trail of 1898 itself, a narrow path clinging to the stony flank of a mountain; Dead Horse Gulch, where 3,000 exhausted pack animals had been left to die; Bennett Lake, where more than 10,000 men had paused to build the boats or rafts that would float

them to the Yukon River and the gold fields of the Klondike. The train made its only stop of the day at the lake, and all the passengers had lunch in the station. The surrounding landscape was bleak, and apart from the railroad buildings, about the only sign of the community that had flourished there was a clapboard church, gray and dilapidated on a hill.

The meal paid fitting homage to the past by its sturdiness and simplicity. It consisted of plain food, plainly cooked: pot roast, yellow beans, boiled potatoes, cabbage, pickles, homemade rolls, black coffee and mountain water, with apple pie for dessert. We ate it at long tables, covered with white oilcloth, and it would have pleased and filled a sourdough.

Pierre Berton, the eloquent Canadian chronicler of the Gold Rush, has argued that there is a whole literature of bad cooking associated with the Far North, so sauced by the storyteller's hunger that it actually succeeds in rousing the appetite. There are descriptions of beans and pork and stale bread that make the reader want to scrape the bottom of a tin plate. There is plum duff, a boiled pudding; one old Gold Rush tale tells how a sourdough made it with moose fat, soaked it with a couple of bottles of Hudson's Bay rum and served it to his companions. "My, what a feed," wrote one of the miners. "We told yarns, smoked and went to bed." And then there was a "butter" concocted from a broth of caribou horns boiled two nights and a day in snow water. When the broth cooled, the "butter"

Four Klondike miners share a supper of pork and beans accompanied by sourdough bread frozen so hard it is sliced with a hatchet. The meal was probably all the gold hunters could afford; in the late 1890s eggs sold in the Klondike for two dollars a dozen, and a 50-pound bag of flour for 20 dollars.

Overleaf: Forested islands, like these near Wrangell, create a sea lane along Alaska's southeastern coast. Through this so-called Inside Passage, cruise ships and car ferries bring tourists every year to a land that is still largely a wilderness.

congealed on top of the water and, except for its white color, passed for the real thing when salted.

One of my own favorite passages from this literature occurs in *Old Yukon,* the reminiscences of a venerable Alaska hand named Judge James Wickersham. He describes a "rabbit stew" that he encountered in a log tavern on the Yukon. "The stew was prepared in a large kerosene can on top of an ancient Yukon sheet-iron stove set on the dirt floor and held in place by a low, rough frame of logs. In this can the famed rabbit stew always simmered. As hungry guests reduced its contents, more water, rabbit, caribou, bear or lynx was added. From early in November when the first ice permitted travel on the great river highway in front of [the landlord's] door, until the following May break-up, the odor and steam from this ragout of wild meats permeated the tavern, glazed the half-window with beautiful icy patterns, and filled the two-inch air-hole above the door with frost."

I suspect that Judge Wickersham's stew must have been terrible—as bad, perhaps, as the boot Charlie Chaplin exquisitely consumed in *The Gold Rush*—but I relish his description nevertheless. Even more do I relish the diary entries of a man who was lost in the snow outside Dawson and actually did eat his boots. It is, in its way, a classic example of food writing that is evocative and to the point:

"October 17: Travelled fifteen miles. Made supper of roasted rawhide sealskin boots. Palatable. Feel encouraged.

"October 18: Travelled all day. Ate more pieces of my sealskin boots boiled and toasted. Used sole first. Set rabbit snares.

"October 19: No rabbit in snare. Breakfast and dinner of rawhide boots. Fine. But not enough.

"October 20: Breakfast from top of boots. Not as good as sole."

In all fairness there are also accounts of *good* eating in the Far North —summer eating, mostly, when the days are long and the nights short, and all living things fill up with sweetness. Descriptions of grilled arctic char, boiled king crab, sautéed scallops three inches across, strawberries the size of teacups—these can set the mouth to watering and leave readers hankering for the real thing.

In Whitehorse, where we spent the night after our trip over the mountains, I met one fellow who set my appetite on edge for sourdough, and especially for sourdough pancakes. He was the first of several strong individualists Liet and I were to meet on the trip who descend from a long line of characters with names like Two Step Louie, Eat-em-up Frank, Malamoot Kid, Hot Air Smith and Cock-eyed Shorty. Yukon Bud Fisher was the name of my new friend, and I noticed that when he wrote it out for me he put quotation marks around Bud rather than Yukon. He wore a chain of gold nuggets sagging across his belly, and had a white beard and a florid face that made him a dead ringer for Santa Claus.

Bud was born in Pennsylvania, but he has lived in the Yukon since 1929 and proudly speaks of himself as a pioneer. Few of the 15,000 inhabitants of this 200,000-square-mile territory have seen more of it or know more about it. The wilderness that encircles Whitehorse is still so untrammeled that the gray-green water of the Yukon River can be drunk safely only a mile upstream from the town. And the people of White-horse live well off the land. Few are without some sort of game in their freezers, and one friend of Bud's "allowed as how" he still had 300 pounds of last season's trout on hand.

Inevitably our conversation turned to sourdough, that manna of the North. Bud has a sourdough starter that is 35 years old; he has kept it going by regularly feeding it flour and water and protecting it from ex-tremes of temperature. He has never had to add yeast to his starter, for the wild yeast cells present in the air continually settle on it. When Bud prepares pancakes he scoops up half a cup of starter and mixes it in a bowl with flour, water, salt and sugar. He covers the batter and allows it to stand overnight in a warm place to work. In the morning he adds an egg (a sea-gull egg, if he has one, for its distinctive flavor), a half tea-spoon of baking soda and perhaps a little moose or porcupine fat. He pours enough of the tangy batter into a small frying pan to fill the bottom, lets it bubble up, flips the pancake over, cooks it some more and then eats it right out of the pan, perhaps with a slush of crushed wild berries spooned over the top.

Liet and I met our next larger-than-life character the following day in Fairbanks, where we flew from Whitehorse. He is Don Sheldon, one of Alaska's most famous bush pilots and already a figure of legend, who was to fly us to one of the major points on our Alaskan itinerary, Tal-keetna. He stood at the airport exit waiting for us, dressed in khaki pants and a khaki parka with a wolverine-lined hood thrown back over his shoulders, and on his head he wore the knitted wool cap that has become his emblem. Don is a man who is not comfortable on the ground. When he walks, he has a rolling gait, and his manner is that of an awkward Mon-tana cowboy. But up in the sky he throws off his earthling's guise and puts on wings. And he seems not merely the master of his plane and pas-sengers, but of the whole state of Alaska as well.

"I hope you've got your spurs with you," Don said, "because it's going to be rough over McKinley tonight." We must have looked uneasy at the prospect of a bumpy night flight over the highest mountain in North America, for in the next breath Don suggested that we spend the night in Fairbanks and fly on to our destination in the morning. "Have you eat-en?" he asked. We told him that we had had only a snack on the plane. "Well, doggone, we've got to do something about that." Don's solution was to call friends and invite us all over to dinner. "But are you sure that's all right?" Liet asked, not yet realizing that Alaskans do not stand on ceremony. "Don't you worry," Don said, and he went off to the tele-phone. He came back a few minutes later and announced, "You'll eat Alaska-style tonight."

We welcomed this chance to see Fairbanks and to have a home-cooked meal. But first we had to find accommodations, and this proved difficult. The city was filled with men on their way to the North Slope, where the recent discovery of oil had set off a great boom, another great rush, the likes of which Alaska had not experienced since 1898. When at last we located what must have been the only available room in Fairbanks and reserved it, we took off with Don in a taxi for his friends' house.

A cabbage from the Matanuska Valley dwarfs Mrs. John Bush, who grew it in her kitchen garden. The 35-pound giant had a stem too thick and tough to cut with a knife or sickle, and had to be sawed through. A hybrid variety grown primarily for display, the cabbage set no records despite its weight; in seasons past Mrs. Bush has raised cabbages of almost 70 pounds.

Continued on page 44

Where Size Also Means Flavor

Because of—*not* in spite of—their short summer, Alaskans raise some of the most magnificent garden produce in North America. Long days of sunshine foster almost incredible plant growth, while comparatively cool temperatures slow down the plants' respiration, so that they store up the starch and sugar that make for quality and flavor. Radishes, beets, carrots, onions, potatoes, peas, salad greens, broccoli, cauliflower—all thrive in these conditions. Rhubarb, in varieties such as the Red Chipman (shown at left with a flowering stem of wild fireweed that sets off its brilliant color), grows three and four feet high. Indeed, rhubarb does so well in the Far North that many Alaskans use it in their desserts and preserves as a substitute for conventional cultivated fruits, which must be imported. But rhubarb must be planted carefully, for its vigorous growth can choke out or weaken other plants on the same plot.

Aglow with freshness, vegetables from a Matanuska Valley truck garden are displayed for sale at a roadside stand.

Decorated by a weathered pair of moose antlers, a four-legged cache near Homer on the Kenai Peninsula is a colorful reminder of Alaska's pioneer days. Elevated caches like this one served early prospectors, trappers and settlers as storehouses for their food, keeping it high, dry and safe from hungry animals.

Don's friends, John and Patty McGee, a middle-aged, comfortably plump couple, met us at the door of their small house. The interior was snug, a good place to be when the temperature drops well below zero. Our host made us a round of "salty dogs"—vodka and grapefruit juice poured into glasses with salted rims—and our hostess produced a plate of homemade caribou salami as an accompaniment. The salami was smooth, spicy and juicy, with the gamy taste of the meat tamed by garlic.

As we sat sipping our salty dogs, I asked the McGees about cooking in the cities of Alaska. Most food, we learned, is shipped in from the "outer 48," as Alaskans refer to the rest of the continental United States, and much of it arrives by boat from Seattle. Store-bought meat is therefore expensive. "To beat the prices," said our host, "we city people hunt. In Alaska we've got more than a dozen different kinds of big game animals, and all sorts of smaller ones. Did you know that kids here can get excused from school to go hunting with their dads in the fall? Lots of families actually depend upon hunting for their meat supply, and I mean folks like ourselves. My wife and I, we like the taste of wild meat."

"Alaskans are great gardeners too," said our hostess. "We love flowers, and we grow a lot of our own vegetables. But it takes special watching to get some things so they'll grow. Like behind the kitchen now—I've got tomato plants and cucumbers inside our glassed-in porch. They like the sun and the extra warmth and they're doing real well."

The proof of all this was in the eating. We had a roast saddle of caribou from the well-stocked freezer, served with a thick, smooth gravy, crisp hashed brown potatoes and a salad of cucumbers, lettuce and tomatoes. The venisonlike flavor of the caribou was complemented by a tart relish of crushed and sugared lingonberries, which our hostess had gathered the previous autumn. The dessert was a deep-dish blueberry pie, made with wild blueberries she had picked that very afternoon, a couple of miles outside town. And as a special ending to the meal, she produced a bottle of her own cranberry wine to go with the black coffee. It was as red in color as it was strong in alcohol, a nightcap to beat all nightcaps.

The next morning we flew south in Don's Cessna 180, through a drizzle that gave the long, flat landscape beneath us a murky cast. Soon we hit snow—this was in August—and for 100 miles we bounced along, hopping, skipping and jumping over Mount McKinley. I was alarmed; but Don was not in the least perturbed. On the other side of the mountain we entered a world of sunshine, summer green and blue skies filled with cauliflower clouds. The tiny plane was approaching the village of Talkeetna.

In retrospect, I am not really sure that Talkeetna exists; somehow a village of log cabins and free spirits seems incompatible with 20th Century America. But I still retain my first impression of the plane touching down on Don Sheldon's grassy, sun-drenched runway, and I must believe that I was there. A jeep took us straight to our destination, a motel at the edge of town, run by a wonderful woman called—I never did learn why —"Evil Alice" Powell. Standing in her front yard against a backdrop of orange and yellow nasturtiums and pink sweet peas was Evil Alice herself, cigarette in hand, and as wide a smile on her face as I have ever seen. Alice is in her sixties, and she makes no bones about it. She does not bother to hide her wrinkles under makeup, or her gray hair under dye —but she does wear stretch pants, and wears them well. And she likes nothing so much as a Daiquiri poured to the very brim of a wide, shallow glass, from which she takes her first sip with delicious concern.

After showing us our room, Alice led us into the dining room for lunch. The meal would be a simple one, she said. She had tossed a salmon into a paper bag and planned to bake it. I must have looked doubtful, because she took me by the elbow to the kitchen and removed a couple of paper clips from the folded end of a brown paper bag. Inside was a fine fat salmon, seasoned with salt and pepper, salved with butter. It had been caught the day before.

The fish needed little time to bake. In a matter of minutes we were seated at a round table with Alice, contemplating a meal of Alaskan freshness. The salmon, cooked in a vapor of its own juices, was a rich clean pink. There was a bowl of green peas, and a bowl of new potatoes swimming in melted butter. The superb vegetables had come from the fabulously productive Matanuska Valley, near Talkeetna.

Alaska's potential as a producer of prime vegetables is not yet widely fulfilled. Of its more than 350 million acres only 17,000 are used to produce commercial crops, and not all vegetables will grow here, but those that do, flourish. Salad greens, kale, Brussels sprouts, beets, radishes and turnips are goaded by the long days and short nights and the relatively low summer temperatures into building up unusually high sugar content. The peas served with the salmon were marvelously sweet, and I learned later to nibble them raw, like candy. Other vegetables from the Matanuska Valley, which was settled only a few decades ago, are famous for their sheer size. There are seven-pound turnips, for example, and oat stalks seven feet long. The most prodigious of all these vegetables, though, are the Matanuska cabbages. A hybrid species to begin with, and prone to vigorous growth, these potbellied giants swell enormously in the fields. Some may weigh up to 60 or 70 pounds. A 30-pound specimen, harvested in our honor, lolled in Alice's yard.

With lunch came sourdough bread (Recipe Index), which looked like ordinary white bread, but had a dense and sturdy texture and a sharp flavor. It was bread with muscle, the kind that demands to be sliced in slabs and thickly buttered. Halfway through the first slice, it occurred to Alice that we might like to try some "squaw honey" a neighbor had given her. "Honey?" I asked, for I knew that honey bees cannot survive Alaska's long winter. She produced a jar, and I spooned some of its viscous contents on my bread. It tasted like honey, and had honey's golden color —but as Alice explained, it was essentially a product of the kitchen. In a nearby meadow her friend had picked a bouquet of red and white clover and pink fireweed, a flower that grows rank throughout Northwestern North America. She had steeped the blossoms in a boiled sugar syrup, clarified with a pinch of alum, and when the blossoms yielded up their fragrance and flavor, she had strained them out and bottled her "honey."

Alice should have cautioned me about eating too much. What with the honey and bread, the salmon, potatoes and peas—and warm rhubarb pie for dessert—I was full, groaningly so. But Alice soon announced with a *Continued on page 48*

The crock of bubbling sourdough is the base for typical Alaskan pancakes; the fresh wild blueberries are an optional addition.

The Sourdough Cook
of Cache Creek

In a cabin on Cache Creek, near Mount McKinley, prospector Phil Brandl *(right)* makes sourdough pancakes every morning for himself and his wife Becky. Phil rises early, takes an earthenware crock *(above)* from its warm spot atop a wood-burning stove and pours some of the contents into a bowl. The crock contains his "starter," a tangy leaven of flour, water and yeast, to which he adds salt, sugar, baking soda and an egg. For the special breakfast shown on these pages, when friends came to visit, blueberries were also added. Brandl's pancakes *(far right)* are unforgettable for their body and pleasantly acid flavor.

"Evil Alice" Powell, a friend of the Brandls, pours mugs of coffee for Phil's wife Becky and a group of guests at a pancake breakfast.

wink of her eye that we were flying off in Don's plane to a gold-mining camp to eat sourdough pancakes. I was coming to feel that Alaskans use planes the way we do taxis. The distance between Talkeetna and Cache Creek, the site of the mining camp, was 50 miles. Driving there over kidney-jolting dirt roads would have taken the greater part of a day. The flight took 20 minutes, and afforded an eagle's-eye tour of the countryside. Looking out of the plane, I saw a lush green world of meadows, swamps and algae-edged ponds, laced by squiggles of blue streams. Half hidden among spruce and cottonwood trees stood moose, and on a hillside, shining in all the beauty of his wild state, was a black bear raking blueberries from a bush with his paw. As we circled over him, he stood up.

It is not often that people drop in on the miners of Cache Creek, and Phil Brandl and his wife Becky, who run the camp, were glad to see us. Phil, a big thunderclap of a man, came to the area in 1938. He walked in from Talkeetna and has been working at Cache Creek on and off ever since. Becky arrived 10 years later, by air, to cook for the camp—and wound up marrying Phil a few months afterward. She still does the cooking—but it is Phil who makes the sourdough pancakes.

We walked along the edge of Cache Creek to the camp, a cluster of ramshackle buildings covered with tar paper and decorated with weather-bleached moose antlers. Becky pointed to a bushy area behind a cabin where, the spring before, she had dropped a bear with one shot. She is a thin, slight woman, and I remarked on her courage, but killing a bear seemed to her a very ordinary thing to do.

We stepped into the Brandls' cabin, where the floors of the three small rooms were covered with linoleum strips. In the living room a shotgun leaned against a cabinet near an overstuffed couch covered with a pink bedspread. On a table were the scales Phil uses to weigh his gold, and next to them stood a kerosene lamp. And in the kitchen, atop the warming oven of the wood-burning range, was the sourdough crock. Phil lifted the lid and I peered at the creamy, bubbling contents. The odor was yeasty, almost malty. Now Phil set about giving us a demonstration of the "proper" way—his way, of course—of making sourdough pancakes.

Sourdough ranks among the world's most controversial foods. Like fried chicken or spaghetti sauce, it has its factions and fanatics, each of whom knows more about it than the next fellow, or thinks he does. There is the old-fashioned type who believes that the only real and effective starter is made from hops, water and flour, and must be at least a couple of decades old—a kind of eternal flame of cooking that should never be extinguished. And then there is the type of aficionado who is convinced that potato water makes a better starter than hops, and still another who uses only raw milk. Phil Brandl holds a more modern view; he begins his starter by the method described in this book *(Recipe Index)*, with a boost from today's active dried yeast, and, though he will concede that a starter *can* improve almost indefinitely as it ages, he tosses his out at the end of each year. About the only point on which Phil and the others agree is that a starter should not be kept in a metal container, for its ingredients corrode almost all metals; thus Phil's kitchen boasts the ubiquitous earthenware crock of the true sourdough devotee.

Phil scooped some batter from this crock into a bowl; then he poured in a little salad oil, flicked in a pinch or two of salt and sugar, and added a couple of eggs and a touch of baking soda "to sweeten things up a bit." Next, he took a slab of brown bacon rind, and slid the fat side over his griddle. When the surface gleamed, he dropped a spoonful of batter on it —and a pancake burst into bloom.

Alice, who has her own definite ideas about sourdough, suggested that we sprinkle some wild blueberries on top. Although Phil likes his pancakes plain, he was not about to get into an argument with a lady and stepped aside. Alice took a handful of berries from a sluice pan on the metal sink and dribbled them a few at a time on each bubbling pancake.

The afternoon was so extraordinarily beautiful—with light and air as palpable and clear as the ice-cold water in the stream beside the Brandls' cabin—that we decided to eat outdoors. In front of a building labeled the Ritz Plaza (it was, in fact, the camp toolshed) a table was set up and a red-and-white checked oilcloth was spread on top of it. Soon I was cutting into a stack of sourdough pancakes swimming in brown-sugar syrup. Here I was, under a satin sky, in the company of gold miners, the creek close by, the hills covered with blueberry bushes. The pancakes were excellent —sourish, but attractively so—and the blueberries were wonderfully sweet and tart.

Flying back to Talkeetna in the late afternoon, we could see the snow-covered hulk of McKinley, the highest mountain in North America,

A raspberry shortcake brings a look of bliss to the face of a hungry Alaskan, Robert O'Malley, a 10-year-old from Anchorage. The berries for the cake ripened under sheets of plastic film draped over the bushes to protect them from frost.

enthroned on a bank of low-lying puffy clouds. Next morning it was wrapped in fog, and we faced the task of turning a rainy day into a productive one. We were delighted when Alice invited us to drive with her to a place she calls the Homestead, to help feed her boys—two young grandsons and two of their friends. All four had been living alone in the house for a week, "looking after themselves"—which meant getting by on hot dogs, hamburgers and peanut-butter sandwiches. Alice thought it was time they had some solid food, and she planned a meal she knew would be a treat for us as well. It included moose, one of the common game animals in Alaska, and one whose meat is staple fare there.

Alaskans have different ways of cooking moose. Many treat it like beef, roasting or broiling it or grinding it for hamburgers. Alice puts the meat to more imaginative use. She may slice it thin for a wild-mushroom Stroganov or marinate it in soy sauce, red wine and garlic and then fry it. On this occasion she chose to make the latter dish. She poured the marinade over small steaks and placed them in plastic bags, then knotted the bags, thus ensuring that there would be no spillage on the trip to the Homestead—a trick that picknickers might do well to copy.

Alice's Homestead lies about six miles from Talkeetna. We drove part of the way over a gravel road, then left Alice's station wagon at a turnoff and boarded a jeep, the only vehicle able to negotiate the pits and bumps in the narrow dirt road leading to the house. Alice and her husband Sherm came to this spot 20 years ago; by working the land and living on it, they were entitled by homestead legislation to 160 acres. Though remote, the location is a good one: the Alaska Railroad (the Moose-gooser, as it is sometimes called) runs right past the front door, and keeps the place in touch with the outside world. One of the remarkable things about this line is that anyone can flag the train down. Whenever Alice wants to go to Anchorage from the Homestead, she stands between the rails and waves a flag. As with a rural bus, the train stops and the conductor lets her on.

The boys were glad to see us. They came tumbling out of the house, and eagerly helped carry in the makings of their dinner. The oldest boy was 15, the youngest 10. While Alice got a good fire going in her stove, I took Robert, the 10-year-old, aside and asked him what it had been like to live without parents for a week. Out poured a breathless story of water fights, duels fought with devil-club stalks, bombardments with rotten apples, peanut butter smeared between someone's toes and a hot dog that had been cremated to a black crisp with lighter fluid. He had not taken a bath in a week and was proud of it. "I don't take baths here," he said emphatically. "I don't get dirty."

At the sizzling sound of meat hitting hot metal we joined the others clustered around the stove to watch Alice deliver the moose steaks one at a time to the griddle. Soon the small kitchen began to fill up with the delicious smell of frying moose. If this was not tantalizing enough, there was the dining table already laden with brimming bowls of potatoes and peas awash in sweet cream, green and purple coleslaw made from Matanuska Valley cabbages, and large ripe rain-washed raspberries plucked by Alice from bushes in her garden.

The moose was excellent, tender and juicy and just a little bit underdone so that a knife running through it revealed a pink center. The soy-sauce-and-wine marinade had reduced the strong meat flavor without fully taming it. The boys had seconds, then thirds—and they might have had fourths had Alice not reminded them that dessert was yet to come. As a special treat for Liet and me Alice had steamed the last of her wild fiddlehead ferns, which she gathers in the forests each spring and freezes. She served them generously buttered, and we ate them as a natural accompaniment to the moose. They had a gentle flavor and a dense, leafy texture, like Brussels sprouts.

We were to have still wilder fare the next day. Mount McKinley had emerged from its wrapping of clouds, and Alice arrived at our door in the morning to announce, "You and Liet are going with Don Sheldon to the mountain." As cheechakos (the Alaskan term for "tenderfeet"), we were completely unprepared for the experience. We would fly to McKinley in a ski plane, land on a glacier, climb to a crag where Don claimed he had a little house, have a picnic and fly back.

The plane flew not so much to the mountain as *into* it; up close, McKinley seems like a whole range of mountains. For a while I was scared, and Don knew it. Casually, he began to tell me of "squirrelly winds," torrents of air that spill off the peak and toss a plane about like a leaf, of crashes and bodies entombed in ice, of avalanches and whiteouts "when you can't tell the air from the ground." His shock therapy worked and I took courage: our lives were in his hands. He was the mountain god lifting us to his home; the cowboy manner had vanished.

We began our ascent over a moraine, a dumping ground of Ruth Glacier, where great boulders lay scattered on the churned, muddy earth like so many pebbles. Don flew higher and higher, under garlands of clouds and between the splintered walls of an enormous canyon, following the white superhighway of the glacier. Ahead loomed the south peak of McKinley, a vast shark's fin of rock covered with snow so blindingly white one could barely look at it. The plane rounded the peak, then zoomed off toward a natural amphitheater that seemed at first no bigger than a football field—until Don pointed to his house, a tiny speck way off below.

Landing seemed incredibly easy, and we hopped out into a world of immense purity. Fresh snow lay underfoot and stretched away in a smooth blanket to walls of gray and tan stone. The walls seemed close, but they were a mile or more away; one of the amazing aspects of a mountain as huge as McKinley is that there is no way of relating to its scale. But we did not feel diminished. My lungs filled with the clean, sparkling air, and my eyes with the blue-white light of the sky and snow.

The environment seemed safe, somehow, but Don cautioned us about hidden crevasses bridged by bands of snow. We strapped snowshoes to our boots and tied mountain climber's rope around our waists, and in single file we marched off toward Don's house, a small six-sided structure lashed to a loaf-shaped outcropping of stone. In order to build it, Don had flown in a total of 10,000 pounds of building materials in his small plane, bringing load after load to one of the most spectacular points in the whole Alaska Range. I am convinced that he did so not for any prac-

Mount McKinley, the tallest peak in North America, is a wild, snowy domain that few men know as well as Don Sheldon, an Alaskan bush pilot. This view from Sheldon's ski plane shows the rugged area where he has built a one-room retreat on a crag overlooking McKinley's Ruth Glacier. He often takes friends there for parties and picnics.

tical reason, but because deep down he felt a need to assert his supremacy over the mountain. Don's house is accessible only by ski plane; storms and those squirrelly winds keep the place from being visited more than a few days every year. Three Japanese skiers whom Don had flown in the week before had been marooned at the site by snow, and only now, with a break in the weather, were they able to go about their business—filming a documentary for television. We searched for them on the slopes, spotted them, three black spots far to our left, and hallooed to them.

Approaching over a ramp of ice and snow, we arrived at the one-room house without mishap, intent on the hedonistic mission that had taken us there. We were going to feast on roasted Dall sheep—and what better place to eat this mountain-dwelling species than in its own domain? There are few people who have tasted Dall sheep, fewer still who have eaten it at a 6,000-foot altitude. The difficulty of shooting this nimble animal, which can spring with ease from precipice to precipice, and the exquisite quality of its flesh have made it a challenge to hunters. Fortunately, not many marksmen have the agility to track it down, much less keep up with it . . . and the Dall sheep, a relatively rare beast, is ensured its survival, at least for a while.

Don built a fire on the rocks outside his front door and eased the chunk of meat, a haunch precooked by Alice and wrapped in foil, into a

large iron skillet, which he set down over the flames. Soon the meat was hissing and crackling, the only sound in an otherwise silent world. The heat made the air shimmer, and melted some of the surrounding snow to reveal black mud in which no plant had ever grown.

Just before the meat was heated through, Don slathered its crusty dark-brown surface with the contents of a bottle of Alice's homemade cranberry ketchup. When Alaskans talk about cranberries they do not mean the large, cultivated variety, but two entirely different species. One is the high-bush cranberry, bearing red currantlike fruit with flimsy skins on shrubs six or more feet tall. The other is the low-bush cranberry, or lingonberry. In Alaska either kind is combined with onions, cloves, cinnamon, all-spice, pepper, celery salt, sugar, salt, water and vinegar to produce a mul-tiflavored relish that is delicious with game. A similar ketchup made with cultivated cranberries *(Recipe Index)* is an excellent condiment for beef, pork, lamb or duck.

As Don prepared to carve the meat, the three Japanese schussed in, and we invited them to share our meal. They had been living on de-hydrated foods reconstituted in snow water, and welcomed a change in their diet. The sheep must have been as foreign to them as it was to Liet and me, but we all wound up loving it. The meat tasted like baby lamb, but it had its own spiciness, imparted to the flesh perhaps by the sweet

After a landing on Ruth Glacier, Sheldon readies the mountain-climbing rope he will loop around his guests' waists for the treacherous climb to his house. The building can be seen on the rocks behind the guests, who include the author of this book and his wife *(red parka)*. At the house, Sheldon will roast a special kind of meat *(overleaf)*.

mountain grass and lichens the animal had eaten. We consumed slices of it with a finger salad of fresh lettuce, orange slices and chunks of raw kohlrabi. Refrigerated by the cool air, the kohlrabi was crisp and full of sparks. A ruby-red California wine wafted our soaring spirits still higher, and we took off our coats and sweaters and rolled up our sleeves to bake in the dry, hot sun. An hour or so later the weather changed and clouds began to pour across the sky. It was time to go—but just before descending to the plane in the amphitheater below, we looked up to see a wind-driven rush of snow fall from a cliff and explode into white plumes, a reminder that the weather was still king on McKinley.

With each new day in Alaska, Liet and I felt ourselves becoming more and more serene. Away from the cities, out in the wilds, our lives seemed to come into balance. In this part of the world people are too few to impinge on the environment; almost everywhere we found it as the pioneers had found the West a century ago, as nature had made it. Yet I was also aware that wherever we went, we were leaving our footprints. Never was I more acutely conscious of that fact than on an excursion we made at the very end of our Alaskan stay.

We went fishing. We did not hike or drive to the fishing creek, but flew to it in a helicopter, over miles of dense forest through which few men have ever walked. Our pilot, a Californian with a beard as crinkly as cigarette tobacco, set us down on a rocky river bed, and then whirled off to pick up another couple. Liet and I stood there, miles from civilization and other humans. For a moment, being inside the fern-scented wilderness rather than peering in from the edge made it seem tame, even friendly. But we had not gone far along the bank when we saw great paw prints—unmistakably those of a bear. From then on we felt uneasy; we recognized ourselves as intruders. I waded into the ice-cold water and felt the swift, rustling current tug fiercely at my rubber boots.

The pilot returned in half an hour, without the other couple; he had deposited them at a more promising pool several miles away and had come to take us there. The new location was little more than a break in the woods, and as we dropped into it, setting the branches around us to swaying, we scared a bald eagle from its nest. For a long while afterward the eagle soared above us, its white head glistening in the sunlight.

I had never been fishing before—and I have been so corrupted by this first experience that I may never go again. For one thing, there are not many virgin pools left in the world. I had no sooner cast my baited hook than I saw a flash of silver and felt a pull on the line. I reeled in a fine 16-inch grayling and, unhooking it, felt the plunge of its strong body in my hand. We ripped fish after fish from the water, like berries from a bush.

By then the light was long and the shadows spilled down the hillsides. In the silence the eagle wheeled overhead. We went over our catch, picking out some of the fish for our dinner that night and setting the rest aside for the freezers of our friends. A little ruefully we realized that our zeal had got the best of us. We would never get to eat all the fish we had taken from that pool, for we had promises to keep; we were scheduled to leave Alaska next morning on a flight to Seattle, far to the south, there to continue our exploration of the Pacific Northwest.

Opposite: One hundred and fifty feet above the snowfields of Ruth Glacier, Don Sheldon serves up a slice of Dall sheep, considered by many the choicest of American game meats. He has covered the roast with Alaskan wild cranberry ketchup, and will serve the meat with a fresh salad, crisp raw kohlrabi and a tart red wine.

Royal Rhubarb Cake

Preheat the oven to 350°. With a pastry brush, spread the tablespoon of softened butter over the bottom and sides of an 8-by-6½-by-2-inch baking dish. Arrange the rhubarb pieces in one layer on the bottom of the dish. Mix ¾ cup of the sugar, 2 tablespoons of the flour, the orange peel and the cinnamon together in a bowl, and sprinkle over the rhubarb.

Combine the remaining cup of flour, 2 tablespoons of the remaining sugar, the baking powder and the salt, and sift them into a bowl. Add the 4 tablespoons of butter bits and, with your fingertips, rub the flour and fat together until they resemble flakes of coarse meal. Pour in the egg-and-milk mixture and mix with your fingers or a wooden spoon until the dough is smooth. Spoon over the rhubarb and smooth the top with a spatula. Bake in the middle of the oven for 25 minutes. Then mix the orange juice and the remaining tablespoon of sugar and brush over the top of the cake. Bake for 15 minutes longer, or until the top is brown and a toothpick or cake tester inserted in the center comes out clean.

Remove the cake from the oven and run a thin-bladed knife around the edges to loosen the sides. Place an inverted serving plate over the cake and, grasping plate and baking dish together firmly, turn them over. Rap the plate on a table; the cake should then slide out easily. If any bits of rhubarb stick to the baking dish, lift them out and replace them on the cake. Serve at once, accompanied by the chilled cream.

To serve 6

1 tablespoon butter, softened, plus 4 tablespoons butter, chilled and cut into ¼-inch bits
1 pound fresh rhubarb, trimmed, washed and cut into ½-inch pieces (about 2 cups)
¾ cup plus 3 tablespoons sugar
1 cup plus 2 tablespoons all-purpose flour
1 tablespoon freshly grated orange peel
1 teaspoon ground cinnamon
2 teaspoons double-acting baking powder
½ teaspoon salt
1 egg, lightly beaten and combined with 3 tablespoons milk
3 tablespoons strained fresh orange juice
1 cup heavy cream, chilled

Sourdough Starter

Because of their flavor and texture, sourdough bread, rolls and pancakes are well worth the trouble they take to make, but it is not possible to ensure predictable results. The success of sourdough starter, which gives the dough its character, depends on a proper blend of yeast and bacterial fermentation. This in turn depends to a large degree on the flour and the amount and types of bacteria in the air. In many parts of the United States and Canada, it is possible to buy sourdough starter from bakeries.

Starting a day ahead, place the flour in a large glass mixing bowl. Make a well in the center and pour in the yeast and water. With a large spoon, gradually stir the flour into the yeast and water, continuing to stir until the ingredients are well combined. Then, with a whisk or a rotary or electric beater, beat vigorously until the mixture is completely smooth. Drape with a kitchen towel and set aside in a warm, draft-free spot (such as an unlighted oven) for 24 hours. If at the end of this time the starter has not bubbled, it must be discarded.

After you have used as much of the starter as you need, transfer the remaining starter to a glass jar or crock equipped with a tight-fitting lid. Covered and refrigerated, it can be stored for several weeks. If used regularly, it may keep indefinitely.

To make about 4 cups

3 cups all-purpose flour
1 package active dry yeast
2½ cups lukewarm water (110° to 115°)

Rhubarb, a plant that thrives in the long, sunny days of an Alaskan summer, finds a variety of uses in the kitchen. Shown here are a rhubarb-and-strawberry ring, a rhubarb cake and a tart rhubarb jam.

To make 3 small loaves

1 cup sourdough starter *(page 57)*
6½ to 7 cups all-purpose flour
2 cups lukewarm water (110° to
    115°)
1 teaspoon salt
3 tablespoons sugar
½ teaspoon baking soda
3 tablespoons vegetable oil
2 tablespoons butter, softened

Sourdough White Bread

Starting a day ahead, place the sourdough starter in a large glass or ceramic mixing bowl and add 2½ cups of the flour and the lukewarm water. With a large wooden spoon, mix the starter, flour and water together until well combined, then continue to stir until the dough is smooth. Drape the bowl with a kitchen towel and place in a warm, draft-free spot (such as an unlighted oven) overnight.

The following day, remove 1 cup of the mixture and refrigerate it, in a tightly sealed glass jar or crock, as your new sourdough starter. Or you can add it to any sourdough starter you may have left.

To the dough remaining in the bowl add 4 cups of the flour, the salt, sugar, baking soda and oil. With a large spoon, stir the ingredients together, and continue to stir until the mixture is smooth and the flour is completely absorbed. The dough should be just firm enough to be gathered into a ball. If it is too soft, add the remaining ½ cup of flour, a tablespoon at a time, beating vigorously after each addition and using only enough of the flour to give the dough its proper consistency.

On a heavily floured surface, knead the dough by pushing it down with the heels of your hands, pressing it forward, and folding it back on itself. Continue to knead for about 10 minutes, or until the dough is smooth, shiny and elastic. Sprinkle it from time to time with a little flour to prevent it from sticking to the board.

Shape the dough into a ball and place it in a lightly buttered bowl. Drape with a kitchen towel and set in the warm, draft-free place for about 2½ hours, or until it has doubled in volume.

With a pastry brush, spread the bottom and sides of three warmed 9-by-5-by-3-inch loaf pans with the softened butter. Punch the dough down with a single blow of your fist and with a large, sharp knife, cut it into three equal parts. Shape each part into a loaf and place the loaves in the loaf pans. Set aside in the warm, draft-free place for about 1 hour, to allow them to double in volume.

Preheat the oven to 375°. Bake the loaves in the middle of the oven for about 1 hour, or until they are golden brown on top and shrink slightly from the sides of the pan. Transfer the bread to cake racks to cool and serve at room temperature.

To make 12 rolls

1 tablespoon sugar
1 package active dry yeast
1¼ cups lukewarm water (110°
    to 115°)
1 cup sourdough starter *(page 57)*
3½ to 4 cups all-purpose flour
1 tablespoon butter, softened

Sourdough Rolls

In a small, shallow bowl, sprinkle the sugar and yeast over ¼ cup of the lukewarm water. Let the mixture stand for 2 to 3 minutes, then stir once or twice and set the bowl in a warm, draft-free spot (such as an unlighted oven) for about 5 minutes, or until the mixture bubbles and almost doubles in volume.

Place the sourdough starter in a large glass or ceramic mixing bowl and pour in the yeast mixture. Add the remaining cup of lukewarm water and 1½ cups of the flour and stir with a large spoon until all of the ingredients are well combined. Then drape with a kitchen towel and set aside in the warm, draft-free place for about 2 hours, or until the mixture bubbles and doubles in volume.

Stir the mixture briefly with a large spoon. Remove 1 cup and refrigerate it in a tightly sealed glass jar or crock, to be used as your new sourdough starter. Or add it to any sourdough starter you may have left.

To the mixture remaining in the bowl gradually add 2 to 2½ cups of the remaining flour, beating vigorously after each addition and using only enough of the flour to make it firm enough to be gathered into a ball. On a heavily floured surface, knead the dough by pushing it down with the heels of your hands, pressing it forward, and folding it back on itself. Continue the kneading for about 10 minutes, or until the dough is smooth and elastic. Sprinkle it from time to time with a little flour to prevent it from sticking to the board.

Shape the dough into a ball and place it in a lightly buttered bowl. Drape with a towel and set aside in the warm, draft-free place for about 1 hour, or until the dough doubles in volume.

Preheat the oven to 375°. With a pastry brush, spread a large baking sheet with the tablespoon of softened butter. Punch the dough down with a single blow of your fist and with a large, sharp knife cut it into 12 equal parts. Shape the dough gently into balls and flatten them slightly with your hands. Place the balls about 2 inches apart on the prepared baking sheet. Bake in the center of the oven for 20 to 25 minutes, or until golden brown and crisp. Serve the rolls at once.

Rhubarb Ring with Strawberries

To serve 6

1 tablespoon vegetable oil
2 pounds fresh rhubarb, trimmed, washed and cut into ½-inch pieces (about 4 cups)
1 cup plus 1 tablespoon sugar
1½ cups water
2 envelopes unflavored gelatin
1 cup heavy cream, chilled
1 tablespoon rum
2 cups fresh ripe strawberries, hulled
Confectioners' sugar

Brush the tablespoon of oil evenly over the inside surfaces of a 1-quart ring mold, and wipe away all excess with a paper towel.

Combine the rhubarb, 1 cup of the sugar and 1 cup of the water in a 2- to 3-quart enameled or stainless-steel saucepan and bring to a boil over high heat, stirring until the sugar dissolves. Reduce the heat to low and simmer partially covered for about 10 minutes, or until the rhubarb is tender but still intact.

Meanwhile, sprinkle the 2 envelopes of gelatin into the remaining ½ cup of water and let it soften for 4 or 5 minutes. Add the gelatin to the rhubarb mixture and stir until it dissolves completely. Then pour the mixture into the oiled ring mold, spreading it and smoothing the top with a spoon or rubber spatula. Cool to room temperature, cover the mold with foil or plastic wrap, then refrigerate for at least 3 hours, or until it is firm to the touch.

Just before serving, pour the cream into a large chilled bowl. Whip with a wire whisk or a rotary or electric beater until the cream is stiff enough to stand in firm, unwavering peaks on the beater when it is lifted from the bowl. Beat in the remaining tablespoon of sugar and the rum, and taste for sweetness.

To unmold and serve the rhubarb ring, run a thin knife around the sides of the mold and dip the bottom briefly into hot water. Place an inverted serving plate on top of the mold and, grasping plate and mold together firmly, turn them over. Rap the plate on a table and the rhubarb ring should slide out easily. Arrange a row of strawberries around the ring and mound the rest of the berries in the center of the mold. Sprinkle the berries with confectioners' sugar. Serve the whipped cream separately from a small bowl.

III

The Bounty of the Pacific Northwest

Flowering pear trees whiten a slope of Oregon's Hood River Valley, one of the great fruitgrowing regions of the Pacific Northwest. Beyond the neat orchards rises snow-tipped Mount Hood, the state's tallest mountain.

Elisabeth, who is three, has a way of putting things in their proper perspective—hers, of course. As our plane neared the Seattle-Tacoma airport, she spied Mount Rainier thrusting through a flat sea of clouds. "It looks like a big lump of ice cream!" she cried. That, I explained, was because the mountain was covered by snow. "I want to eat that plate of snow," she announced.

I can understand why Elisabeth reduced Rainier to edible proportions. It is almost too big—a vast presence even when hidden by an overcast. But then, everything about the Pacific Northwest is big. The region sprawls over 600,000 square miles, 10 times the area of New England. It includes three huge states, Washington, Oregon and Idaho, along with western Montana and British Columbia. It is all muscle and brawn, like a flexed arm of the North American continent bulging with mountains and strapping hills. Dense blue-green forests crowd in from the coast, massing in the valleys and sweeping up the steep slopes. Only east of the mountains do the trees thin out, giving way to bare dry lands and deserts that seem as wide as the sky is high.

The people of the Pacific Northwest actively enjoy its breadth and grandeur. They make endless use of the outdoors, sailing the coves and inlets, clamming along the shores, picnicking on the beaches, climbing and skiing in the mountains, fishing the rivers and lakes, hiking and backpacking through the woods. They are continually exploring the landscape around them—and continually coming upon the unexpected. When my wife and I had dinner with the Portland journalist Carl Gohs, who has written the text for two lavishly illustrated books about Oregon and Washington, he enthusiastically described a "new" place that he and some friends had recently found. "We packed into the mountains back of the Columbia Gorge and picnicked next to a smooth, clear pool where the water spilled over about a hundred feet down, into a straight-walled rock gorge. I thought I had seen all of Oregon, but this was the best spot yet." Carl went on to tell us how he and his companions had celebrated their discovery with a picnic lunch, Pacific Northwest style—onion and cheese rolls, hunter's and liver sausage, chunks of Cougar Gold, a rich cheese developed at Washington State University, and a tart pool-chilled wine from the Yakima Valley. (That wine, interestingly enough, was the product of a group of professional men who recently—and mostly for the fun of it—became serious vintners.)

For visitors from New York *all* of the Pacific Northwest is a discovery. We traveled up and down and across it, trying not to measure our cramped existence in the city against the open life of the people we met, but we could not help making pained comparisons. As parents, we envied the mothers and fathers who could let their children run free. As nature lovers, we wished we could escape Manhattan as effortlessly as they do their own cities. And we coveted the green oases that Pacific Northwesterners have at their disposal when they stay home. In Vancouver's Stanley Park we wandered for hours along tree-shaded paths and took tea and crumpets in a flower-fringed cottage. In Portland we were staggered to find a 3,500-acre wilderness park within the city limits—a forested park with tall columns of Douglas fir, hemlock and Western red cedar, among which deer nonchalantly picked their way. And in Seattle we marveled at the site of the 1962 World's Fair, now reincarnated as a lovely recreation and amusement park resembling Copenhagen's Tivoli Gardens.

Seattle may be the city that best sums up the mood of the Pacific Northwest and the one where the flavor of the area best comes through in the cooking. As often happens, it was drizzling the day we arrived, but no matter. Like all the cities of the Pacific Northwest, Seattle is a friendly place, and it is a place where we have good friends. One of them, Grace Brynolson (who is the picture editor of this book), was on hand at the airport, and as she drove us to our hotel the sun broke through the clouds and tinseled the skyline. In any light, Seattle is beautiful, rising tower upon tower from the shimmering waters of Puget Sound; but in this light it was spectacular, and the moment was punctuated by the shuddering bellow of a ferry whistle coming from the harbor.

Dinner that first evening was at a restaurant called the Farm House in Port Townsend, 50 miles from the hotel, some of it by ferry. John and Dorothy Conway, who run the restaurant, are not restaurateurs in the usual sense. John teaches drama at the University of Washington in Seattle, and Dorothy is a portrait photographer. When classes are over for the week, they make the long trip to Port Townsend and step into their weekend roles of host and hostess to entertain as many as 80 guests for dinner on Friday, Saturday and Sunday nights. What impressed me most about the arrangement was the fact that neither John nor Dorothy seemed to find it particularly strenuous. Indeed, John Conway—who does most of the cooking for the restaurant—insisted to me that he finds his way of life refreshing.

The friendly atmosphere of the Farm House was apparent the moment we stepped from our car. Dorothy led us into a glass-walled dining room and seated us at a table with a sweeping view of the Strait of Juan de Fuca. A sea gull, its wings edged with light, dipped against the evening sky and swept out over the blue and amber water. Somewhere over there was the little town of Dungeness, which gave its name to Dungeness crab. Now John Conway, who had been pouring wine, came up with a big green bottle in his hand and introduced himself. He invited us to the salad table, urging us to eat as much as we wanted.

There were 15 platters and bowls on that table, each with a different kind of salad or appetizer. John recommended the Farm House salad, the restaurant's specialty, containing diced red Delicious apples, sliced green grapes, bits of fresh pale-yellow pineapple, raisins, Spanish peanuts, pine nuts, sweet-pickle relish and an oil-and-tomato-paste dressing. I helped myself and then dipped into three other salads. The first was made of cold rice, cold salmon and curried mayonnaise. The second consisted of sliced cucumbers and shrimp, with a sweet-sour dressing of rice vinegar, honey, sesame oil and sherry. The third had the same dressing, but was made up of a mixture of chicken, celery, agar-agar (a gelatinous product made from seaweed) and ginger. All four salads were excellent, their textures as interesting as their flavors.

I asked John how he came to use such exotic ingredients as agar-agar, rice vinegar and sesame oil. He admitted to being under the influence of the Orient, having lived there, and went on to say that the influence is common in the Pacific Northwest. "We face the Far East here," he explained. "That predisposes us to many things Oriental. We're lucky, too, in having large Japanese and Chinese populations. I sometimes think that of all the ethnic groups that have settled in this region they're the ones who've had the most far-reaching effect on cooking."

After the salad course I had a bowl of soup, and here again a subtle Oriental influence was evident. John explained that "I've learned the Chinese way of mixing meats in the soup base—chicken with beef, veal with chicken, chicken with clams." Our soup had been made with chicken and beef, and the stock had been cooked slowly for two days on a wood-burning stove. John had added white wine, Parmesan cheese and oregano to round off its richness.

Our main course was roast beef and Yorkshire pudding, which belong to the Pacific Northwest almost as much as they do to England. Oregon was originally settled by Easterners and Southerners of British descent; to the North, British Columbia contains Victoria, one of the most English cities anywhere outside of England. The beef was the Idaho grain-fed (rather than corn-fed) variety, with fat whiter than any I had seen before, and a good, deep flavor. The vegetable course—the one that at most restaurants is steamed to mealiness and mush—was perfect at the Farm House: tiny fresh green peas simmered briefly with sliced mushrooms and water chestnuts.

We relaxed in the quiet sunset, watching the room turn pink and eat-

Continued on page 66

Crisp Rings of Pickled Kelp, a Gift of the Sea

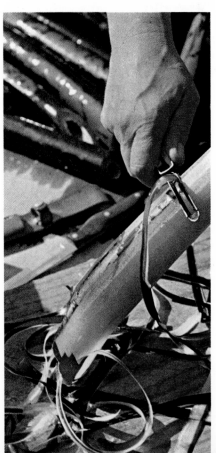

The giant kelp, a tubular seaweed 20 to 30 feet long that floats in Washington's Strait of Juan de Fuca, has long fascinated John and Dorothy Conway, who run a Port Townsend restaurant called the Farm House. Knowing that the Japanese eat kelp, Dorothy hit upon the idea of pickling it as a relish. She starts her recipe by fishing kelp from the water *(above)*, then cuts away and discards the thick bulb and peels off the tough outer covering of the tube *(left)*. The sliced rings *(right)* are ready for immersion in a vinegar, water and sugar solution, spiced with a combination of ingredients known only to Dorothy Conway. After steeping for several weeks, the rings will be as crisp and refreshing as watermelon pickle—but with a subtle marine flavor all their own.

A logger's breakfast is laid out at dawn on a steel-top table at the Hoko logging camp, located on Washington's Olympic Peninsula. The meal is huge, but so is a logger's appetite: after consuming this food (it usually takes about 10 minutes) the logger can then call for seconds—and he usually does.

ing our dessert of fresh raspberries picked from bushes outside the window. There was no one to hurry us, no one to thrust a check at us; we could stay as long as we liked. Now Dorothy joined us, and we talked for a while about local foods. John said that the best strawberries he had ever eaten came from nearby Sequim. Dorothy described the giant mushrooms called puffballs, "as big as basketballs," which she picks in the pasture above the Farm House. "We slice them—each slice is a foot across—and sauté them. Sometimes we dip them in egg and fry them."

The talk of wild food reminded Dorothy of her kelp pickles. She went over to the salad table and came back with a bowl of honey-colored translucent rings, each about an inch across. I had heard Alaskans tell how they peel and slice tubes of giant kelp and preserve the rings in a sweet-sour pickle solution, and I asked Dorothy whether she used the same kind of kelp. "I do, and I get it right out there," she said, pointing to the water, "but I have my own secret recipe." I tried one of the rings; it was crisp and spicy, rather like pickled watermelon rind, but with a coppery tang all its own.

The next morning revealed another facet of the region. After a drive along dark forest roads, I sat down to breakfast at a long steel-topped table in the cookhouse of the Hoko logging camp. The air was thick with the warm odor of buckwheat pancakes, and the room was jammed with wool-shirted loggers hunched over their food. I had imagined the log-

gers as a rough crew surrounded by tough women. But many of them turned out to be college boys earning money for next year's tuition, and the women who waited on them in the cookhouse were wives, mothers and even grandmothers.

The breakfast, however, was no surprise. It was huge—the Mount Rainier of morning repasts—and one needed a lumberjack's appetite to get through it. A slice of melon, grapefruit sections in a bowl, cereal, two fried eggs and four sausages, toast and pancakes, a doughnut and a chunk of buttered hardtack proved my limit, and I shoved back my half-finished plate and settled for some conversation with the cook. He had been up since 3:30, and had cooked no fewer than 12 dozen eggs, 15 pounds of sausages and 800 pancakes for 80 men, and had just finished off his morning's work with a "horse blanket," a two-foot-wide pancake made from the leftover batter.

Enormous though it was, that breakfast took the loggers little more than 10 minutes to eat. The table at which I sat was soon deserted, except for the wreckage they left behind them—ripped-open cereal boxes, empty bowls and syrup-splattered plates yellow with egg yolk. I noticed that each man stopped on his way out to pick up a brown paper bag from a huge collection of bags near the door. "What are they doing?" I asked the cook. "Oh, that's their lunch," he replied, and went on to list the contents of each bag: two sandwiches, a piece of cake, a wedge of pie, cookies

Four men of the Hoko camp have lunch on the logs they have felled. Every lunch packed by the camp cook includes two sandwiches, wedges of pie and cake, cookies, fruit and coffee. Loggers who find this ration insufficient can pick up extra food when they leave the dining room after breakfast.

and fresh fruit. "And that's not all. You see that stuff on the trays over there? They can fill out their lunch with that—anything they want." I watched one of the college boys help himself to a couple of hard-boiled eggs and a banana. "Oldtimers just aren't in it compared with these college kids," said the cook with deep satisfaction.

Lumberjacks and fishermen once dominated the economy of this region, and they have left an indelible mark on it. Both industries are now in decline; breakfast at the Hoko Camp represented a way of eating that may vanish in a few years. I went up the mountain behind the camp to view the logging operation. Fog sealed off the sky along the narrow dirt road, which climbed higher and higher through a landscape of splintered stumps, broken branches and salmonberry bushes dangling low with fruit. But then I emerged into sunshine, and saw the Pacific Northwest as it might have been in the beginning. The rips and tears on the mountain's flank, the logged-over patches, the camp below—all lay hidden under a thick white blanket of clouds. Two peaks, edged with spruce, floated like islands before me, and far beyond, a streak of blue, was the Pacific. The air smelled of Christmas trees.

I love to roam markets, so when I got back to Seattle Liet and I went to the Pike Place Market, one of my favorites. It is beautiful, in a down-to-earth way that has been attracting local painters for years, and it has none of the anonymity of the modern supermarket, for the people behind the stands take an aggressive pride in their produce. (When I asked one woman whether her peas were really good, she nodded and said firmly, "I should know—I picked them myself.") The vegetables and fruit are brought in fresh each morning during the summer; the prices remain surprisingly low, considering the quality of the food; and the range of goods is wide—everything from oregano, lemon mint and catnip at 15 cents a bunch to "doughnut holes" (the punched-out centers of doughnuts, fried to a turn) at 19 cents a dozen.

At one stall we saw purple berries almost as big as my thumbs and stopped to ask what they were. Nectarberries, we were told. The woman in charge gave me one to eat, and as it broke open in my mouth and flooded it with juice I thought of those little liqueur-filled chocolate bottles that are the delight and indulgence of Europeans. Next to the nectarberries stood boxes of plump black and red raspberries at their peak of ripeness. At another stall the stacked vegetables looked as though they had been meticulously combed into place—each string bean parallel to every other, the carrots side by side—and even the signs were beautiful, the work of the Japanese proprietor who had painted his prices on paper bags with the large strokes of an ink-dipped brush. Lettuce was of the purest white and green, and in this market iceberg lettuce really deserved its name, for it had the crispness of ice and snow and the coloring as well. Mushrooms were brown-capped, rather than white, and suggested a kinship with wild places and wild foods. Long stalks of rhubarb glowed strawberry red, in contrast with bunches of dripping white icicle radishes just washed by a garden hose.

Close by were the fish stands, mercifully free of the odor that clings to seafood too long out of the sea. The salmon—that *sine qua non* of the Pacific Northwest—glittered, and its flesh was deep pink, suffused with orange. On a neighboring bed of ice was another essential of the good life: red and cream-colored Dungeness crab, each as much as 10 inches across, with thick claws that promised tender eating.

Luckily we were to do better than look: we had an invitation to the beach house of Stewart and Rosemary Ballinger at Enetai, on the other side of Puget Sound, to lunch on Dungeness to our hearts' and stomachs' content. This meant taking one of the ferries that crisscross Puget Sound. Ferries are different here; they have class. Ours gleamed with fresh white paint, her railings were a vibrant green, her brasses were newly polished and her deep-throated whistle had loud authority. We headed into the wind leaving a trail of hissing foam behind us, and soon landed at Bremerton, where we were met by our hosts. The Ballingers took us to their wide-decked house, facing east across the water. Their children were down on the beach, clustered around a small muddy hole, obviously hunting buried treasure. They were, in fact, digging our first course, tiny native littleneck clams, and while we watched they filled their bucket and staggered up to the house with it.

Waiting for the clams to steam, we sat on the deck sipping gin and tonic. A light breeze swept the deck and the spruces and firs around the house sparkled in the brilliant light of the Pacific Northwest.

The steamed clams clattered onto our plates, and we dipped them one by one into cups of melted butter and popped them into our mouths. The clams provided only the appetizer. After them we had cracked Dungeness crab, served with swirls of homemade mayonnaise *(Recipe Index)*. With the cool, juicy, tender crab we had hot garlic bread and a chilled white wine, in each glass of which I could see the blue-green world around us reflected upside down. The dessert was a fresh boysenberry pie, another specialty of the Northwest, with its big purple berries swelling under a flaky crust.

Our dinner the following night was another demonstration of natural

Joe Desimon, an Italian-born truck farmer, sits at the wheel of his 1914-1915 Buick delivery truck, his vegetables piled high in back. When this picture was taken in the early 1920s, Joe was selling his produce at a stall in Seattle's Pike Place Market *(overleaf)*. By 1927, he had gained a controlling interest in the entire market, and today, as a gesture of good will, Desimon's heirs lease the produce section of the market to the city for one dollar a year. Thus, because of Joe Desimon, the city can charge nominal rents for these stalls, and truck farmers can still sell their wares at relatively low prices.

69

The Pike Place Market, a colorful Seattle landmark since the early 1900s, offers shoppers a wide range of fine foods, ranging from locally grown fruits, vegetables and herbs to specialty meats and fresh seafood. Most of the produce sold at stands like these comes from about 50 truck farms in the vicinity of the city. The stands rent for 85 cents a day with water or 50 cents without —and one has been occupied by the same farmer for 50 years.

flavors and easy preparation. We were invited to a salmon barbecue by Richard White, a Seattle businessman who has a lodge near Agate Pass, a pleasant cruise from Seattle across Puget Sound and around the northern tip of Bainbridge Island. At the dock, where we paused to await the launch to Dick White's Kiana Lodge, the masts of sailboats at their moorings fenced off the sky. There must have been several hundred, and their number could have been duplicated at any of the thousand other marinas in the Seattle area. We were nearly an hour getting over to the lodge, passing through bays and inlets and hearing the voices of people enjoying themselves along the tree-shaded shores. It was one of those evenings of perfect visibility when Seattleites say that "the mountains are out." Mount Rainier, now the color of butterscotch, rode high above the horizon to the southeast; Mount Baker, frosty and imperious, stood off to the northeast. Even after sunset both peaks glowed like embers.

We walked the length of a long dock and followed a path along the water's edge to the lodge, a low log building. Dick White, an ebullient fellow with an equally ebullient Great Dane at his side, greeted us at the front door. Then he took us, drinks in hand, on a tour of the place, which —as is so often the case in the Pacific Northwest—involved going right outdoors. In the blue twilight around us all colors were intensified. The flowers had richer, deeper hues than they ever seem to have in full light. White's hobby is raising begonias and fuchsias. Red, yellow, pink, white begonias as big as saucers hung from baskets suspended in the trees, and the fuchsias arched out of their pots like explosions of red and purple fireworks. The grounds have an Indian motif, with tall totem poles standing here and there among the trees; and at some distance from the lodge,

nestled in a grove of cedars, there is a replica of an Indian long house.

Now Dick led us through the twilight to the lawn behind the lodge. Here he was preparing a salmon barbecue, one of the great culinary institutions of the Puget Sound area. He anointed a cut-up salmon with herbed butter, and laid piece after piece on a wire grill; over the fish he fixed another grill so that the salmon slices were sandwiched between. Then he lowered the grills over the white-hot ashes of a fire of green alder wood. The key to the success of a salmon barbecue is timing. After a couple of minutes, Dick lifted the grill high above his head. Satisfied that the fish was cooked on the underside, he turned it over. Two minutes later the salmon was done, and we hurried back to the lodge to eat it. The fish was crusty on the outside, hot, tender and moist inside, permeated slightly by smoke. The pie we had for dessert was equally simple and good: a baked crust into which fresh raspberries had been poured and covered with a quilt of whipped cream.

Each day we became more aware of how much the cooking of the Pacific Northwest is predicated on freshness. Like the seafood, the vegetables were fresh and full of flavor, and the fruit was irresistible. Indeed, one of the most striking of the many meals we ate consisted largely of fruit. It was a brunch at Snoqualmie Falls Lodge, perched above the thundering falls a few miles east of Seattle. The view there was so distracting —with the torrent gushing from the cliff and plunging 270 feet to the pool below, where it burst into mist and rainbows—that we did not at first notice the inordinate number of plates and glasses on our table. Then our waitress wheeled up a cart and began to arrange before us the bountiful morning repast: pitchers of cold orange juice, big bowls of

At Snoqualmie Falls Lodge, a famous restaurant 26 miles from downtown Seattle, brunch is a rousing meal with a special emphasis on fresh fruit, usually locally grown. Along with bacon, ham, eggs, hashed brown potatoes, biscuits, toast and pancakes, there are blueberries, strawberries, raspberries, grapes, pineapple, melon and—the bruncher's appetite willing—baked apples.

strawberries, blueberries and sliced peaches, platters with crescents of watermelon, cantaloupe and Cranshaws, plates with bunches of green and purple grapes, and a pan of baked apples from which the juice was beginning to ooze.

While we tried to make our choices from all this, the waitress confounded us by saying that she would be back soon with "the rest of the brunch." I followed my daughter Elisabeth's example by having a little of almost everything. Her younger sister Marissa, for whom strawberries and blueberries were new experiences, devoted herself to mastering the difficult art of picking blueberries up in her fingers without dropping them—not a simple task.

When the waitress reappeared I asked her where the fruit had been grown. Most of it—at least the apples, peaches, grapes and melons—had come from Yakima, she said, about a hundred miles away. Then she laid before us, as she had promised, the rest of the brunch: hot oatmeal, followed by fried eggs and bacon, fried ham, sausages, corn fritters, hashed brown potatoes and pancakes. Our waitress then passed around a basket of hot biscuits and invited us each to take one, as part of the ceremony of the fireweed honey, a ritual for which Snoqualmie Falls Lodge is famous. She dipped into a pot of honey with a spoon, and wound some of the honey around it; then she stood back and poured the honey onto my plate from a height of about three feet. It fell off the spoon in a thick, wavering ribbon—a fall of honey that is supposed to simulate the flow of the waterfall—and came to rest in a cone on my plate. The honey was viscous, almost chewy; it had been cooked for seven hours to thicken it and concentrate its flowery flavor.

The combination of natural beauty with nature's bounty of food seemed to epitomize the Pacific Northwest. And while the scenery cannot be moved, the food is something everyone can experience. The food of the Pacific Northwest is one of the most movable of feasts, and far more people partake of it outside the region than most of us realize. Nearly half the pears and a quarter of the apples grown in the United States come from there, as well as tons upon tons of strawberries, raspberries, blackberries, sweet cherries, peaches, apricots, plums, walnuts and filberts. In addition, the Pacific Northwest raises 85 per cent of the nation's soft wheat and 100 per cent of its lentils. Even America's beer depends for its flavor on the hops grown in Washington, Oregon and Idaho. An irony of this gargantuan productivity is that only about 15 per cent of the entire region (excluding British Columbia) is cultivated; mountains and lack of sufficient rain render the rest of the land unusable or fit for little besides cattle and sheep raising.

The abundance of fresh fruit has had a direct effect on the cooking of the Pacific Northwest. More good preserves, relishes and chutneys are produced here than in almost any other part of North America. The desserts are some of the richest turned out anywhere. Cakes, cookies and breads are all the tastier for the inclusion of apples, pears, cherries and other fruit. The pies run with juice. Among the Swiss-Americans of the region it is still the custom to dry their own pears and plums and use them in a spicy, rolled *Kuchen*—and pears drying in a slow oven for a couple of

Continued on page 76

73

Dining Alfresco in the Pacific Northwest on Food from the Beach

Perhaps nowhere in America do people eat outdoors more often and more easily than in the Pacific Northwest. Natural beauty, a mild, refreshing climate and an abundance of good local foods combine to make alfresco meals a rich experience for families like that of the Stewart Ballingers of Seattle, who regularly lunch on the deck of their summer house at Enetai in Puget Sound. For the Ballingers, part of the fun lies in gathering much of the food themselves from the beach outside their home. As their contribution to one meal, the Ballinger children and their friends dug the first course, native littleneck clams *(left, top)*, and washed off the mud *(left, bottom)*. Mrs. Ballinger cooked the clams in a steamer and served them with melted butter. The rest of the meal *(opposite)* consisted of cracked Dungeness crab, homemade mayonnaise *(Recipe Index)*, garlic bread, chilled white wine, fresh fruit and boysenberry pie, a popular dessert in the Pacific Northwest. And at the end, there were few dishes to clean—the luncheon plates were paper.

The Oregon Cheddar cheese called Tillamook, one of the finest of all Pacific Northwest cheeses, is produced by the Tillamook County Creamery Association, a dairy cooperative. Made from the rich milk of cows that graze almost all year long on green grass, Tillamook is generally aged from six to 12 months. It goes well with such local fruit as the Delicious apple and table grapes shown here.

days can fill a house with sweet odors. Perhaps the most famous candies of the Pacific Northwest are the sugar-dusted Aplets and Cotlets. They are made from either apples or apricots (hence their names), sugar and walnuts, and resemble the Middle Eastern confection called Turkish delight; in the Aplets I think I detect the slightest trace of rose water, a favorite flavoring of the Middle East.

Many of the fruits and vegetables are grown inland, east of the Cascades. To have a look at apple and pear country I headed for the Wenatchee Valley, Washington's chief apple-producing district. From the air the thick carpet of forest covering the Cascades seemed to fray away as the mountains changed from green to arid brown. The Yakima region, source of the fruit at our Snoqualmie brunch, presented a desert landscape, green only where irrigation waters had penetrated. And Wenatchee itself looked like the wide-open West of cowboy movies, complete with sagebrush. Could this be apple-growing country? It was entirely different from the verdant orchard regions of New York State.

Now I could understand why people speak of two separate Pacific Northwests—a wet one and a dry one. Running north and south, the Cascades form a great barrier that cuts off the flow of damp air from the Pacific and leaves the inland region parched. Some sections receive as little as seven or eight inches of rain a year (the apple-growing districts of New York get over 40), yet the lack of rainfall does not hurt fruit production. The extended sunshine and warmth help keep down blight. Massive irrigation systems bring water to the trees when water is needed, and in the correct amount. These factors, plus a deep, fertile soil, rich in minerals, make the zone between the Cascades and the Rockies one of the world's finest fruitgrowing basins.

Wenatchee, a city of 17,000 people, sits in the middle of a sea of orchards. It is a town that apples built, and apples are everywhere in evidence, on signs, on postcards, and in baskets and boxes. The air smells of them and in the spring, at the annual Apple Blossom Festival, the whole valley is saturated with the perfume of the white and pink flowers. When I visited the orchards, harvesting had not yet begun, but the fruit hung heavy on the trees, ripe and firm, dragging down whole branches that had been propped up to keep them from breaking. The apples were mostly Delicious and Winesap, which account for 85 per cent of Washington's apple production.

The red Delicious apple, easily recognized by its bright red color, tapering body and five knobs at the blossom end, came into existence more than a century ago, almost by chance. Jesse Hiatt, a farmer in Madison County, Iowa, chanced upon an apple seedling of unknown origin during the late 1860s. In 1870 he cut down the tree because it had grown "out of the row"—but the next year it was up again, stronger than ever. "If you must live, you may," said Jesse, and over the years he nurtured the tree to blossom and fruit. The apples, like none that he had seen or eaten, were of remarkable sweetness and flavor, and in 1893 he entered some in a competition sponsored by a nursery. The judges were entranced by the new apple, but when they went to look for the name and address of the entrant, they saw that the label had come off his basket. Convinced that such an apple could revolutionize the fruit industry, they held a similar competition the following year in the hope that the same man would enter his apples again. He did—and the rest is apple history.

The Winesap, the other prime apple of the Pacific Northwest, also has a red skin, sometimes tinged by shades of greenish yellow; it can be eaten raw, baked whole or in a pie, or cooked into fluffy sauce. Another important variety, the well-named Golden Delicious, has a tender rich-yellow skin, sometimes touched with a blush of delicate red; this apple is becoming increasingly popular as a delicately flavored fruit to eat whole or slice into salads. Three other major apples produced in the Pacific Northwest are the crimson Rome Beauty, the rosy-red Jonathan and the greenish-yellow Newtown. The Rome Beauty is the best of baking apples, while the Jonathan and Newtown are excellent both fresh and cooked.

None of these apples is easy to grow, and in the Pacific Northwest they are coddled rather than merely cared for. The orchards are laid out according to a plan and schedule, and the stock is selectively uprooted and renewed to assure superb crops. In the spring, beehives are taken to the orchards so the bees can help pollinate the blossoms. After fertilization has taken place, each tree is meticulously sprayed with a chemical that destroys all but the "king blooms." A king bloom is the largest flower in each cluster of five, and it ordinarily produces the biggest and finest apple; with its competition eliminated, it can do even better. Later on, after fruiting, the smaller apples are removed by hand to provide extra nourishment and energy for those that remain. (Pomology, the study of fruit cultivation, is an exact science; orchard owners know and use such information as the fact that for each apple there must be 30 to 40 leaves for maximum fruit development.) When the apples begin to ripen and are ready to fall, they may be sprayed with a hormone that keeps them on the tree another two weeks or so, allowing them to store up every last bit of goodness. Picked at the peak of perfection, with a gentle twist of the hand and an upward thrust of the thumb, the apples are washed, buffed, sorted and—in especially precious varieties—individually wrapped in tissue. The process is much the same for pears, with one major difference. Pears do not ripen to perfection on the tree; they must be picked when they are slightly immature and allowed to grow soft and juicy at room temperature. A pear that is left on the tree too long may become mushy, gritty and inedible.

From Wenatchee and Yakima I went to Oregon's Rogue River Valley, the Pacific Northwest's greatest pear country. The area had a gentility about it that might seem out of character but is not, for in this valley fruit-growing once was considered a gentleman farmer's occupation. The dream of the earliest growers was to plant an everbearing orchard, go off around the world and then drop by for the annual harvest; the trees were supposed to do all the work. With such a plan in mind, many young scions of Eastern establishment families went west to live off the fruit of the land—and soon were jolted into reality. Raising fruit is a year-in, year-out, never-ending job. Those who stayed in the valley left the mark of their culture on the region, for few of them ever had all that time for travel. Ashland is partly a resort town; every summer it holds an outdoor

At the home of Wally Huntington, a Portland, Oregon, landscape architect, an all-Pacific-Northwest meal receives its last-minute touches. The menu includes tiny Oregon shrimp, Columbia River caviar, Dungeness crab, Olympia oysters, broiled Columbia River sturgeon, baked Idaho potatoes and Brussels sprouts. Every dish is made with special care; the sprouts, for example, shown being served to Mrs. Mirza Dickel (*opposite*), are peeled *after* cooking so that their hearts remain crisp and green.

Shakespeare festival that is one of the oldest events of its kind in North America, and one of the finest. Close by is the town of Jacksonville, a well-preserved piece of Victoriana, lovingly maintained. Medford, the shipping and canning center of the Rogue River Valley, is an attractive, well-laid-out city that brings New England to mind.

Located in Medford are the Bear Creek Orchards, home of the successful mail-order food business called Harry and David's, which has done much to spread the reputation of Pacific Northwest fruit all over the United States. To visit this operation is to see the *crème de la crème* of the orchards. There are Comice pears as big as softballs, with their greenish-yellow skins brushed with red and their flesh so juicy and so soft that they are best eaten with a spoon. Their full French name, *doyenne du Comice*, means "the best of the show." But many people are just as impressed by the plump golden Bartletts, the yellow Anjous and the russet Boscs, all fine eating pears, and perfect companions for cheese and wine. While we were sampling pears, the pickers were at work in the orchards, standing on tapered aluminum ladders and reaching through the leaves to get at the fruit. They plucked the pears as if they were fragile jewels, gently depositing them in canvas bags.

The Northwest's fruit industry grew out of the homesickness of the people who first settled there. This remote corner of Western America was a new and alien world to them, and they missed the cultivated fruit that they had taken for granted back home. According to some accounts, the first apple tree in the Pacific Northwest sprang from a seed brought

all the way from London in 1824 by Captain Aemilius Simpson. At a farewell banquet in his honor a young lady, more or less as a joke, slipped some apple seeds into his pocket and bade him plant them in the wilderness. Some time after his arrival at Fort Vancouver, in what is now the state of Washington, Captain Simpson handed the seeds over to Dr. John McLoughlin, who was then the chief agent of the Hudson's Bay Company in the Pacific Northwest. Delighted by the gift, Dr. McLoughlin entrusted the seeds to his gardener, who planted and nurtured them under glass. The lone tree that grew from these seeds was carefully protected. "At first there was one apple on it," recalled Dr. McLoughlin's daughter in later years, "and that everyone must taste . . . but the second year we had plenty."

Though Dr. McLoughlin's apple tree was the progenitor of many others, the real Johnny Appleseeds of the Pacific Northwest were two enterprising Iowans, Henderson Luelling and William Meek. Luelling headed west in 1847, carrying the stock for a nursery in soil-filled boxes in his wagon. Transporting the delicate cargo across country was not easy. Every night the plants had to be watered; when the oxen pulling the heavy wagons grew tired and footsore, Luelling and his family fell back behind the wagon train and traveled on alone at a slower pace. In the settlement of Milwaukie, at the head of the Willamette Valley, he went into partnership with Meek, who had arrived with stock of his own and a bag of apple seeds. Together they founded a nursery.

So strong was the craving of the pioneers for familiar fruit that people

Dessert at Wally Huntington's dinner is a Bartlett pear *(above)*, poached in ginger sauce and topped with a mixture of brandy and whipped cream; the rich dish is complemented by a glass of sparkling champagne. Pacific Northwest pears are famous for their taste; the area produces a quarter of all the pears that are sold in the United States.

RED BARTLETT
Marketed only in recent decades, the Red Bartlett is similar to its better-known older cousin *(right)* in all ways but the color of the skin. Not widely grown, this pear fetches a premium price.

BARTLETT
Lord of all pears, the Bartlett occupies 75 per cent of American pear-producing acreage. Sweet, juicy and tender, it is as versatile as it is popular—equally good when canned, baked or eaten raw.

FORELLE
Of French origin, the Forelle turns a predominantly golden yellow color as it ripens, and acquires a faint blush and tiny red freckles. It is prized for its decorative effect rather than its tart flavor.

BOSC
With its graceful taper and its unmatched sweetness, the Bosc has become the nation's third-best-selling pear, after the Bartlett and the Anjou *(right)*. Its long season lasts from September to March.

Each a fit candidate for a Cézanne still life, the eight varieties of pear seen here include time-tried as well as as experimental strains produced by growers in the Pacific Northwest. The right combination of soil and weather helps make the region ideal for cultivating the fruit in a great range of shapes, tastes and textures.

came from all over the region to view the first apples to be produced on a Luelling-Meek tree; when new stock became available, many paid as much as a dollar apiece (good money in those days) for the trees. By the early 1850s, enough trees had been planted and were bearing fruit to supply a booming California market. Fruit shipped to San Francisco in theft-proof ironbound crates fetched almost incredible prices; in 1853, for example, a shipment of four bushels was sold for $500 there. But the Californians soon began to plant orchards of their own; the demand for the fruit of the Pacific Northwest waned and prices dropped. A new industry might have been nipped in the bud had not the coming of the Northern Pacific Railroad in 1883 made it possible to ship Pacific Northwest fruit to other markets. As the industry prospered, the orchards spread out from the eastern mountain valleys into the dry interior, where irrigation made fruitgrowing possible.

Idaho's long and twisting Snake River plain was dismissed by Washington Irving as "vast desert tracts that must ever defy cultivation." A bad prophecy: much of the plain is now one vast vegetable garden, watered by a network of irrigation canals and ditches. (In the mountains behind Boise, I saw an enormous reservoir literally drained dry by the crops; the water had gone down like beer in a glass, leaving successive rings around the sides.) As in the fruitgrowing regions of Oregon and Washington, the soil is a rich volcanic ash, ideally suited for raising those giant Idaho potatoes that bake into fluffy softness.

Elsewhere in the plain was more abundance. Large sweet onions with

ANJOU
Like the Bosc, a winter pear, the Anjou was first developed either in France or Belgium. When ripe it may be yellow, yellowish green or green. Its buttery flesh gives it appeal as a fresh dessert fruit.

COMICE
Another favorite during the cold months, although easily bruised, the Comice is the juiciest of all pears, often eaten with a spoon. Its full name—*Doyenne du Comice* —means, roughly, "best in show."

SECKEL
By a fluke of history the Seckel is so called for its second discoverer, not its first, a Pennsylvanian named Jacobs. This miniature pear wins its warmest kudos when it is either pickled or brandied.

ELDORADO
A newcomer, the Eldorado is a native of California. Its tree is hardy and blight resistant, and the fruit can be stored even longer than the Bartlett, which it may some day challenge in popularity.

white papery skins lay in the fields in long parallel rows like twisted ropes of pearls; the air smelled as though a great pot of delicious soup was on the boil. Close by was a field of emerald peppermint, ready for cutting; in the warm sunshine it, too, threw off a pleasant bouquet. Beyond the mint lay another field, with a pungency of its own—the tangy, unmistakable scent of hops. Strung on wire trellises, the hop vines rose 20 feet into the air, and the ruffled green flowers dangled down. Across the road a red harvesting machine advanced slowly, ferreting out potatoes. The odor of damp, freshly turned earth somehow reminded me of the rich smell of potatoes baking in an oven.

Everywhere it was a land of plenty, bearing food for millions of mouths. But the most interesting demonstration of what man, machinery and water had wrought was in a custom cannery in Nampa, 20 miles from Boise. Here some of the women of the area were dealing with the problem of what to do with the surplus produce of their kitchen gardens and fields. Their solution was to can it—but not for storage on the shelves of their own pantries. Instead, they were sending it overseas for distribution among the needy of foreign countries. Only a few decades ago this Snake River plain was an out-of-the-way corner of our nation, locked between high mountains and almost empty of man and his works. Lonely American farmers had struggled here to tame a wilderness. Now their descendants had food enough and to spare—enough to send as a gift beyond the mountains, beyond the continent, to share with people struggling to survive in other lands.

Yellow Rice with Cold Fruit and Curry Sauce

To serve 6

FRUIT

1 pint (about 2 cups) fresh ripe
    strawberries
1 pint (about 3 cups) fresh ripe
    blueberries
1 pound (about 3 cups) fresh ripe
    sweet cherries
1 small ripe honeydew melon or
    cantaloupe
4 medium-sized firm ripe peaches
1 tablespoon fresh lemon juice

YELLOW RICE

2 tablespoons butter
2 cups uncooked long-grain white
    rice (not the converted variety)
1 quart boiling water
¼ teaspoon finely crumbled saffron
    threads or ground saffron
8 whole toasted almonds

CURRY SAUCE

1 cup dry white wine
2½ cups chicken stock, fresh or
    canned
2 tablespoons curry powder
2 tablespoons cornstarch
2 tablespoons cold water
¼ cup seedless raisins

Pick over the strawberries, blueberries and cherries one at a time, removing any stems or caps and discarding any fruit that is badly bruised or shows signs of mold. If you like, pit the cherries. Wash the fruits separately in a sieve or colander under cold running water, then shake them dry and spread on paper towels to drain.

Cut the melon in half crosswise, and scoop out the seeds with a spoon. With a melon baller, shape the melon meat into balls.

With a small knife, peel the peaches and cut each of them lengthwise into quarters. Discard the stones. Drop the peach quarters into a small bowl, add the lemon juice to prevent discoloration, and turn the peaches about with a spoon until they are evenly coated. Then combine the strawberries, blueberries, cherries, melon balls and peach quarters in a serving bowl, cover with foil or plastic wrap and refrigerate until ready to serve.

In a heavy 3- to 4-quart saucepan, melt the butter over moderate heat. When the foam begins to subside, add the rice and stir for 2 or 3 minutes, until the grains glisten with butter. Do not let the rice brown. Stir in the boiling water and saffron, and bring to a boil over high heat. Cover tightly, reduce the heat to low, and simmer for about 20 minutes, or until the rice is tender and has absorbed all the liquid in the pan.

While the rice is simmering, prepare the sauce in the following fashion: Combine the wine, chicken stock and curry powder in a small enameled or stainless-steel pan and, stirring frequently, bring to a boil over high heat. Reduce the heat to low and simmer for 2 or 3 minutes. In a small bowl or cup, stir the cornstarch and cold water together to make a smooth paste. Then, stirring the curry mixture constantly, pour in the cornstarch in a slow, thin stream and simmer until the sauce thickens lightly and is smooth. Stir in the raisins.

Spoon the rice into a 1-quart mold or deep bowl, packing it in firmly with the back of the spoon. Then place an inverted serving plate over the mold and, grasping plate and mold together firmly, turn them over. Rap the plate sharply on a table and the rice should slide out easily. Arrange the toasted almonds attractively on top of the rice. Pour the sauce into a bowl or sauceboat and serve it with the yellow rice and the fresh fruit.

Chop Suey Dessert Sauce

To make about 1½ cups

¾ cup sugar
1½ cups water
¼ teaspoon red food coloring
½ cup coarsely chopped pitted
    dates
½ cup coarsely chopped dried figs
½ cup coarsely chopped walnuts

Combine the sugar and water in a 1- to 2-quart enameled or stainless-steel saucepan and bring to a boil over high heat, stirring until the sugar dissolves. Cook briskly, uncovered, until the syrup reaches a temperature of 220° on a candy thermometer. Stir in the food coloring.

Combine the dates, figs and walnuts in a bowl, pour in the hot syrup, and stir until all the pieces are evenly moistened. Spoon the sauce into a jar equipped with a tight-fitting lid. Cover and store at room temperature. The sauce will keep up to 3 weeks. Serve it with ice cream.

A selection of fruit—cherries, blueberries, peaches, strawberries and melon balls—is served with saffron rice and curry sauce. The recipe was created at the turn of the century for the family of James Beard.

The Farm House Restaurant near Port Townsend, Washington, features a buffet service of salads in an almost infinite variety.

To make about 2 dozen 1-inch
round drop cookies

2 tablespoons butter, softened
2 tablespoons cornstarch
½ pound filberts (1½ cups)
1 cup sugar
3 egg whites

Filbert Macaroons

Preheat the oven to 350°. With a pastry brush, spread the softened butter over two large baking sheets. Then sprinkle each of them with a tablespoon of the cornstarch, tipping the sheets from side to side to spread the cornstarch evenly. Turn the sheets over and rap them sharply on a table to remove the excess cornstarch. Set them aside.

Spread the filberts out on a cookie sheet or jelly-roll pan and roast in the middle of the oven for 20 minutes. Transfer to a damp kitchen towel and rub with another damp towel to remove the skins. Pulverize the peeled nuts in a blender or nut grinder.

With a large mortar and pestle or in a deep bowl with the back of a wooden spoon, pound the pulverized filberts and sugar together. When they are well combined, beat in the egg whites one at a time and continue to pound until the doughlike mixture is smooth and thick enough to hold its shape almost solidly.

Reduce the oven temperature to 300°. Drop the dough by the tablespoonful onto the prepared baking sheets, spacing the macaroons about an inch apart. Bake in the middle of the oven for about 30 minutes, or until the macaroons are a delicate golden brown and firm to the touch. With a large metal spatula, immediately transfer the macaroons to wire racks to cool. In a tightly covered jar or tin, the filbert macaroons can be kept safely for several weeks.

Great Northern Bean Salad

To serve 10

If you plan to use canned beans, drain them of all their canning liquid, wash them thoroughly under cold running water, drain again and pat dry with paper towels. If you plan to cook the beans yourself, place them in a large saucepan and pour in enough cold water to cover them by at least 2 inches. Bring to a boil, let them boil for 2 minutes, then turn off the heat and let the beans soak for 1 hour. Bring back to a boil, lower the heat, partially cover the pan, and simmer as slowly as possible for 1½ hours, or until the beans are tender but still intact. Drain the beans in a fine sieve and place them in a large bowl.

With a wire whisk, beat the garlic, mustard, salt, pepper and vinegar together in a small bowl. Add the oil gradually and continue to beat until the dressing is smooth and thick. Pour over the beans, cover with plastic wrap, and refrigerate for at least 2 hours.

Taste for seasoning. Just before serving, gently fold in the celery, pickles, onions, sour cream and mayonnaise.

2 cups dried Great Northern beans, or 5 cups canned white beans
2 teaspoons finely chopped garlic
2 teaspoons prepared mustard
1 teaspoon salt
¼ teaspoon freshly ground black pepper
2 tablespoons red wine vinegar
6 tablespoons olive oil
1 cup coarsely chopped celery
1 cup finely chopped sweet gherkin pickles
1 cup finely chopped red onions
1 cup sour cream
2 cups freshly made mayonnaise (*Recipe Index*)

Spinach Soup

To serve 6 to 8

In a 3- to 4-quart enameled or stainless-steel saucepan, bring the chicken stock to a boil over high heat. Add the spinach, reduce the heat to low, and simmer partially covered for 7 to 8 minutes. Then pour the contents of the pan into a sieve set over a large bowl. Press down hard on the spinach with the back of a wooden spoon to extract all of its juices. Set the stock and the drained spinach aside separately.

Melt the butter in the saucepan and stir in the garlic and onions. Cook over moderate heat for 3 to 4 minutes, stirring frequently, until the onions are soft and translucent. Add the reserved chicken-spinach stock and bring to a boil, then stir in the spinach, nutmeg, salt and pepper. Partially cover the pan and simmer the soup over low heat for about 5 minutes, stirring occasionally. Taste for seasoning and serve at once from a heated tureen or individual soup bowls, garnished with chopped egg.

2 quarts chicken stock, fresh or canned
2 pounds fresh spinach, washed and coarsely chopped
4 tablespoons butter
½ teaspoon finely chopped garlic
1 cup finely chopped onions
⅛ teaspoon ground nutmeg
1 teaspoon salt
¼ teapoon white pepper
2 hard-cooked eggs, finely chopped

Oriental Salad

To serve 4

Place the rice, chopped anchovies, scallions, pimiento and tomato in a serving bowl and toss together thoroughly with a fork.

With a wire whisk, beat the vinegar, mustard, salt and a few grindings of pepper in a small bowl until the mustard has dissolved. Add the oil gradually and continue to beat until the dressing is smooth and thick. Taste for seasoning, pour the dressing over the rice mixture, and stir with a fork until the ingredients are well combined.

For each serving, arrange several lettuce leaves to form a cup on a chilled plate and spoon the salad into the lettuce cup.

If you prefer, you may pack the salad firmly into a 2-cup mold, cover tightly with plastic wrap, and refrigerate for 2 hours, or until thoroughly chilled. Just before serving, remove the plastic wrap and place an inverted plate over the mold. Grasping plate and mold together firmly, quickly turn them over. The molded salad should slide out easily. Surround with the lettuce and serve at once.

½ cup raw long-grain white rice, boiled, drained and cooled
A 6-ounce can flat anchovy fillets, drained, rinsed under cold water and coarsely chopped
½ cup finely chopped scallions
½ cup finely chopped pimiento
1 firm ripe tomato, sliced ¼ inch thick and cut into ¼-inch dice
2 tablespoons red wine vinegar
½ teaspoon dry mustard
1 teaspoon salt
Freshly ground black pepper
6 tablespoons olive oil
Chilled crisp lettuce leaves

To serve 4 to 6

1½ teaspoons salt
1 pound fresh green string beans,
    trimmed and washed
3 tablespoons red wine vinegar
½ teaspoon dry mustard
Freshly ground black pepper
½ cup olive oil
12 firm ripe cherry tomatoes
1 large red onion, peeled and cut
    crosswise into ⅛-inch-thick
    slices and separated into rings

To make about eighteen 3½-inch
pancakes

1½ cups uncooked rolled oats
2 cups milk
1 cup flour
2 tablespoons dark-brown sugar
2 teaspoons double-acting baking
    powder
1 teapoon salt
3 eggs, lightly beaten
4 tablespoons butter, melted and
    cooled
¼ cup vegetable oil

To serve 8 to 10

2 tablespoons butter
1 cup finely chopped onions
1 teaspoon finely chopped garlic
2 quarts chicken stock, fresh or
    canned
2 cups (1 pound) dried lentils
1 medium-sized firm ripe tomato,
    chopped and puréed through a
    sieve or food mill, or substitute
    ½ cup canned tomato purée
½ teaspoon crumbled dried basil
Freshly ground black pepper
2 hard-cooked eggs, finely chopped
½ cup finely sliced or chopped red
    radishes
½ cup finely chopped scallions
    (optional)

Green Bean Salad

Bring 3 quarts of water and ½ teaspoon of salt to a boil in a large enameled or stainless-steel pan. Drop in the beans and boil briskly, uncovered, for about 10 minutes, or until they are tender but still slightly
resistant to the bite. Drain the beans and transfer them to a serving bowl.

With a wire whisk, beat the vinegar, remaining salt, mustard and pepper together in a small bowl. Still whisking, slowly pour in the oil; continue to whisk until the mixture is smooth. Pour the dressing over the
beans, and add the tomatoes and onions. Toss the ingredients together
lightly with a wooden spoon, then cover the bowl with plastic wrap and refrigerate for at least 2 hours before serving.

Oatmeal Pancakes

Place the oats in a deep bowl, pour in the milk, stir well, and set aside
until all the milk has been absorbed. Meanwhile, combine the flour, brown
sugar, baking powder and salt, and sift them together onto a plate or a
sheet of wax paper.

Add the eggs to the oats mixture and mix with a large spoon. Then
sprinkle the flour mixture over the top and stir it in. Add the melted butter and stir only long enough to blend the batter. Do not overmix.

With a pastry brush dipped in the vegetable oil, grease a griddle or
heavy skillet lightly and heat it until a drop of water flicked onto it splut-
ters and evaporates instantly. Pour the batter from a pitcher or small
ladle into the hot pan to form pancakes about 3½ inches in diameter.
Cook for 2 or 3 minutes over moderate heat, until small, scattered bubbles have formed and begun to break on the surface of the cakes. Immediately turn them with a spatula and cook for a minute, until the other
side of the pancake is brown. Stack on a heated plate or platter and repeat the whole procedure, stirring the batter gently and oiling the pan
for each batch of pancakes until they are all cooked. Serve the pancakes
hot, accompanied by butter and maple or fruit syrup.

Cold Lentil Soup

In a heavy 3- to 4-quart saucepan, melt the butter over moderate heat.
When the foam begins to subside, add the onions and garlic and, stirring
frequently, cook for about 5 minutes, until they are soft and translucent
but not brown. Stir in the chicken stock, lentils, puréed tomato, basil and
a few grindings of pepper, and bring to a boil over high heat. Reduce the
heat to low and simmer partially covered for 1 hour.

Rub the soup through a fine sieve into a bowl with the back of a spoon,
or put it through the finest blade of a food mill. Cool to room temperature, cover with foil or plastic wrap, and refrigerate the soup for at least
2 hours, or until it is thoroughly chilled.

To serve, ladle the soup into a chilled tureen or individual soup plates.
Mound the chopped hard-cooked eggs, radishes and scallions (if used) attractively in separate bowls and present them with the soup.

Green beans, sweet red onions and lentils are three of the important
vegetables of the Pacific Northwest. Here the beans and onions have
gone into a crisp salad, the lentils into a cold, creamy summer soup.

IV

Blessings from the Sea

The rocky coast of the Pacific Northwest offers a great variety of seafood treasures. Along beaches like this one, near the Hecata Head Lighthouse in Oregon, there are clams and oysters; in the offshore waters are crabs, shrimp and fish, including five species of salmon.

My family and I ventured to the edge of the cliff for a view of the Pacific at Otter Rock, Oregon. We looked out—and then down, our eyes drawn by the activity of another family, their heads bent, moving as aimlessly as sleepwalkers among the tidal pools. If they spoke, we could not hear them in the roar of the surf.

It did not take long to find out what they were doing. A steep path took us down to the beach, a great stretch of clean white sand broken by sea-green boulders. Soon we too were engaged in that delightful Pacific Northwest occupation—beachcombing. Our take was small: a few stones, a fragment of blue glass worn smooth by sand and water, a sliver of driftwood; but every item was a treasure. We would even have carried away some of the dried tubes of giant kelp lying about, if there had been room in our car. Such kelp does not exist in the East, and we remembered being told that the Indians of the Pacific Coast once used the tubes as containers for seal and fish oil.

Had there been time we would have pursued even rarer treasure, the colored glass floats that break loose from fishermen's nets and drift to shore. All along the shores of Oregon and Washington we saw houses and shacks decorated with them, and the owners could tell us which had come from Japan and which from Russia.

But if the glass balls eluded us, another kind of coastal treasure was within our reach. The beaches and offshore waters of the Pacific Northwest contain many hidden riches—clams, oysters, crabs, shrimp and fish of all sorts, sizes and flavors. The coastline, if Alaska and British Columbia are included, runs some 45,000 miles. It is indented with innumerable bays and fjords and dotted with islands that offer the shallow sheltered places needed by many fish and shellfish to grow and reproduce. Below the ocean's ruffled surface the continental shelf provides a vast platform on which all sorts of aquatic life can flourish.

It is on the beaches, however, that a newcomer becomes aware of Pacific Northwest seafood. They offer some of the most dramatic scenery in the West, with wind-whipped cliffs and outcroppings of rock; behind them rise tree-clad hills and mountains or, in Oregon, billowing dunes of white sand. The people who wander the shore know its many moods but are ever amazed by the way these moods can shift from hour to hour.

In winter a bizarre army, bundled up and armed with "clam guns," takes to the beaches. The guns are no more than slender shovels, yet they are weapons nevertheless, used to capture one of the most elusive and delicious of all shellfish, the Pacific razor clam. The razor clam lives along sandy, wave-washed shores from California's Pismo Beach north to the Aleutians. At maturity, it measures about five inches long and from one and a half to two inches wide. It has a thin, lacquerlike shell with sharp edges; diggers must grasp it from the hinged side, which always faces toward the ocean. What makes the razor difficult to seize is not its cutting edge but its ability to work its way down into wet sand as fast as nine inches a minute. (This rate may not seem speedy—but just try to capture a razor clam with water streaming into the hole.) To beat its hasty retreat the clam extends an appendage resembling a leg and strong muscles pump water into the tip, which flares out like a nailhead. Using the tip as an anchor, the clam pulls itself down with another set of muscles and slips deeper and deeper into the sand.

Razor clams are generally sought at low tide, and they are difficult to locate under the smooth sand. But they can be made to "show," as local people say, if the digger jumps up and down or pounds the sand with the clam gun—which adds a touch of madness to a scene already surreal. As the clam retreats, it leaves a small depression—the "show"—in the sand, and the moment this is spotted the digging begins. The shovel is plunged in on the ocean-side of the show, and the sand quickly lifted out. One or two shovelfuls are usually enough to bring the prize into sight—and then the trick is to grab the clam before it disappears.

The clams may be opened by dipping them briefly in a pot of boiling water. Some people say this toughens the flesh and pry them open instead. They are then plunged into cold water, and the delicate white meat is scooped out. Since the meat is slippery, most cooks dry it with paper towels; they then dip it in beaten egg, roll it in cracker crumbs, and sauté it quickly in a quarter inch of oil or butter or both. Some cooks prefer to dredge the clams in dry pancake flour. The idea is to cook the meat as little as possible—just to the point where it is pale gold on the outside. The flavor is subtle yet rich, like that of scallops.

Hardly as nimble as the razor but a lot more difficult to come by nowadays is the geoduck, a ridiculous clam with an impossible name, pronounced "gooey duck," from a Nisqualli Indian word meaning "dig deep." And dig deep is what people must do to get these clams. They hide in muddy or sandy areas at depths anywhere from 18 inches to three feet. The ridiculous thing about them is their enormous neck, or siphon, which may stretch as much as three feet long. The necks are too long and big to be withdrawn fully into the geoducks' shells, but they can be retracted so quickly that geoducks sometimes give the illusion of retreating swiftly into the sand when actually they are not moving at all.

Heavy digging has reduced the numbers of these clams, and they are now generally found only on beaches laid bare by very low tides, from California to British Columbia's Queen Charlotte Islands. Catching them is an even more absurd-looking sport than pursuing razor clams. A favored method calls for the use of a 10-gallon can open at both ends. The can is driven down around the clam and the sand dug out. This often requires the digger to get down on more than hands and knees; some people lie flat, then disappear head and shoulder into the can. What is more, grasping a geoduck is quite a sensation; not for nothing is it called "gooey."

In the state of Washington, a clam hunter is legally permitted to take three geoducks daily, but one may prove more than enough. Some weigh three pounds, and there is little waste. The neck, which is tough, is usually ground for chowder, and the body is sliced into thin steaks, pounded to tenderize the meat, and fried.

The shore of the Pacific Northwest is much more than a cabinet of shellfish curiosities; plenty of less exotic clams exist and all are fun to dig and eat. At least three native types abound. There are the littlenecks, or rock clams, which measure no more than two and a quarter inches across. (The East Coast littleneck is actually a quahog.) There are butter clams, which are similar to quahogs but not so tough, and live up to their name in taste. Amid the native clams live some others that were introduced to the Pacific Northwest either by intent or accident. One is the Japanese littleneck; another is the Eastern softshell, or mud clam, which, despite its popularity in its original habitat, is often overlooked here.

The thought of an Eastern clam like the softshell settling happily into Western waters pleases me, for it may inspire more people to adopt the fine old New England custom of the clambake. Actually, there are good grounds for calling the clambake a Western institution, too. The Indians of the Pacific Northwest used to build large fires in which they heated stones. After the flames died down they would place leaves on the stones, add clams, mussels and fish, pour water on them, and cover them with a mat to steam. Cooked in this fashion, the fish and shellfish were from all accounts delicious, perhaps the finest of Indian foods.

Euell Gibbons, a nature writer who apparently will eat anything so long as it is wild, conjures up a vision of what a true Pacific Northwest clambake might be like in his book *Stalking the Blue-eyed Scallop*. He would fill a "steaming trench of Rockweed with Western Razors, sweet Washington Butter Clams, Dungeness Crabs, boneless strips of king salmon each wrapped with a sliver of onion in a corn husk, and maybe a mighty Geoduck as the *pièce de résistance*, surrounded by new white potatoes and tender young sweet corn." Sounds possible; sounds good.

While native clams abound, only one oyster is native to the Pacific Northwest. It is the prized Olympia, an inch and a half long, with a thim-

Continued on page 95

A Furious Treasure Hunt for Fine Fat Clams

The five-inch Pacific razor clam (*right*) is a bizarre-looking creature, but there is nothing odd about its meat, which is white, rich and somewhat like that of scallops in flavor. To capture this prize, hordes of earnest diggers pursue the razor clam on the sandy beaches of Oregon and Washington. Few diggers are more avid than those who compete in the Great International Clam Prix every spring at Ocean Shores, Washington. At the crack of a starting gun, they rush down to the beach and begin to dig frantically (*left*); the first contestant to get back to the starting line with 18 clams wins $250. Corraling those 18 clams is no easy feat: a razor clam can burrow into the sand at the rate of nine inches a minute, and the edges of its thin, lacquered shell are as sharp as its name suggests.

Nets and shovels flying, participants in the Great International Clam Prix tear up a stretch of beach in their search for elusive razor clams. To flush out their quarry, some diggers jump up and down on the beach or pound the sand with their "clam guns," or shovels. A disturbed clam will retract its neck, causing a telltale little dimple called a "show" to form in the sand.

bleful of meat inside. I have watched these tiny oysters being shucked, and I could see that it was tedious work, which explains why so few people bother to gather them. But what the Olympia lacks in size it more than makes up in flavor—a distillation, seemingly, of all the world's oysters. It is grand when eaten raw, with a drop of lemon juice and black pepper.

Olympias cling to rocks in sheltered tidal waters of the Pacific Northwest (outside of Washington, in British Columbia, Oregon and northern California, people call them native oysters). They are raised commercially in the southern Puget Sound area behind dikes that offer protection from extremes of weather. Such coddling pays off: in their plump maturity, Olympias fetch up to two dollars for a four-ounce jar.

Over the years other kinds of oysters have been transplanted to the Pacific Northwest and done well; in fact the Pacific oyster, which arrived from Japan in 1902, is now the mainstay of the oyster industry. It is about three times the size of the Olympia and has gone wild wherever conditions favor its reproduction. In the Strait of Georgia, in British Columbia, yachtsmen go ashore and literally rake in their suppers.

Clams and oysters are only part of the Pacific Northwest's shellfish riches. Scallops also exist along the coast and are rightly prized by cooks with the good sense—and good taste—to gather them. The deep-water scallops of southern Alaska are so big—about eight to the pound—and so numerous that they have led to the development of a new industry at Seward, which now calls itself the Scallop Capital of the Pacific.

One kind of shellfish I had not expected to encounter in the Pacific Northwest was abalone. Having eaten it only in California, I had somehow assumed that this pearly-shelled mollusk wanted no part of colder waters. But abalone grow all the way north to Alaska, and though they are smaller and darker-fleshed than those found to the south, they are every bit as good to eat. We had sautéed abalone served to us in British Columbia by a couple who go down to the beaches at "minus tide," when the water is at its lowest level, and pry a few from the rocks with tire irons.

The horde of shellfish does not stop at the low-tide mark. Out in the deeper waters of the Pacific live the crabs—the Dungeness, the Alaska king crab and the snow crab. Many people rate the Dungeness as the finest crab not only of the Western Seaboard, but of all North America. An argument is easy to develop on this score, but even I—an Easterner and a lover of flaky blue crab—must concede that the Dungeness has points in its favor. Its size (in Washington a Dungeness must measure at least six and a quarter inches across its shell before it can be legally taken) is really the least of its virtues. Its meat is sweet and firm, whether it is eaten plain or enveloped in the creamiest of sauces.

Dungeness is the basis of a flourishing industry on the West Coast. California, Oregon, Washington, British Columbia and Alaska all compete for it. Californians tend to think it belongs to them, forgetting that it is named for the town of Dungeness on the Olympic Peninsula in Washington, where commercial fishing for this crab is said to have started. I must admit that when I visited the place, I almost felt like bowing.

While the reputation of the Dungeness crab is confined largely to the West Coast, that of the Alaska king crab has spread across the continent

Clams found on both the West and East Coasts lend themselves to a variety of dishes. Combined with sweet corn, they can be used in either a creamy chowder or a light soufflé (*opposite*); a spoonful of the hot, fluffy soufflé is shown above.

95

The edible crabs of the North Pacific include the succulent Dungeness *(above)*, about nine inches across the shell and the most popular crab along the West Coast; the snow, with meat-filled legs a foot or more in length *(right)*; and the king, a prickly-shelled giant, shown on the aproned lap of an Alaskan cannery worker *(opposite)*. The king leads the three in sales across the country, largely because its meat is adaptable to the freezing methods that make shipping over long distances possible; but its numbers are declining. Fishermen are turning to the snow, which is now being taken in greater numbers. Some connoisseurs rate its sweet meat above that of the king.

and even to Europe. Part of this success story has to do with smart merchandising and the fact that the meat freezes well and can be shipped long distances, but another part has to do with the king crab itself. It is an amazing creature: males weighing 15 pounds with leg spans of four or five feet are still caught, and occasionally a 25-pound giant measuring six feet across will turn up. I have watched king crabs scrambling around in a tank at the Wakefield Seafoods plant in Seldovia on the Kenai Peninsula in Alaska. They hobbled over each other, brown prickly legs flailing and claws scissoring at the air like monsters in a science-fiction movie.

Unlike the Dungeness, the king crab lives only in the cold waters off Alaska's southern and northwest coasts and seems not at all discomfited by temperatures that may fall below 32°F. in the ice-covered Bering Sea. The few daring skin-divers who have braved the deep to take a look at them have brought back startling tales. During their first two or three years of life the crabs have the habit of piling one on top of another to form a structure called a pod. As many as 6,000 may thus assemble, with the top layer disbanding and crawling down over the others to feed on the ocean floor. A diver who approached a disbanded pod found he could herd the crabs in any direction he wanted, but when he came too close, they reared up on their third and fourth pairs of legs and slashed out at him with their claws.

At the Wakefield plant I watched king crabs being processed. Dispatched one at a time by a steel blade that also eviscerated them, they were briskly boiled for 25 minutes, then relayed by conveyor belt into a

96

large, clean, well-lit room. Here a small army of men and women in yellow aprons and red rubber gloves handled the cooked crabs on an assembly-line basis. One girl did nothing but squeeze segments of crab legs through a wringer device that popped white meat out of the fiery red shells. (Most of the meat is in these legs; a single segment can yield a chunk seven inches long and an inch and a half wide.) In minutes, the crabs were reduced to their edible parts—legs, tails, claws and tidbits—and packed in boxes, ready for freezing. Surrounded by so much crab, I found myself getting hungry, and helped myself to a chunk of leg. It was mild and juicy, still warm from cooking and very similar to lobster.

Another crab of Northern Pacific waters, smaller than the king, is the snow crab. Its long spindly legs are also filled with snowy meat. Nobody knows how many snow crabs there are in Alaskan waters; the number may well be in the hundreds of millions. This resource is only beginning to be tapped. Eventually, it may be the basis of a fishery as flourishing and lucrative as that of the king crab.

Last but not least of the Northern Pacific's shellfish attractions are shrimp—in several varieties and sizes. The largest is the prawn, which can grow nine inches long; the smallest and by far the most numerous is the tiny pink shrimp, a succulent nugget that occurs in two separate species, one off the coast of Oregon, Washington and British Columbia, the other from British Columbia north to Alaskan waters. I especially favor the pinks; in my opinion the tinier they are the finer they taste. To bring out the best of their flavor they should be shelled one by one—and the work is worth the trouble. I still vividly recall eating Alaskan pink shrimp at Kodiak the way I like them—and the way a great many Westerners cook them. My host tossed them by the handful into boiling salted water, let them rise to the top and scooped them off, an operation that took a minute. We sat with a pink mound of rosy shrimp in front of us, nudging off the shells with our fingers and devouring crescent after crescent of sweet flesh until all were gone.

While the shrimp of the Pacific Northwest are available year round, many fish of the region seem to come and go—disappearing for months on end, then suddenly reappearing out of the depths, fat and ready for the pot. For me, this makes them all the more precious. With all the frozen foods we have at our disposal—indeed, with all the vegetables and fruits that seem to be more plentiful out of season than in—a lot of the excitement has been drained from eating. I like seasons and what they bring —in food as well as weather—and in this respect Northwestern cooks are blessed. They live close to nature and the sea; they know when the salmon are running and when the smelts are spawning. They avail themselves of the ocean's riches as these riches become available.

When my wife and I last visited the Pacific Northwest, we saw signs announcing salmon derbies almost everywhere we went, and the newspapers were filled with the names of anglers and the weights of the fish they had caught. The lure of a big salmon—and of the even bigger prize money —had men, women and children thronging the riverbanks and cluttering the tidal waters in dories. At towns like Westport, Washington, the activity began well before sunrise, almost as though a D-Day launching was in progress, and built to a crescendo, punctuated by the cries of sea gulls, the metallic clatter of tackle boxes being shifted about and voices that went shrill as rackety outboard motors started up.

"The salmon are running!"—and what could be more exciting? The very thought that these noble fish are stirring out there, under the blank black surface of the water, stirs me. The idea that the salmon will soon crowd up the rivers kindles my appetite. There are few things more deliciously rewarding to eat than fresh-caught fish of any kind, and fewer still that can match the taste and texture of a bright-eyed, red-gilled, silver-scaled, clean-smelling salmon only an hour or two out of the water.

No fewer than six kinds of salmon abound in the Pacific, and five of them can be found on the North American side of the ocean, from Alaska to California. Where salmon are so numerous and so varied, it is only natural that they should be known by several names, but these names can be confusing. Within a single species, for example, the Chinook is also called the king, spring, quinnat and tyee. What one calls each species of salmon, in fact, depends to a large extent on where one lives—or what one does. Scientists refer to the five species as *tschawytscha* (commonly called Chinook), *kisutch* (coho), *gorbuscha* (pink), *keta* (chum) and *nerka* (sockeye). I mention these scientific names not because they are tongue twisters, but because they are Russian—a reminder that the Russians once roamed this coast in search of fish as well as furs.

Of these five salmon species, the Chinook is the biggest. A ravenous feeder, it weighs on the average between 15 and 20 pounds and is a fantastic fighter; a man with a 30-pound tyee on the line is in for a battle (any Chinook 30 pounds or over is called a tyee, the Chinook jargon for chief). The Chinook ranges from California's Sacramento and San Joaquin Rivers to the Bering Sea, but it occurs in greatest concentration in the Columbia River. The explorers Lewis and Clark, canoeing down the Columbia in October, 1805, literally shoved their way through fish that had returned to the river to spawn. "The number of dead Salmon on the Shores & floating in the river is incredible to say," wrote Clark (who was a lot better at exploring than he was at spelling), "and at this Season [the Indians] have only to collect the fish Split them open and dry them on their Scaffolds."

Smaller than the Chinook but almost as impressive a fighter is the coho, or silver, salmon, a beautiful sight to behold as it leaps glittering from the water. It can weigh between six and 15 pounds, which makes it an ideal fish to cook whole. The third salmon to interest the sportsman is the pink, or humpback, named for the ridge of cartilage that forms on the male's spine just before spawning time. Averaging three to five pounds, it is the smallest of the five species, but scrappy nonetheless. The pink can be tasty eating; many cooks in the Puget Sound area wrap it in cheesecloth, poach it in salted water with bay leaves and then serve it with a creamy egg sauce.

The two remaining salmon species are the chum, or dog, and the sockeye. Both feed on tiny marine plants and animals, and are rarely taken by anglers. The flesh of the chum is pale pink or yellowish white; that of the sockeye is dark red. The sockeye makes a particularly fine product for canning because of its oily richness and excellent flavor.

In Washington alone nearly 850,000 pounds of salmon are caught each year by sport fishermen. What cannot be eaten fresh is preserved, mostly by canning or smoking. This practice has given rise to a delightful institution, unique to the area, the custom cannery. Here people bring their catch, leave it and come back later to pick it up, packed in tins. I visited one such place, capable of turning out 1,500 cans of salmon a day, at Sekiu on the Olympic Peninsula. The young man and woman who run it charge 20 cents a can—slightly more if the customer wants the fish smoked first—and provide labels with blanks for the fisherman to fill out. Many people save this personalized product to give away at Christmas or send to friends living outside the Pacific Northwest.

Salmon is often smoked at home, in smokers ranging from old refrigerators and barrels to specially equipped sheds. Two methods of smoking, hot and cold, are employed. For both, salmon fillets are first steeped in brine for two or more hours, drained, and then dredged in salt. After the desired degree of saltiness is reached, they are rinsed and placed on racks to dry in the open air. (Drying allows a pellicle—a thin skin or film—to form on the flesh, sealing in the moisture that would evaporate during the smoking.) Then, for hot smoking, the fillets are placed close to a fire of hickory or other hardwood for a couple of hours at temperatures between 150° and 250°. Hot-smoked salmon is delicious, but since it is cooked it will not keep. Cold smoking involves a much longer process and yields a product that can be stored without re-

A translucent sidestripe shrimp caught at Seldovia, Alaska, displays the red banding that gives it its name. The species, which inhabits waters from Alaska to California, grows as long as five inches. Though of excellent quality, the sidestripe is so perishable that it must be cooked soon after being taken.

frigeration as long as the weather remains fairly cool. In this method, the fillets are hung or placed on racks as far from a low, smoldering fire as the size of the smokehouse permits, and left there for several days at temperatures ranging from 70° to 90°—hence the term cold smoke. A salmon cured either way is one of the finest delicacies of the Pacific Northwest.

One of the oldest methods of preserving salmon is simple salting. This involves layering salmon fillets in a crock or keg with a quarter inch of coarse salt in between. After three days the fillets are taken out and washed, and the container is drained; then the fillets are put back in and covered with a strong brine. Salmon preserved this way must be soaked before being eaten, but are excellent cooked for breakfast or a light supper and served in pink, flaky wedges with boiled potatoes.

Salmon can also be pickled, as I happily discovered on a visit to Astoria, Oregon. Dr. Ed Harvey, of the state's Otter Trawl Commission, takes some of the fresh salmon it is his great good fortune to receive each year from fishermen friends, cuts it in pieces, and puts the pieces down in jars with vinegar, onions, bay, peppercorns, mustard seed and cloves. The richly spiced sour chunks *(Recipe Index)* are marvelous to chew—exuding a juice that incites the appetite all the more.

If salmon reigns supreme, it has its challengers in other fish of the Pacific Northwest. Certainly as far as fighting fish go there is none to match the steelhead, a kind of rainbow trout that, unlike its fresh-water brethren, spends most of its life in the sea. The steelhead is related to the Atlantic salmon, and shares with that distant kin the ability to spawn more than once. When it begins its winter run, a Northwestern malady known as steelhead madness sweeps through the populace. Streams and rivers fill with fishermen in waders, ready to face bone-chilling water and driving rain for the chance of hooking a "steelie." Rod Belcher, a Seattle sports announcer on TV and radio, speaks with fervor about his first encounter with a steelhead. "Unlike most of the breed, my steelie decided to head upstream. Up and up he went, tearing out yards of singing line, up over rapids, around a bend—and suddenly my line went limp. So did I. I had never seen the fish, but I had felt its surge of wild energy, and then and there I became a dedicated steelheader. It was a month later that I landed my first steelie—a six-pound beauty that was traveling up the Skykomish —and now, instead of being just dedicated, I was a hopeless addict."

Halibut, too, has its partisans, though it is not commonly caught by anglers. An Indian woman once told me that her ancestors had held halibut in higher esteem than salmon, perhaps because this big, floppy flatfish with its bulging eyes was harder to catch. Halibut were, and still are, plentiful in Northwestern waters, but they dwell along the bottom of the sea. They support a thriving commercial fishery second only to salmon, and their firm, dry, clean-tasting meat, either fresh or frozen, is shipped all over the continent. Halibut range in weight from so-called "chickens," weighing from five to 10 pounds, up to "whales" of 80 pounds or more. Some may weigh as much as 400 pounds and measure eight feet long; invariably these specimens are females. The big halibut are filleted or sliced into steaks, while smaller ones are occasionally sold whole.

More than a dozen other kinds of flatfish also live on the ocean floor.

Opposite: A sleek silver salmon lies with red roe in a basket on the wharf of a cannery in Kodiak, Alaska. The salmon will be processed for domestic consumption, and the roe will be shipped to Japan (in boxes like the one at top, supplied by Japanese importers), where it is prized as a great delicacy.

In the Pacific Northwest, sports fishermen who have caught more salmon than they can eat often take the surplus to "custom canneries." The can shown here, packed at a small cannery at Sekiu on the Olympic Peninsula, carries a typically personalized label.

Chief among them, as far as cooks are concerned, are the petrale sole, the sand dab, the lemon, or English, sole (it has a delicate lemon flavor) and the Dover sole. Just to confuse matters, not one of these is a true sole; all belong to the flounder, or dab, family. They are mild, lean fish, with delicate flesh that is best cooked simply and quickly. I remember with some amusement a petrale sole amandine that I was served in Oregon. The cook meant well, but the brittle slivers of almond encrusting the fish formed a coating almost as hard and thick as a pavement. How much more enjoyable is an Oregon variation on the same dish, in which the delicate filberts or hazelnuts grown there replace the almonds.

Even more varied than the flatfish are the rockfish. At least 50 species exist in the northeastern Pacific, 33 off Washington and Oregon alone. They are strange looking, with large heads and spiny dorsal fins that can inflict painful wounds when handled carelessly, but they are excellent eating. Some of the most popular are the orange, red and black, and the "Pacific Ocean perch"—which is, of course, not a perch. All have white, solid flesh, bland in flavor, and when filleted may be sautéed in butter, broiled, fried or poached.

There is cod aplenty in the Pacific as well—but not all of it is really cod. Both the tom cod and the true, or gray, cod are correctly designated, the true being closely related to the Atlantic species that was long a mainstay of the poor people in Southern Europe. But neither the lingcod nor the black cod are related to their namesake, or to each other. Lingcod is a long, narrow fish that may grow as long as five feet and weigh 20 pounds or more; its meat is lean and white. The so-called black cod—its correct name is sablefish—has extremely fatty flesh and is absolutely marvelous when smoked. I had it whenever I could find it in Alaska and British Columbia, where it is poached in milk and served in golden flaky pieces, with melted butter glistening in the crevices.

The surf, or silver, smelt and the Columbia River smelt, or eulachon, are two other fish of renown. There must be billions of them in the Pacific Northwest. Surf smelts are netted on sandy beaches when the tide is at its highest, and a legal limit—generally no more than 25 pounds—is imposed upon the daily catch. (That can still add up to a lot of fish, since a smelt weighs only about an ounce.) The eulachon come sweeping into rivers and smaller streams in glittering hordes so thick that people can scoop them up with anything from dip nets to cooking pots. Both types of smelt become crisp on the outside when fried—the usual way of cooking them—but remain soft and moist inside.

Manifestly, fishing is one of the great industries of the Pacific Northwest. Clustered all along the coast are fishing towns with sheltered harbors and rows of canneries that lend color as well as flavor to the entire area. My wife's oldest brother Ernie lives with his Australian wife Mollie in just such a town, Prince Rupert, in northern British Columbia. They love the place, and I can understand why. There is an exhilaration to life here, something about the blueness of the sea and the endless activity of boats coming and going that gets under one's skin. The view from Ernie's house unfolds across the bay; the eyes sweep past forest-covered mountains and islands to the high, cloud-filled sky. We have sat in the rich honey-tinted

102

light of long summer evenings eating supper and watching the fishing boats return to port against the backdrop of the setting sun. Seen from miles away, they inch forward as in a slow-motion film, minting a trail of gold behind them.

The first time Liet and I visited Prince Rupert we had visions of all the fresh fish we were going to eat—only to be confronted by a great irony. As far as Ernie and Mollie knew, there was no fish available in this community of 2,000 fishermen. But they had moved to Prince Rupert only recently; failing to see any fish in the markets, they had assumed that it was all being canned or frozen for shipment elsewhere. They have since learned otherwise; what they do not catch themselves from their own sailboat they now buy for a small sum at the Fishermen's Co-operative.

Imagine the joy of going to a pier and getting a fish from the man who caught it! I accompanied Ernie to the co-operative a couple of times, and on our first visit we sought out Pete de Greef, a young fisherman of sturdy Dutch stock. He was a little late getting back from the fishing rounds, and we took advantage of the wait to look around. Tied up at the pier were some of the tidy, compact boats we had seen from Ernie's house as they streamed into the bay. None was really large; most fell into the 35-foot class, while the largest might have been 45 feet long.

As we walked along the pier we caught sight of Pete's boat, the *Lilimak II,* chugging across the bay to its berth beside an unloading platform. It is a troller, a type of vessel much used in British Columbia waters to harvest salmon. Trollers are equipped with six steel lines, with as many as seven lures attached to each line. As the boat plows slowly ahead the lures sweep through the water at different levels; when a salmon strikes, the line is reeled in and the fish taken off the hook. Trolling differs from

Juicy pickled salmon provides a refreshing, unexpected cocktail snack or light meal. For the version shown here, a hot marinade that includes onions, vinegar, olive oil, peppercorns, mustard seeds, cloves and bay leaves is poured over chunks of fresh salmon, and the fish is allowed to steep for 24 hours.

103

In the clear, fresh light of early morning, a commercial fishing boat called a troller glides to its berth at Prince Rupert, a major fishing port in northern British Columbia. Like all fishermen, a troller captain takes his chances; in a single tour at sea, which can last up to a week, he may take as few as a hundred or as many as a thousand pounds of salmon. Because they are taken individually with hook, line and lure rather than a net, troller-caught salmon have a high reputation for quality and are generally free of the bruises and scrapes of net-caught fish.

such other methods of commercial salmon fishing as gill netting and purse seining in that the fish are caught individually. In gill netting, fish simply swim into the meshes of a net that is hung like a curtain behind the drifting boat; their gills become entangled as they try to escape, and the catch is then hauled on deck. In purse seining, a huge net is dropped into the sea around a school of fish and the bottom is drawn shut like a string purse. Large numbers of salmon are captured by purse seiners, and there is often a handsome profit for the crew of three to eight men to divide. But there are risks, too: a lost or badly damaged net can cost $5,000 to $10,000 to replace.

Pete saw us standing on the platform and waved. He was the stereotype of the fisherman—big, red-cheeked, raw-knuckled, dressed in yellow oilskins and black boots with the glitter of fish scales on them. He opened the hatch and we went down into the hold. There lay several dozen Chinook and coho salmon, bright bars of polished silver, and partially visible through a thin covering of crushed ice were the milk-white bellies of halibut. With the help of his younger brother Billy, serving temporarily as his deckhand, Pete began to unload. I had not expected that halibut to be so large—but when they slithered onto the platform, I stepped back. Some were four or five feet long. The man whose duty it was to sort them out by size lifted each fish into his arms as though he were cradling a mermaid and tossed it gently into one of several waiting carts.

Fish need proper handling from the moment they are caught, and the Fishermen's Co-operative has laid down strict rules for its members to follow. Sport fishermen, especially those who value good food, could learn from these rules. Pete stuns a fish while it is still in the water, to prevent it from thrashing about and damaging itself as it is hauled onto the deck.

104

Along with salmon, white-bellied halibut is an important commercial fish of the North Pacific. In the picture above, a worker at the Prince Rupert Fishermen's Co-operative sorts halibut by length before putting them on the scales. Though some of these halibut are half as long as the sorter himself, they fall into the 40-to-60-pound, or medium, range. Smaller specimens, weighing from five to 10 pounds, are called chickens; giants of 125 pounds or more are called whales.

He deals it another blow to end its struggles, and promptly bleeds it to enhance its firmness and keeping power. He cleans it as quickly as possible, knowing that to wait is to invite disaster—for within an hour, stomach acids will begin to eat into the flesh. He is also careful to cut away the gills and remove any blood clinging to the throat, the spine and the V-shaped cavity near the vent.

The salmon Pete picked out for us was, of course, a beauty. He first held up a 30-pound Chinook, which next to his own bulk seemed smaller than it really was. But 30 pounds was a lot more than we needed, and we gladly settled for a six-pounder. Pete would not let us pay for it but insisted that we take it, a gift from the sea.

We accompanied him into the plant where his catch was being weighed and I asked about his life as a fisherman. Laughingly he suggested I talk to his brother Billy about that. Billy had recently won local fame by having his one-man boat sink under him, swamped from astern by a wave. Certain he was a goner, he had strung a red float around his neck and climbed the mast. When a search party found him he was still clinging to that mast—to the very tip of it, up to his neck in icy water.

Actually the life of a fisherman in British Columbia is never easy. The season gets under way as early as February and lasts until August, and the boats are out all day, sometimes for days on end, in every kind of weather. Pete and Billy start off by fishing for Chinooks—springs, they call them. In May they troll the sea bottom, looking for halibut as well as salmon. By mid-June, the cohos are running. When I talked to the brothers, it was August, and they were bringing in whatever they could get. During a regular season, Pete can gross between $20,000 and $25,000, but from this he must pay his expenses, including the salary of a deckhand. Billy,

with his smaller boat, can gross $10,000 to $12,000. In the rare year when tuna appear off the coast, their income can soar.

That night Ernie and I, rather than our wives, did the cooking. We took the salmon Pete had given us and prepared it in a paper bag according to Evil Alice Powell's method, as I had learned it in Alaska. But Alice had not told me how long to leave it in the oven, and my sister-in-law then stepped in with a foolproof rule worked out by the Canadian Department of Fisheries. No matter what the fish or how you are going to cook it, measure the body at its thickest part and cook it 10 minutes to the inch. Our salmon was three inches thick, and we gave it 30 minutes, at 450°. We ate it in butter-dripping sections, with a dressing of sour cream and freshly snipped dill. And the fish that had been swimming in the sea that morning was soon reduced to a pile of bones.

The seafood we enjoyed in the Northwest was once revered by the Indians as their virtual staff of life. Fish and shellfish made up three quarters of the coastal Indians' diet, and three quarters of this seafood was salmon. Being so dependent upon it, the Indians prayed each year for its return. Some believed that the salmon belonged to a race of tiny people who swam to them from a magic place under the ocean. But the Indians had no qualms about eating it, doubtless because they were sure the force that had guided it from the ocean would enable it to return as a spirit.

All sorts of superstitions sprang up around the year's first salmon run. The Chinook Indians believed, for instance, that anyone involved in preparing a corpse for burial could drive the fish away, and to avert this danger they went so far as to bury the infirm alive. They also believed that menstruating women—as well as girls who had just reached physical maturity—were tainted, and would not permit these women and girls to partake of the salmon lest the fish retreat from the river or disappear altogether. The first salmon caught in the first run was cooked according to a time-hallowed method, by roasting the head, roe and back on separate spits. Even after the end of the first run, the Indians continued to treat salmon respectfully. "Upon catching a fish," an observer wrote, "they immediately take out his heart and conceal it until they have an opportunity to burn it, their great fear being that this sacred portion . . . may be eaten by dogs, which they shudder to think would prevent [the salmon] from coming again to the river."

At the Portland Art Museum I gained some impression of how much the ocean's bounty had meant to the Indians when I came upon a dish they had used to hold seafood. It was two feet high and more than 14 feet long. Not only was it the biggest dish I had ever seen, but the strangest, and I walked around it to take it all in. It had been carved from a single cedar log, in the shape of a reclining woman, with her elbows, buttocks and feet resting on the ground. Her chest, abdomen and head had been hollowed out to serve as receptacles, and her head was covered by a mask that doubled as a lid. On her knees rested two wooden bowls; at her feet were three more, each at least two feet long. The whole wonderful, bizarre creation served a ceremonial function at the feast of giving called the potlatch, once common among coastal tribes from northern California to southern Alaska.

Opposite: A version of bouillabaisse, the great seafood stew of France, is prepared at Cannon Beach, Oregon, with local ingredients that give it a new and piquant character. The Oregon dish *(see seafood stew, Recipe Index)* contains salmon, lingcod, halibut, shrimp, native littleneck clams and Pacific crabmeat. A meal in itself, the stew is accompanied only by hot garlic bread and icy white wine.

The potlatch was a curious institution. It left bare not only the host's cupboard, but often his house as well. He gave his guests almost everything he owned, for the more he gave the more important he would seem. But he also knew that eventually he would be repaid in kind—and with interest—when his guests invited him to *their* potlatches. Gifts ranged from canoes to animal skins, and though these were distributed according to the recipients' rank in the social order, no one, no matter who he was, ever left a potlatch empty handed.

Certainly no one left hungry. Food was laid out in abundance, more than could possibly have been eaten. The dishes were varied, and at this distance in time, a certain poetry attaches to the menu. There was salmon, of course, and halibut, roasted or boiled; if boiled, the fish would be wrapped in leaves or birch bark to keep the flesh from flaking apart in the cooking water. Herring or salmon roe sometimes were eaten with tender sprouts of berry bushes, acorns and fern root. There were also eulachon, which were so fatty that when they were dried and threaded with cedar-bark wicks they burned like candles.

A missionary who attended several potlatches wrote a less than romantic account of what the food was actually like. First came berries, "preserved in grease and mixed with snow." Then came dried salmon and halibut, which the guest was expected to eat with oil, accompanied by boiled seaweed mixed with fish and fish oil. This course was followed by a dessert of bitter berries beaten to a froth. The Indians spooned up the white foam, squeezed it through their lips to expel the air and sucked the mash back in—a technique, the missionary observed, that produced "an unusual sound." He felt constrained to add that a European attempting to follow the Indians' example "is seldom successful, and must be prepared to be greeted with salvos of laughter at his failure."

The traditional potlatch died out generations ago, victim in part of its own conspicuous consumption; the Indians long since have adopted many of the white man's methods of preparing food—and the white man some of theirs. The Indians now may cure salmon lightly, as Europeans have done for centuries; white men may leave it in the smokehouse a couple of weeks to darken, the way the Indians used to do. Or it can be cut into strips, salted, smoked and dried to make a preparation called squaw candy, which is as chewable as a licorice stick and a lot more satisfying. But surely one of the pleasantest ways of preparing salmon is to cook it, Indian style, in front of a fire. An Indian woman from Vancouver Island showed me how her people did this. She took two thin strips of alder wood wired together top and bottom, slipped a split salmon between the strips, and flattened the fish by inserting splints across the front and back. So arranged, the salmon looked like a large pink leaf, and the woman planted it in front of a pile of embers to cook. She deviated from tradition in only one way: instead of dowsing the fish in strong-flavored eulachon or seal oil, she slathered it with butter and lemon juice. When the salmon was done, she served me the choicest piece. To my surprise, it turned out to be not the middle section but the thin flat part closest to the tail. "It has no bones," she explained with a smile, and never did an old tradition seem more practical—and more gracious.

Opposite: At Blake Island State Park, a 45-minute boat ride from Seattle, Nellie George, an Ahousaht Indian from British Columbia, demonstrates her ancestors' way of cooking salmon. After cleaning and flattening the fish, Nellie inserts it between two upright poles and braces it with splints. The poles can be slanted toward or away from the fire to regulate the speed of cooking.

Pickled Salmon

Combine the vinegar, water, olive oil, onions, bay leaves, mustard seeds, cloves, and white and black peppercorns in a 2- to 3-quart enameled or stainless-steel saucepan. Bring to a boil over high heat, reduce the heat to low, and simmer partially covered for 45 minutes.

Meanwhile, spread the salmon pieces in one layer on a strip of wax paper. Sprinkle the fish evenly with the salt and let it rest at room temperature for about 30 minutes. Then drop the salmon into a colander and run cold water over it to rinse off the excess salt.

Pat the fish dry with paper towels and pack the pieces tightly into glass or earthenware jars or crocks. Pour the hot vinegar-and-spice mixture over the salmon, ½ cup at a time, allowing the liquid to seep down slowly to the bottom of the jar before adding more.

Cool to room temperature, tightly cover with foil or plastic wrap, and refrigerate the salmon for at least 24 hours before serving. Tightly covered, it can safely be kept in the refrigerator for about a week.

To serve 12 as a first course

2 cups white distilled vinegar
2 cups water
¼ cup olive oil
2 small onions, peeled, sliced into
   ¼-inch-thick rings
2 medium-sized bay leaves,
   crumbled
2 teaspoons mustard seeds
2 teaspoons whole cloves
2 teaspoons whole white
   peppercorns
1 teaspoon whole black peppercorns
5 pounds fresh salmon, boned,
   skinned and cut into 1-inch pieces
1 tablespoon salt

Deviled Oysters

Preheat the broiler to its highest setting. With a pastry brush, spread 1 tablespoon of the melted butter evenly over the bottom of a shallow baking-serving dish large enough to hold the oysters in one layer. In a shallow bowl, beat the egg lightly with a fork or wire whisk. Spread the crumbs over a sheet of wax paper and set aside.

Combine the mustard and water in a heavy 6- to 8-inch skillet and stir to a smooth paste. Bring to a simmer over moderate heat, then drop in the oysters and turn them gently about for 2 to 3 minutes, until they are evenly coated and their edges begin to curl. With a slotted spoon, transfer the oysters to a plate.

When the oysters are cool enough to handle, immerse them one at a time in the beaten egg, then roll them in the bread crumbs. Arrange the oysters side by side in the buttered dish and dribble half of the remaining butter over their tops.

Broil the oysters 3 to 4 inches from the heat for about 30 seconds, until they brown lightly. Turn them over, pour on the remaining melted butter, and broil 30 seconds longer. Serve at once, from the baking dish.

To serve 4

6 tablespoons butter, melted
1 egg
1 cup soft fresh crumbs made from
   homemade-type white bread
2 tablespoons dry mustard
¼ cup cold water
24 shucked medium-sized oysters,
   thoroughly defrosted if frozen,
   then drained and patted dry

Remoulade Sauce

Combine the mayonnaise, mustard and anchovy paste in a deep bowl, and beat vigorously with a spoon until they are thoroughly blended. Stir in the garlic, capers, parsley and tarragon, then gently fold in the chopped egg. Taste for seasoning.

Remoulade sauce may be served as an accompaniment to oysters or clams on the half shell.

To make about 1 cup

1 cup mayonnaise, freshly made
   (Recipe Index) or bottled
2 teaspoons prepared mustard
¼ teaspoon anchovy paste
2 medium-sized garlic cloves, peeled
   and very finely chopped
1 tablespoon capers, drained and
   rinsed in a sieve under cold water
1 tablespoon finely chopped fresh
   parsley
2 teaspoons finely cut tarragon, or
   substitute 1 teaspoon crumbled
   dried tarragon
1 hard-cooked egg, finely chopped

Tiny Olympia oysters, and Pacific oysters as well, may be eaten with lemon juice, Tabasco or horseradish—or dipped into the remoulade, tomato or mignonette sauces shown here *(Recipe Index)*.

To serve 6

2 cups water
¼ cup finely chopped shallots
2 cups fresh watercress leaves,
    tightly packed
½ cup finely chopped fresh parsley
2 teaspoons crumbled dried
    tarragon
4 teaspoons unflavored gelatin
3 egg yolks
4 teaspoons dry mustard
2 teaspoons salt
¼ teaspoon ground white pepper
1½ cups olive oil
2 tablespoons tarragon vinegar
2 tablespoons strained fresh lemon
    juice
1½ pounds freshly cooked king-
    crab meat, cut into 1-inch chunks,
    or substitute 1½ pounds
    thoroughly defrosted and drained
    frozen or canned king-crab meat,
    cut into 1-inch chunks
½ cup finely chopped celery
Bibb or Boston lettuce (garnish)
Watercress (garnish)

To serve 6

1 cup freshly shucked or canned
    minced clams, drained, with
    liquor reserved
½ to ¾ cup milk
4 tablespoons unsalted butter
¼ cup finely chopped onions
5 tablespoons all-purpose flour
5 egg yolks
2 tablespoons finely chopped
    pimiento
1 teaspoon salt
⅛ teaspoon cayenne
6 egg whites
1½ cups corn kernels, cut from
    about 3 large ears, or substitute
    1½ cups canned or frozen
    kernels, drained and thoroughly
    defrosted if frozen

King Crab Salad Ring

Bring 1½ cups of the water to a boil in a small saucepan, drop in the shallots, and cook briskly for 2 minutes. Stir in the watercress, parsley and tarragon, and boil for 1 minute longer. Drain the herbs through a fine sieve, pressing down hard with the back of a spoon to extract all their juices, and discard the juices and cooking water. Chop the drained herbs fine with a knife, then purée them through a food mill into a bowl.

Pour the remaining ½ cup of water into a heatproof measuring cup, sprinkle in the gelatin, and let it soften for 2 or 3 minutes. Then set the cup in a skillet of simmering water and, stirring constantly, cook over low heat until the gelatin dissolves completely. Remove the cup from the heat and let the gelatin cool to room temperature.

Warm a large mixing bowl in hot water, dry it quickly but thoroughly, and drop in the egg yolks. With a wire whisk or a rotary or electric beater, beat the yolks vigorously for about 2 minutes, until they thicken and cling to the beater. Stir in the mustard, salt and white pepper. Beat in ½ cup of the oil, ½ teaspoon at a time; make sure each addition is absorbed before adding more. By the time the ½ cup of oil has been beaten in, the mayonnaise should be the consistency of very thick cream. Beating constantly, pour in the remaining oil in a slow, thin stream. Stir in the vinegar and lemon juice, and taste for seasoning. Then incorporate the herb purée and mix in the cooled but still fluid gelatin.

Fold in the crabmeat and celery thoroughly, and ladle the mixture into a 1-quart ring mold, spreading it and smoothing the top with a spatula. Cover with foil or plastic wrap and refrigerate for at least 3 hours, or until the salad is thoroughly chilled and firm to the touch.

Just before serving, unmold the salad ring in the following fashion: Run a long, thin knife around the edges of the mold to loosen the sides and dip the bottom briefly in hot water. Invert a chilled serving plate on top of the mold and, grasping plate and mold together firmly, turn over. Rap the plate on a table and the mold should slide out easily.

Arrange lettuce leaves around the mold and fill the center of the ring with watercress. Serve at once. If you like, you may further garnish the salad with chunks of cold crabmeat.

Corn and Clam Soufflé

With a large, sharp knife, chop the clams as fine as possible and set them aside. Strain the clam liquor through a fine sieve lined with a double thickness of cheesecloth. Measure the liquor, add enough milk to make 1 cup, then pour into a small saucepan and place over moderate heat. When bubbles appear around the edge of the pan, remove from the heat.

Preheat the oven to 400°. With a pastry brush, coat the bottom and sides of a 2-quart soufflé dish with 1 tablespoon of the butter. Melt the remaining butter in a heavy 1½- to 2-quart saucepan, add the onions, and cook over moderate heat for about 3 minutes, until the onions are soft but not brown. Off the heat, mix in 4 tablespoons of the flour and stir the mixture to a smooth paste. Add the lukewarm milk-and-clam-liquor mixture all at once and beat vigorously with a whisk. Cook over moderate heat, whisking constantly, until the sauce is smooth and very thick. Re-

To make a cool summer salad, tender chunks of Alaska king crab are folded with bits of chopped celery into an herb-flavored mayonnaise. Gelatin is added, and the savory mixture is poured into a mold and allowed to set. For an extra fillip of texture and color, the center of the ring is heaped high with watercress and the dish is presented on a bed of crisp lettuce.

move the pan from the heat and, one at a time, beat in the egg yolks. Stir in the pimiento, salt, cayenne and chopped clams, and taste for seasoning.

In a separate bowl, preferably one of unlined copper, beat the egg whites with a large whisk or a rotary or electric beater until they are stiff enough to form unwavering peaks on the beater when it is lifted out of the bowl. Stir 3 heaping tablespoons of the whites into the clam sauce. Toss the corn with the remaining tablespoon of flour and stir it into the sauce. With a rubber spatula, gently but thoroughly fold in the remaining egg whites until no white streaks show. Be careful not to overfold.

Pour the mixture into the soufflé dish and smooth the top with a spatula. Reduce the oven heat to 375° and bake the soufflé undisturbed in the center of the oven for 35 to 40 minutes, or until it is puffed and lightly brown on top. Serve at once.

Spicy Tomato Sauce

Combine the oil, lemon juice and Tabasco or Pickapeppa sauce in a deep bowl, and beat vigorously with a wire whisk to blend the ingredients. Add the mustard, salt and white pepper, and continue beating until smooth. Then stir in the tomatoes, green peppers, horseradish and shallots, and taste for seasoning. Serve as an accompaniment to cracked crab, or to oysters or clams on the half shell.

To make about 2½ cups

⅓ cup olive or vegetable oil or a combination of the two
3 tablespoons strained fresh lemon juice
2 or 3 drops Tabasco or Pickapeppa sauce
1 tablespoon dry mustard
2 teaspoons salt
1 teaspoon white pepper, preferably freshly ground
6 medium-sized firm ripe tomatoes, peeled, seeded and finely chopped (*see lingcod with garlic and tomatoes, Recipe Index*)
½ cup finely chopped green bell peppers
¼ cup freshly grated horseradish, or substitute ½ cup bottled horseradish, thoroughly drained and squeezed dry in a towel
2 tablespoons finely chopped shallots

113

Shad-Roe Pâté

Wash the roe under cold running water and pat them completely dry with paper towels. With scissors or a small, sharp knife, slit the membranes connecting the pairs of roe. Roll the roe gently in ½ cup of flour to coat them evenly, then shake gently to remove the excess flour.

In a heavy 8-inch skillet, melt the butter with the oil over moderate heat. When the foam begins to subside, add the roe and cook them for about 6 minutes on each side, turning them with a slotted spatula and regulating the heat so that they color richly without burning. Transfer the roe to a bowl and, with the back of a table fork, mash them to a smooth but granular paste.

Add the onions to the fat remaining in the skillet and, stirring frequently, cook for about 5 minutes, until they are soft and translucent but not brown. Stir in the remaining 2 tablespoons of flour and mix well. Then, stirring the mixture constantly with a wire whisk, pour in the cream in a slow, thin stream and cook over high heat until the sauce comes to a boil, thickens heavily and is smooth. Reduce the heat to low and simmer for about 3 minutes. Beat in the lemon juice, garlic, celery seeds, marjoram, tarragon, basil and salt, and taste for seasoning.

Add the sauce to the mashed roe and, with a wooden spoon, beat until the mixture is smooth. Cool to room temperature, cover tightly with foil or plastic wrap, and refrigerate for at least 3 hours, or until thoroughly chilled. Serve the shad-roe pâté as a first course, accompanied by crisp crackers or warm toast.

To make about 2½ cups

2 pairs shad roe (about 1½ pounds)
½ cup plus 2 tablespoons flour
4 tablespoons butter
1 tablespoon vegetable oil
2 tablespoons finely chopped onions
1 cup heavy cream
2 tablespoons strained fresh lemon juice
½ teaspoon finely chopped garlic
¼ teaspoon celery seeds
¼ teaspoon crumbled dried marjoram
¼ teaspoon crumbled dried tarragon
⅛ teaspoon crumbled dried basil
1 teaspoon salt

Marinated Oysters

Place the shucked oysters and their liquor in a 10- to 12-inch skillet and cook uncovered over moderate heat for 2 or 3 minutes, until the oysters are plump and their edges begin to curl. Immediately pour the contents of the pan into a fine sieve set over a large bowl and let the oysters drain. Set the liquid aside. Arrange the oysters in a glass or enameled dish just large enough to hold them in one layer, and scatter the onion and lemon slices evenly over the top.

In a 1- to 1½-quart enameled or stainless-steel saucepan, combine the vinegar, drained oyster liquor and pickling spice, and bring to a boil over high heat. Then reduce the heat to low and simmer uncovered about 8 minutes. Strain the mixture through a fine sieve, discard the spices, and let the liquid cool to room temperature before pouring it over the oysters. Sprinkle them with the salt, pepper, parsley and olive oil, cover tightly with plastic wrap, and refrigerate for two days before serving.

To serve 4 as a first course

2 dozen fresh medium-sized shucked oysters and their liquor
1 medium-sized onion, thinly sliced in rings (about ½ cup)
1 lemon, sliced crosswise into paper-thin slices
½ cup white wine vinegar
1 teaspoon mixed pickling spice
1 teaspoon salt
⅛ teaspoon freshly ground black pepper
¼ cup finely chopped fresh parsley
¼ cup olive oil

Mignonette Sauce

Combine the vinegar, salt and pepper in a mixing bowl, and beat with a wire whisk or a spoon until the salt dissolves completely. Stir in the shallots, then taste for seasoning and serve at once.

Mignonette sauce is served as an accompaniment to oysters or clams on the half shell.

To make about ½ cup

½ cup white distilled vinegar
1 teaspoon salt
2 teaspoons white pepper, preferably freshly ground
2 tablespoons finely chopped shallots

Introduced to the West Coast in 1871, Eastern shad has flourished there ever since. A shad-roe pâté is served here with marinated oysters.

A fresh six-pound salmon is stuffed with a heady mixture of onions, tomatoes and parsley, then covered with strips of bacon.

To serve 6 to 8

2 tablespoons butter, softened, plus
   2 tablespoons butter, chilled
1 teaspoon finely chopped garlic
6 medium-sized firm ripe tomatoes,
   peeled, seeded and finely chopped
   (*see lingcod with garlic and*
   tomatoes, Recipe Index), or
   substitute 2 cups chopped drained
   canned tomatoes
⅛ teaspoon crumbled dried thyme
⅛ teaspoon sugar
3 teaspoons salt
Freshly ground black pepper
A 5- to 6-pound fresh salmon,
   cleaned and scaled but with head
   and tail left on
2 tablespoons strained fresh lemon
   juice
2 large firm ripe tomatoes, peeled
   and cut crosswise into ¼-inch-
   thick slices
1 large onion, peeled, cut crosswise
   into ¼-inch-thick slices and
   separated into rings
1 large green bell pepper, seeded,
   deribbed and cut lengthwise into
   ¼-inch-wide strips
2 tablespoons finely chopped fresh
   parsley
4 thin slices lean bacon

Baked Stuffed Salmon

Preheat the oven to 425°. With a pastry brush, spread the 2 tablespoons of softened butter evenly over the bottom of a shallow baking-serving dish large enough to hold the salmon. (If you prefer to serve the fish from a platter, line a shallow baking pan with a wide strip of heavy-duty foil and let 2 inches extend over the pan at each end. Brush the softened butter over the foil.)

Melt the 2 remaining tablespoons of butter over moderate heat in a 2- to 3-quart enameled or stainless-steel saucepan. When the foam begins to subside, add the garlic and stir for 1 minute. Then add the chopped to-matoes, thyme, sugar, 1 teaspoon of the salt and a few grindings of pepper. Stirring from time to time, cook briskly until the sauce is thick enough to coat the spoon heavily. Taste for seasoning, then remove the sauce from the heat and set aside.

Wash the salmon under cold running water and pat it completely dry inside and out with paper towels. Combine the lemon juice with 1 tea-spoon of salt and rub the mixture into the cavity of the fish. Let the salmon rest at room temperature while you prepare the stuffing.

Combine the sliced tomatoes, onion rings, green-pepper strips, pars-ley, the remaining teaspoon of salt and a liberal grinding of black pepper in a deep bowl. Toss together gently but thoroughly, then fill the salmon with the stuffing. Close the opening with small skewers and crisscross with kitchen string as you would lace a turkey, or sew the opening se-curely shut with a trussing needle and white thread.

Place the salmon in the buttered dish. With a sharp knife, score the top of the fish by making four ½-inch-deep slashes each about 4 inches long and spaced about 1½ inches apart across the body. Insert a thin slice of bacon into each slash, then spoon the reserved tomato sauce evenly over the salmon.

Bake uncovered in the middle of the oven, basting the fish from time

116

The stuffed salmon comes from the oven with a coat of garlic- and thyme-flavored tomato sauce applied just before baking.

to time with the juices that accumulate in the pan. In 40 to 50 minutes the salmon should be just firm when pressed lightly with a finger. Serve at once, directly from the baking dish. Or, using the long ends of foil as handles, carefully lift the salmon out of the pan. Gently slide it from the foil onto a large heated platter and moisten the top with a few spoonfuls of the sauce remaining in the pan.

Seafood Stew

In a heavy 6- to 8-quart casserole, heat the olive oil over moderate heat until a light haze forms above it. Add the onions, celery and garlic and, stirring constantly, cook for about 5 minutes without allowing the onions and celery to brown. Stir in the bay leaves, thyme or basil, saffron, orange peel, parsley and tomato paste, mix thoroughly, then pour in the clam juice, wine and chicken stock. Bring to a boil over high heat, then partially cover the pan, reduce the heat to low, and simmer undisturbed for 30 minutes.

Strain the contents of the casserole through a fine sieve set over a large bowl, pressing down hard on the vegetables and herbs with the back of a spoon to extract their juices before discarding the pulp.

Shell the shrimp. Devein them by making a shallow incision down their backs with the tip of a small, sharp knife and lifting out the black or white intestinal vein with the point of the knife.

Return the strained stock to the casserole and, over high heat, bring to a boil. Then drop in the clams, lingcod, halibut and salmon, lower the heat and simmer uncovered for about 6 minutes before adding the shrimp and crabmeat. Simmer an additional 3 to 4 minutes, or until all the clams have opened and the fish flakes easily when prodded with a fork. Taste for seasoning and serve directly from the casserole or, if you prefer, transfer the stew to a heated tureen or serve in individual soup bowls.

To serve 8

STOCK
¼ cup olive oil
1 cup finely chopped onions
½ cup finely chopped celery
2 teaspoons finely chopped garlic
2 small bay leaves, crumbled
½ teaspoon thyme or sweet basil
⅛ teaspoon powdered saffron
½ teaspoon grated orange peel
2 sprigs parsley
¼ cup tomato paste
1½ quarts clam juice, fresh or
    bottled
2 cups dry white wine
2 cups chicken stock, fresh or
    canned

FISH AND SHELLFISH
½ pound small shrimp
1½ pounds (15 to 20) small hard-
    shell clams, washed and
    thoroughly scrubbed
1 pound lingcod, cut in 2-inch
    pieces
1 pound halibut, cut in 2-inch pieces
1 pound salmon, cut in 2-inch pieces
1 pound lump crabmeat

117

V

The Pleasures of Field and Stream

"The steaks are on!"—and a party on an overnight pack trip into Montana's Glacier National Park waits hungrily at the fire. Arrayed on the rocks is the rest of the meal: tossed green salad, sweet corn, hashed brown potatoes and watermelon—the kind of food that always seems to taste better when it is eaten in crisp mountain air.

Theodore Roosevelt, who hunted often in the vast plains and mountains of the Northwest, once said that only a hunter "can understand the keen delight of hunting in lonely lands." There would come, said Roosevelt, "forever to his mind the memory of endless prairies shimmering in the bright sun; of vast snow-clad wastes lying desolate under gray skies; of the melancholy marshes; of the rush of mighty rivers; of the breath of the evergreen forest in summer; of the crooning of ice-armored pines at the touch of the winds of winter; of cataracts roaring between hoary mountain masses. . . ."

Indeed, with some of the wildest forests, bluest lakes, clearest streams, tallest peaks and broadest prairies on the continent, the Northwest is a sportsman's paradise. Deer roam everywhere; moose, elk and bear live not only in Canada and Alaska, but in the mountain states of Idaho, Montana and Wyoming as well; and on the high crags there are wild sheep and goat. Pronghorn antelope, the swiftest of all American game animals, dart across the flatlands. Pheasant, grouse and prairie chickens scrabble through the grass and grain; migrating waterfowl alight on lakes and rivers in the spring and the fall. Beneath the surface of Wisconsin's waters alone, no fewer than 170 different kinds of fish await the angler —and the cook's decision to pan-fry, poach, broil, bake or smoke.

Almost all these animals and fish were a part of the Indians' diet, and wildlife in untold numbers throughout the entire region helped the first white men to gain a foothold in the wilderness. It may be that there never has been a hardier or healthier breed than the mountain men—the

fried them, and these glorified meatballs now sat piled in a pan awaiting the sour-cream sauce with which they would be cooked *(Recipe Index)*.

Two side dishes had been prepared earlier and needed only reheating. One was wild rice, into which Bud had stirred pearl onions, chopped olives and sliced mushrooms. The other, called sauerkraut pheasant scrap, was largely of Bud's own devising, like many of his dishes. After removing the breasts and thighs of the pheasants, he had boiled the carcasses with celery, onion, thyme, rosemary and chervil, picked the loosened meat from the bones, and added it, with a little of the broth, to a bowl of sauerkraut and whole small onions.

Before things became frenzied in the kitchen, I asked Bud how he had become interested in cooking. "My wife just didn't want to cook the game I shot," he said. "It was as simple as that." (And so it has been for a great many other hunters.) Bud's wife Margaret was standing by, and she nodded. "Margaret's a real good sport—and I've always tried to keep the kitchen neat." Indeed, it was neater than I could have kept it if I had been preparing a meal for a lot smaller guest list than 26. "I'd say we've gotten along pretty good in the kitchen, wouldn't you, Mom?" But then Bud caught sight of his wife's recipe for mulled wine, the drink that was going to be her contribution to the dinner. It was sitting in full view on the counter. "Get that piece of paper out of here," he said mockingly. "Someone'll think I'm cooking from recipes!"

Many things about that dinner were impressive, but nothing more so than the reverence with which Bud prepared it. Not only had he seasoned his dishes judiciously; he watched over them all while they were cooking. "There's real beauty in wild meat," he said. "The delicate flavors ought to be brought out." Few connoisseurs think of wild meat as possessing delicate flavors, but I know now that game need not be gamy. In fact, gaminess is often the mark of the careless or ignorant hunter —the hunter who doesn't know how to dress the animal he has shot and to care for it properly afterward. Needless to say, Bud Jensen is not a careless hunter, and under his tutelage I learned something about this part of the hunter's craft.

Ideally, a game animal should be dressed immediately after it is killed. The job involves bleeding and eviscerating the animal, and in the case of a deer, removing the musk glands from the hind legs, for these glands can taint the meat. Special care must be taken not to pierce the internal organs, especially the intestines; any spillage will give the flesh an unpleasant flavor that the cleverest of cooks cannot disguise. Some hunters cut the throat to drain the blood; others simply turn the eviscerated animal belly down to let the blood escape, then swab out the body cavity with moss, leaves, a clean cloth or paper towels. Quick cooling is crucial; both bleeding and gutting help bring down the temperature, but a careful hunter will take the additional step of propping the carcass open and letting the air in, or of hanging the carcass in the breeze. Skinning the animal can hasten cooling, but this step is practical only when the air is free of dust, flies or rain; meat that has been rained on but not carefully dried will sour in a few hours.

Once the carcass has been cleaned and cooled, it can be brought in from the field, either whole or quartered for easier transportation. The hunter who slings an animal over the hood and bumper of his car may be showing off his trophy, but he is also showing that he knows nothing about the handling of game. The heat and fumes of the engine and the dust and dirt kicked up by the tires can only hurt the meat. The hunter who wants to enjoy his meat will store the carcass in the trunk of the car, wrapped in a sleeping bag or some other insulating material to keep it cool. At home, it should be hung up to age, usually for a period of 10 days or two weeks, and preferably in a room with a temperature between 35° and 40°. Game improves as it hangs; the animal's own enzymes break down the muscle tissue and tenderize the meat.

When the time comes to cook the meat, the most meticulous preparation is important. Game differs from ordinary beef, pork or poultry in that it has little fat, but even this small amount of fat is best removed, since it carries much of the gamy flavor. Then, to assure that the meat will not dry out in the cooking, it should be larded or basted or both. Many people are conscientious about doing so but make the mistake of leaving the meat in the oven too long, in the erroneous belief that very well done game will be less gamy. Actually, the opposite is usually the case. Most game is best served rare, especially venison; and this rule applies not only to all cuts of deer, but to moose, elk and caribou as well.

If eating properly prepared wild meat can come as a revelation, so can hunting. Few hunters are handy with words; as a rule, little of the beauty of the sport comes through in their accounts of their experiences. Many talk about hunting as a way of answering an atavistic need. (No doubt it does for some; "Buckskin" Schaefer, a man I met in Oregon, lives in a log cabin, dresses from head to toe in buckskin he cures and sews himself, and hunts with bows and arrows of his own manufacture.) Others use such abominable clichés when they talk about the sport that I cannot listen to them. For me, at least, the excitement lies not so much in the chase or in the pride of bringing home the meat as in the penetration of nature—in seeing the animals' world as they see it, and even feeling, perhaps, a little of what they feel.

My own hunting experience took place in a great hunting state, South Dakota. It was late fall, and migrating geese on their way down from Canada had settled on the Missouri; one estimate put their number at 10,000. Sticky with sleep, a friend and I rose before dawn and drove out onto the prairie on a twisted ribbon of road. The night was one of the blackest I've seen—a great smudge of carbon, as though the whole sky had fallen, stars and all. We arrived at our destination, the ranch of a man who permits hunters to use his land, and walked to the warm-up shack. Inside, an electric coffee percolator snorted like a sleeping dog. A dozen men sprawled about in chairs and broken-down sofas, huddled into their rumpled clothes; some drowsed, some dreamed with open eyes of the geese they were going to shoot. "Just have patience, boys," one said suddenly. "They'll come. And when they come, we'll get them."

At the announcement that the truck was ready to pick us up and drive us to the blinds, the hunters came to life and shuffled out of the shack into the darkness. We bumped over a dirt road, clutching the cold metal

Continued on page 130

A Hunt at Dawn in South Dakota for Migrating Canada Geese

Every autumn great flocks of Canada geese fly across South Dakota on their way south. Here and there the migrating geese come to rest on water (one flock is shown below on a pond near the state capitol in Pierre, where it is against the law to shoot them). At the sight of the birds, in the air or on the water, local hunters grow tense with expectation. Some, like those seen at far left, take to blinds and patiently wait for geese to lift off the Missouri River and fly in their direction. On the day these pictures were taken flock after flock came close to the blind—but luck was not with these hunters. They bagged only a single bird, the goose at left.

sides of the truck for support, then jounced across the range and up a hill. At the crest were two blinds. Half of us hopped into one.

With the faint light of dawn we could begin to pick out details in the misty landscape. Grass-covered hills lay around us, cold and frosted. Down below, a couple of miles away, was the pale-blue Missouri. From the water came the first honkings of geese, a cacophony that grew in intensity; the birds' cries sounded like Indian war whoops in the movies, eerie to hear in what was once Sioux country. Fog rolled by, gradually taking on the sulphurous color of the sun. And then up rose a flock of geese.

They wiggle-waggled across the sky in a V formation, and disappeared into the incandescent fog. Others followed. We waited tensely for a flock to fly in our direction. When at last one did, we crouched in the blind in order not to be seen, and pressed ourselves against the crumbling earth, our shotguns raised and ready. But the geese swerved. "They must have seen us," said one disgusted hunter.

While we waited for other geese to approach, a man reached into a duffel bag and produced goose sandwiches for us all. His wife had simmered the breast meat in "sour wine"—that is, in a somewhat acrid dry wine —seasoned with bay leaf and thyme. The goose was savory, and the butter clung to it in hard, waxy bits.

Now the hunters began to complain about the weather. Already the fog and mist had burned off, and the sky had opened up big and wide. Geese are better hunted on an overcast day; fog or low-lying clouds force them down within range of the hunters' guns. But then the geese came, a wedge of them, flapping and honking overhead, and clearly within range. A blast of shot flew up to meet them. There was sudden disorder and squawking in the flock, and the V stretched out into a long, flailing kite tail. One bird spun off from the rest to fall on a hill behind us. Then the whole countryside was silent.

A long while passed before other geese flew near—and they were far too high for us to shoot. Disappointment settled over the hunters; but none seemed frustrated. We sat on top of our hill, looking out at our grass-level view of the world, and the morning grew more beautiful.

When the time came to go, I stood up against the sun's low rays, casting a long-legged shadow that seemed a mile or more in length. With two of the hunters I went down our hill and up the one behind to find the wounded goose. The frost on the grass had begun to melt, and each blade sparkled. We caught sight of the bird—and it of us. It began to run as fast as its leathery feet could carry it, but they were not fast enough. One of the hunters caught up with it and snapped its neck. A moment later the goose lay on its back on the ground; its legs jerked for a moment, then stopped moving.

I picked up the warm, soft bird—the wild bird that only one other man had touched—and carried it down to the waiting truck. We drove off, over the hills and back to the warm-up shack. As we passed a field of unharvested corn, we could hear some of the geese that had come off the river. They were feeding noisily among the stalks, and they sounded positively joyous.

The thrill of hunting in the Northwest can be matched only by that of

Opposite: Bud Jensen, a Cedar Rapids businessman and—in season —an enthusiastic hunter, cooks all the game he shoots. Putting the finishing touches on a game dinner for 26 men, he lightly bastes elk meatballs with a parsley "brush" dipped in melted butter. Other dishes for the dinner include tiny quail and two mallard ducks *(foreground, left and right);* behind them are pheasant tidbits in sauerkraut *(oval casserole, center)* and pheasant breasts with mushrooms in a white-wine sauce; ranged in the background are plump loaves of white bread baked by Jensen earlier in the day.

Winnipeg goldeye, one of northwestern Canada's greatest delicacies, is soaked in brine *(right)* to enhance and help preserve its flavor, then smoked from four to seven hours *(above)*. The traditional golden-red sheen of the final product comes from a vegetable dye added to the brine by present-day Winnipeg processors. Originally, goldeyes were smoked over willow fires, which gave their grayish flesh a reddish cast. When supplies of willow ran low, fires of oak and birch (which do not color the flesh) were substituted, and the processors hit upon the idea of using a dye.

fishing in the wilderness. Opportunities exist everywhere for anyone with a hook, line and determination—from the clear, rushing streams of the Cascades and Rockies to the deep waters of the Great Lakes. Montana claims to be the No. 1 trout-fishing state; Minnesota, with its 10,000 to 15,000 lakes, advertises itself as the fresh-water fishing capital of the nation. Even prairie states like the Dakotas offer exciting fishing, for reservoirs and artificial lakes built there in recent decades have made angling almost as much a part of the sportsman's scene as the goose and pheasant shooting. South Dakota's Oahe Reservoir, a 250-mile-long stretch of sky-blue water in the midst of rolling grasslands, is on the way to becoming one of America's best spots for northern pike. Skin divers exploring the 210-foot depths of the reservoir claim to have seen catfish as big as themselves, and fishermen have brought up one of the oddest of living fossils, the paddlefish, whose only relative, *Psephurus,* lives halfway around the world in the waters of China.

The king of the fresh-water fish of the Northwest is, of course, the trout. Somehow trout is synonymous with wilderness, and it is available in several species, including the indigenous rainbow and cutthroat, the Dolly Varden, the lake and the brook; there are also such imports as the Greek and brown (or Loch Leven) species. Finally, there are some hybrids such as the splake, a cross between the brook and lake.

Of all the trout, however, it is the rainbow that is best known and most often caught. Indeed, the rainbow is the region's greatest single contribution to the gastronomy of the world. Once restricted to West Coast mountain streams and to anglers' feasts on the banks of forest pools, it has been successfully transplanted to the waters and tables of Eastern North America, Europe, South America, Asia, Africa, Australia and New Zealand. Ironically, some of the frozen rainbows sold in American supermarkets now come from abroad.

Other game fish also abound in the region. Among them are the muskellunge, big, scrappy and good to eat, and the walleye, one of the most delicious of all fresh-water fishes. The lakes of Minnesota and Wisconsin are full of walleyes, and so are some lakes in Canada, where the species is known as the yellow pickerel (which it is not—it is actually a perch). Two other popular fish are the largemouth and smallmouth bass, both a challenge to the angler's skill. Some of the smaller fish of renown in the region are the perch, crappie (whose name is locally pronounced "croppy"), bluegill, pumpkinseed and rockbass.

The presence of so many fresh-water fish in the Northwest has led to some odd and picturesque customs. Normally, for example, winter might be regarded as a good time for sport fishermen to stay at home—but not in Minnesota and Wisconsin, where hundreds of thousands of hardy anglers stand around holes hacked in the frozen lakes and dangle lines in the freezing water. Some of these ice fishermen take to the shelter of portable shacks, which can be fairly elaborate affairs, with kerosene stoves mounted on platforms, a couple of chairs and a table, whiskey and cards. The most devoted ice fishermen are probably the sturgeon spearers of Wisconsin. These men wait all day, and sometimes days on end, to make a single thrust at their peculiar-looking prey, another living fossil, with bony plates for armor and a tubelike mouth. The meat is delicious, and in the female there may be a bonus of roe to turn into caviar.

Sturgeon were once common throughout the Great Lakes and in many of the large lakes of the Northeast, but their numbers have declined almost everywhere. The fish population of Wisconsin's Lake Winnebago is now probably the largest of any lake in the United States; in 1967 a record 1,424 sturgeon were caught there during a 26-day season. The fish are long-lived, and can attain great size; one speared in Lake Winnebago in 1954 weighed over 150 pounds and was 83 years old. (The age is reckoned by counting the rings of hard flesh deposited annually at the base of the pectoral fin.)

Spearing sturgeon may seem a strange way to catch fish—but there is a stranger one practiced in Minnesota during the spring. Armed with bows and arrows, fishermen wade the shallows of rivers and streams in search of carp. When one is sighted, they fire away at it, then grab the line attached to the arrow's barbed tip to play the fish and draw it in. Spring is also the time for smelt fishing, and Minnesotans and Wisconsinites participate in this sport almost as a rite. These little fish, originally from the Atlantic, came down the St. Lawrence; after their introduction into the Great Lakes they grew so numerous that they now support a commercial fishery. They generally begin their spawning run in early April, and as they dart by night into the streams and rivers along Lakes Michigan and Superior, thousands of people are on hand to catch them in nets. As many as 100 pounds—about 1,600 smelts—can be taken by a single fisherman in a few minutes. Cleaned and dipped in thin batter and then crisply fried in butter or oil, the smelts are marvelous. At a smelt fry, one of the great institutions of the area, the main objective is to eat as many as possible; 25 smelts are considered a modest number.

Another great institution is the fish boil, particularly in Door County, the beautiful Wisconsin peninsula that juts out into Lake Michigan. A

For two or three weeks in February and March, ice fishing is the sport on Wisconsin's Lake Winnebago. Most fishermen take to the shelter of heated shacks like the ones shown on this page, and spend hours and even days hunched over door-sized holes in the ice, hoping to spear one of the sturgeon that swim in the lake's shallow waters. Since the only light inside the shack is the faint glow that filters up through the hole in the ice, sturgeon spearing has been likened to "looking at a blank picture on a 90-inch TV set and waiting for a shadowy image to cross the screen."

typical fish-boil recipe calls for 100 pounds of fish (usually lake trout or whitefish, cut in pieces), 100 pounds of potatoes, 40 pounds of salt, a great caldron of water—and a gallon of kerosene. John Dobie, a Minnesota conservationist and appreciator of fine foods, told me how his Wisconsin friends go about setting up such a fish boil. They suspend a huge cast-iron pot (the kind of kettle that early settlers used in making soap) over an open fire, and fill it with the salt and water. When the water boils, they lower a basketful of unpeeled potatoes into it. Twenty minutes later they add the fish, also in a basket. The fish cooks quickly, and at the very end the gallon of kerosene is tossed onto the fire. All at once the flames leap up and the pot boils over, carrying away the scum floating on the surface; the cooks can now remove the contents without danger of coating them with scum. A great many people who normally do not care for fish like it the Door County way—and like it all the more when it is sloshed with melted butter and eaten with tossed salad and beer. One Madison man, for instance, told me that he actually hated fish until he ate it in Door County; now he and his wife drive to the peninsula every year to enjoy one of the many fish boils given there during summer. Oddly, the fish is not at all salty or mushy; on the contrary it is juicy, firm and fresh tasting.

Many people of Scandinavian descent in the Northwest preserve and cherish the custom of harvesting fresh-water crawfish, tiny crustaceans that are sometimes called bay crabs or crawdads, and boiling them in dill-flavored water. Usually, they eat them cold, with buttered toast and vodka or, following the Old World habit, shots of icy aquavit. But some cooks simmer the tails in a mixture of butter and water and serve them on rice, while others use the crawfish meat in a variation of lobster Newburg.

The fresh-water delights of the Northwest also include the succulent fish taken by commercial fishermen in Lakes Michigan and Superior. Two of the best, to my mind, are whitefish and chub. Most cooks think of the whitefish as a fine fish to plank or broil, but few know that it also provides a kind of poor-man's caviar. The commercial processors have to color the pale eggs a dark gray, usually with cuttlefish ink, to make them look like the real thing; but the final product is surprisingly good. Smoked whitefish is still another delicacy, though many people say that they prefer smoked chub, which acquire a beautiful golden sheen and a light, delicate flavor in the smoking process. But to my mind, the finest smoked fresh-water fish is surely the Winnipeg goldeye. In itself the goldeye is rather dull; but once it has been hung in the smokehouse for a slow cure, it changes its character, acquiring a firm texture and a nutty, sweet taste. The curing process is carried on exclusively in Winnipeg, Manitoba; smoked goldeye is rather hard to come by elsewhere, but it is well worth seeking out. The flesh is wonderfully smooth and moist, and those who eat it generally wind up picking at the bones. Winnipeg goldeye was a special favorite in the dining cars of the Canadian Pacific Railroad during the heyday of the passenger trains.

Yet what may well turn out to be the most important fish in Lakes Michigan and Superior is, of all things, the coho salmon—the salmon that is one of the mainstays of Pacific Northwest fishermen. Introduced to the lakes as recently as 1966, it has caught on in the lakes' fresh waters and has flourished. It is already providing excellent sport fishing, and may one day be the basis of a large commercial fishery. Living, as it now does, at both the eastern and western edges of the Northwest, the coho serves to tie a diverse region together.

Some ice fishermen use lures to attract a sturgeon *(left)*, while others drive posts into the mud for it to scratch its back on. When a sturgeon does appear, the fisherman hurls a three-pronged spear at the fish—and then the battle begins. Weighing up to 100 pounds, a speared sturgeon can send a man flying with a slap of its tail or break a hole through the wall of a shanty. Fishermen lucky enough to land a sturgeon often have the meat smoked by professionals like John Croyke, who is shown above removing carp from his smokehouse on the shore of Lake Winnebago.

To serve 4

4 pounds fish trimmings: the heads,
    tail and bones of any firm white-
    fleshed fish
2 quarts water
2 medium-sized onions, peeled and
    coarsely chopped
1 medium-sized bay leaf, crumbled
½ teaspoon crumbled dried
    tarragon
2 teaspoons salt
4 ten-ounce brook trout, cleaned but
    with heads and tails left on,
    thoroughly defrosted if frozen
4 envelopes unflavored gelatin
2 cups dry white wine
4 egg whites
4 egg shells, finely crushed

GARNISH
1 or 2 large green leaves from the
    top of a leek or scallion
1 medium-sized carrot, scraped and
    sliced into ¼-inch-thick rounds
The white of 1 hard-cooked egg
4 sprigs of watercress

Trout in Aspic

Combine the fish trimmings and water in a 5- to 6-quart enameled or stainless-steel pot. The water should cover the trimmings completely; add more if necessary. Bring to a boil over high heat, skimming off the foam as it rises to the surface. Add the onions, bay leaf, tarragon and salt, reduce the heat, and simmer partially covered for 20 minutes.

Strain the contents of the pot through a fine sieve into a heavy 12-inch skillet, pressing down hard on the fish trimmings to extract all their juices before discarding them. Set the pot aside.

Let the stock cool to lukewarm, then wash the trout inside and out under cold running water and place them in the skillet. Bring to a simmer over moderate heat, reduce the heat, and simmer uncovered for 5 minutes, or until the fish feel firm when prodded gently with a finger.

With a slotted spatula, arrange the trout side by side on a flat platter or jelly-roll pan. While they are still warm, skin each of the fish in the following fashion: With a small, sharp knife, cut the skin crosswise about an inch above the base of the tail and about an inch below the gill. Gently pull off the skin in strips from tail to gill, then turn the fish over and peel the upturned side. Drape a dampened kitchen towel over the trout and refrigerate them while you prepare the aspic.

Measure 6 cups of the fish stock remaining in the skillet into the reserved pot and let it cool to room temperature. Sprinkle the gelatin evenly over it and let it soften for a few minutes. Add the wine, egg whites and egg shells and, stirring constantly, bring to a boil over moderate heat. When the mixture begins to froth and rise, remove the pot from the heat and let the stock rest for 10 minutes. Then pour the entire contents of the pot into a fine sieve lined with a double thickness of dampened cheesecloth and set over a shallow enameled or stainless-steel pan. Allow the liquid to drain through undisturbed. Season with more salt if needed.

Set the pan in a large bowl half filled with crushed ice or ice cubes and water, and stir the aspic with a metal spoon until it thickens enough to flow sluggishly off the spoon. Pour aspic to a depth of about ¼ inch into a chilled serving platter large enough to hold the four trout attractively, and refrigerate the platter until the aspic is firm.

Keep the remaining aspic at room temperature so that it remains liquid and ready to use; if it begins to set, warm briefly over low heat to soften it, then stir it over ice again until it is thick but still fluid.

Meanwhile, prepare the garnish. Drop the leek or scallion leaves into boiling water for 1 or 2 minutes. Transfer them to a sieve, run cold water over them, then spread them on paper towels and pat them dry. Cut the leaves into a dozen or more long, thin strips to use as stems.

Boil the carrot rounds briskly in the same water for about 5 minutes, until they are barely tender. Drain, run cold water over them, then spread the rounds on paper towels and pat them dry. With a lily-of-the-valley truffle cutter or with the tip of a sharp knife, make carrot flowers. Slice a ¼-inch-thick round from the egg white and cut out four small circles from the round to cover the eyes of the trout.

Usually fried, trout of the Northwest make a formal meal when simmered in stock, chilled and served in wine-flavored aspic.

Set stems, flower and egg-white circles aside, covered with wax paper.

Arrange the trout on the aspic-coated platter and glaze them with a few tablespoonfuls of the liquid aspic. Refrigerate until the glaze is firm. Dip the carrot flowers and green leaf stems into the aspic and arrange them fancifully on top of the fish. Dip the egg-white circles in the aspic and place them over the eyes. Chill again until the decorations are anchored firmly. Then carefully spoon aspic over the trout two more times, chilling the fish after each coating to set the glaze.

Melt the aspic remaining in the pan over low heat, and pour it into a small loaf pan. Refrigerate until the aspic has set firm. Run a thin knife around the edges to loosen them and dip the bottom into hot water.

Place an inverted plate over the pan and, grasping pan and plate together firmly, turn them over. The aspic should slide out easily. Cut the aspic into paper-thin slices, and then into fine dice. Scatter the dice around the edge of the fish platter. Garnish the top with sprigs of watercress and refrigerate the trout in the aspic until ready to serve.

Fresh Minnesota walleyed pike is at its best when it is broiled, basted with melted butter and sprinkled lightly with paprika.

To serve 4

7 tablespoons butter, plus 4
   tablespoons butter, softened and
   cut into ¼-inch bits
¼ cup vegetable oil
½ pound uncooked shrimp
1 cup soft fresh crumbs made from
   homemade-type white bread,
   pulverized in a blender or finely
   shredded with a fork
1 tablespoon very finely chopped
   fresh parsley
⅛ teaspoon ground mace
½ teaspoon salt
Freshly ground black pepper
1 egg yolk
A 2½- to 3-pound pike, cleaned
   but with head and tail left on

Shrimp-stuffed Baked Pike

Preheat the oven to 375°. In a small pan, melt 4 tablespoons of the butter with the oil over moderate heat. Remove the pan from the heat and, with a pastry brush, spread about 1 tablespoon of the mixture evenly over the bottom of a baking-serving dish large enough to hold the fish comfortably. Set the remaining butter-and-oil mixture aside.

Shell the shrimp. Devein them by making a shallow incision down their backs with a small, sharp knife and lifting out the black or white intestinal vein with the point of the knife. Chop the shrimp as fine as possible and place them in a mixing bowl.

Melt 3 tablespoons of butter in a 6- to 8-inch skillet and brown the bread crumbs, stirring them frequently until they are golden. With a rubber spatula, scrape the entire contents of the skillet over the shrimp. Add the parsley, mace, salt and a few grindings of pepper, and beat vigorously with a wooden spoon until the mixture is a thick, smooth paste. Beat in the egg yolk and the 4 tablespoons of butter bits.

Wash the fish inside and out under cold running water and dry it thoroughly with paper towels. Loosely fill the cavity of the fish with the shrimp stuffing, then close the opening with small skewers, crisscrossing them with kitchen cord as if lacing a turkey. Place the fish in the prepared baking dish and brush the top with 1 or 2 tablespoons of the butter-oil mixture. Bake uncovered in the middle of the oven for 30 minutes, basting every 10 minutes with the remaining butter-and-oil mixture. Serve at once, directly from the baking dish.

138

Fried Cornmeal Squares

To make 8

With a pastry brush, spread the softened butter evenly over the bottom and sides of a shallow baking dish 8 inches long and 5 inches wide.

In a heavy 2-quart saucepan, bring the water and salt to a boil. Stirring constantly with a wooden spoon, pour in the cornmeal in a slow, thin stream so that the water continues to boil as the cornmeal is absorbed. Then reduce the heat to low and, stirring frequently, cook the cornmeal for 2 or 3 minutes, until it is very thick and smooth.

Immediately remove the pan from the heat. With a rubber spatula, spread the hot cornmeal into the buttered dish to a thickness of ½ inch. Cover with wax paper and refrigerate for at least 30 minutes, or until the cornmeal is firm to the touch.

With a small, sharp knife or pastry wheel, divide the cornmeal into 2-inch squares and lift them out of the dish with a small metal spatula.

In a heavy 10- to 12-inch skillet, melt the 6 tablespoons of butter bits over moderate heat. When the foam begins to subside, add the cornmeal squares and fry them for about 2 minutes on each side, turning them over with a metal spatula and regulating the heat so that they color richly and evenly without burning. Transfer the fried squares to paper towels to drain for a few seconds, then serve at once.

2 tablespoons butter, softened, plus 6 tablespoons butter, cut into bits
1 cup water
1 teaspoon salt
1½ cups yellow cornmeal

Elk Meatballs in Sour Cream

To make about 4 dozen 1-inch meatballs

In a heavy 10- to 12-inch skillet, melt 2 tablespoons of the butter over moderate heat. Add the onions and garlic and, stirring frequently, cook for about 5 minutes, until they are soft and translucent but not brown.

With a rubber spatula, scrape the contents of the skillet into a deep bowl. Set the pan aside. Add the elk, pork, bread crumbs, egg, milk, parsley, thyme, salt and pepper to the onion-garlic mixture and knead vigorously with both hands. Then beat the mixture with a wooden spoon until it is smooth and fluffy. To shape each meatball, pinch off about 1 tablespoon of the mixture and roll it into a ball 1 inch in diameter.

Melt the remaining 4 tablespoons of butter with the oil in the reserved skillet and brown the meatballs, 10 or 12 at a time. Turn the balls frequently with a slotted spatula and regulate the heat so that they color richly and evenly without burning. As they brown, transfer them to a plate.

Pour off the fat remaining in the skillet and in its place add the chicken stock. Bring to a boil over high heat, meanwhile scraping in the brown particles that cling to the bottom and sides of the pan. Return all the meatballs to the skillet together with the liquid that has accumulated around them and turn the balls about to moisten them evenly. Reduce the heat and simmer partially covered for 20 minutes, or until no trace of pink shows when a meatball is pierced with the point of a knife.

Transfer the meatballs to a heated platter and drape foil over them to keep them warm. With a wire whisk, beat the sour cream, flour and mustard together in a bowl until they are well blended. Then add the sour-cream mixture to the liquid remaining in the skillet and, whisking constantly, cook over low heat for 4 to 5 minutes, until the sauce is smooth and lightly thickened. Taste for seasoning, then pour the sauce over the meatballs. Serve at once with hot buttered noodles or rice.

6 tablespoons butter
½ cup finely chopped onions
1 teaspoon finely chopped garlic
2 pounds ground elk or other ground venison
1 pound lean ground pork
1 cup soft fresh crumbs made from homemade-type white bread, pulverized in a blender or finely shredded with a fork
1 egg, lightly beaten
½ cup milk
¼ cup finely chopped fresh parsley
1 teaspoon crumbled dried thyme
1 tablespoon salt
¼ teaspoon freshly ground black pepper
2 tablespoons vegetable oil
2 cups chicken stock, fresh or canned
1 cup sour cream
2 tablespoons flour
2 teaspoons dry mustard

To serve 4

2 one-pound oven-ready pheasants,
    split lengthwise into halves
1 teaspoon salt
¼ teaspoon freshly ground black
    pepper
½ cup plus 2 teaspoons flour
4 slices bacon
3 tablespoons butter
½ cup finely chopped onions
The livers, hearts and gizzards of
    the pheasants, finely chopped
1 cup chicken stock, fresh or canned
2 firm unpeeled cooking apples,
    cored and quartered
2 tablespoons brandy
½ cup sour cream

Pheasant and Apples with Sour-Cream Sauce

Pat the pheasant halves dry with paper towels and sprinkle them with the salt and pepper. One at a time, dip each half in ½ cup of the flour, turning it to coat both sides, and vigorously shake off the excess flour.

In a heavy 12-inch skillet, fry the bacon over moderate heat until the slices are crisp and brown and have rendered all their fat. Set the bacon slices aside on paper towels to drain, then crumble them into bits.

Pour off all but about 2 tablespoons of the fat remaining in the skillet and add the butter. Melt the butter in the fat and then brown the pheasant halves, one or two at a time. Turn the pheasant frequently and regulate the heat so that it colors richly and evenly without burning. As each half browns, set it aside on a plate.

Add the onions to the fat remaining in the skillet and, stirring frequently, cook for about 5 minutes, until they are soft and translucent but not brown. Add the pheasant livers, hearts and gizzards, and stir for 2 to 3 minutes. Stir in the stock and return the birds and the liquid that has accumulated around them to the skillet. Bring to a boil over high heat, reduce the heat to low, and simmer partially covered for 20 minutes.

Place the apple quarters in the skillet and spoon the cooking liquid over them. Then simmer partially covered for about 10 minutes longer. To test for doneness, pierce the thigh of a pheasant with the point of a small, sharp knife. The juice that trickles out should be clear yellow; if it is tinged with pink, simmer the birds for a few minutes more. Arrange the pheasants and apples attractively on a heated platter and drape foil over them to keep them warm while you prepare the sauce.

Skim the fat from the surface of the cooking liquid, pour in the brandy and bring to a simmer over moderate heat. Reduce the heat to low and cook for 1 to 2 minutes. Meanwhile, with a wire whisk, beat the remaining 2 teaspoons of flour into the sour cream. Stirring the sauce with the whisk, pour in the sour-cream mixture and simmer slowly for 4 to 5 minutes, until it is smooth and slightly thickened. Taste for seasoning, then pour the sauce over the pheasants. Sprinkle the pheasants with the reserved bacon bits and serve at once.

To serve 4

4 fresh rainbow or brook trout,
    about ½ pound each, cleaned
    but with head and tail left on, or
    substitute 4 frozen trout,
    thoroughly defrosted and drained
1 teaspoon salt
Freshly ground black pepper
8 slices lean bacon
½ cup flour
1 lemon, quartered

Fried Trout with Bacon

Wash the fish under cold running water, pat them dry inside and out with paper towels, and sprinkle the cavities with the salt and a few gridings of black pepper.

In a heavy 12-inch skillet, fry the bacon over moderate heat until the slices are crisp and brown, then transfer them to paper towels to drain.

Spread the flour over a sheet of wax paper, coat the fish on both sides, and then shake off any excess flour. Fry two trout in the fat remaining in the skillet for about 4 minutes on each side, turning them carefully with a large spatula. Place the trout on a heatproof platter and keep them warm in a 200° oven while you fry the remaining fish.

Serve the fried trout at once, accompanied by the reserved bacon slices and the lemon quarters.

140

Pheasant, abundant in much of the Northwest, is simmered in chicken stock with apples to moisten the meat and enhance its flavor; the bird is served with a brandy-and-sour-cream sauce and fried cornmeal squares.

2 tablespoons butter
1½ cups finely chopped onions
1 medium-sized carrot, scraped and
    finely chopped
¼ cup finely chopped celery
1 teaspoon finely chopped garlic
3 cups dry red wine
1 cup plus 1 tablespoon cold water
1 medium-sized bay leaf, crumbled
6 whole juniper berries and 10
    whole black peppercorns,
    wrapped in a towel and coarsely
    crushed with a rolling pin
1 tablespoon salt
A 10- to 11-pound leg of venison
1 tablespoon cornstarch

3 cups flour
1 teaspoon salt
¼ teaspoon ground nutmeg,
    preferably freshly grated
4 eggs, lightly beaten
1 cup milk
2 quarts water
2 tablespoons butter
1 cup ¼-inch cubes white bread,
    preferably cut from day-old
    French or Italian bread
2 tablespoons finely chopped parsley

Roast Leg of Venison

In a 3- to 4-quart enameled or stainless-steel saucepan, melt the butter over moderate heat. When the foam begins to subside, add the onions, carrot, celery and garlic and, stirring frequently, cook for about 5 minutes, until the vegetables are soft but not brown. Stir in the wine, 1 cup of the water, the bay leaf, the juniper berries and peppercorns, and the salt, and bring to a boil over high heat. Remove the pan from the heat and let the marinade cool to room temperature.

Place the venison in a roasting pan large enough to hold it comfortably, pour the marinade over it, and turn the meat in the marinade to moisten it on all sides. Cover tightly with foil or plastic wrap and refrigerate for at least 12 hours, turning the meat two or three times.

Preheat the oven to 425°. Insert the tip of a meat thermometer at least 2 inches into the thickest part of the meat, and roast the venison on the middle shelf of the oven for 15 minutes. Reduce the heat to 375° and continue roasting for 1 hour and 15 minutes longer, basting the venison every 15 minutes with the liquids in the bottom of the pan. When done, the meat thermometer should register 140° to 150°, and the roast should be slightly pink. Transfer it to a large heated platter and let it rest for 10 minutes or so for easier carving.

Meanwhile, prepare the sauce. Strain the cooking liquid through a fine sieve set over a bowl, pressing down hard on the vegetables to extract all their juice before discarding them. Measure the liquid, pour it into a small saucepan and skim the fat from the surface. You will need 2 cups of liquid for the sauce. If you have more, boil it briskly until it is reduced to that amount; if you have less, add as much water as you need to make the required amount. Make a smooth paste of the cornstarch and the remaining tablespoon of cold water.

Bring the cooking liquid to a simmer over moderate heat and, stirring constantly with a wire whisk, pour in the cornstarch mixture. Continue to simmer until the sauce thickens lightly and is smooth. Taste for seasoning, pour the sauce into a bowl or sauceboat, and serve at once with the roast venison.

Spaetzle
TINY DUMPLINGS WITH FRIED CROUTONS

To make the dumplings, combine the flour, ½ teaspoon of the salt and the nutmeg in a large mixing bowl. Make a well in the center and drop in the eggs and milk. With a large spoon, stir the flour into the liquid ingredients and continue to stir until the dough is smooth.

Bring 2 quarts of water and the remaining ½ teaspoon of salt to a boil in a heavy 4- to 5-quart saucepan. Set a colander, preferably one with large openings, over the saucepan and, with a spoon, press the dough a few tablespoons at a time through the colander into the boiling water. Stir the dumplings gently to prevent them from sticking to each other, then boil briskly 5 to 8 minutes, or until they are tender. Drain through a sieve or colander and transfer to a large heated serving bowl. Cover the bowl with foil to keep the dumplings hot while you prepare the croutons.

Melt the butter in a heavy 10- to 12-inch skillet and add the bread

Roasted venison with a German accent is marinated in tart red wine before cooking and served with spiced plums and spaetzle.

cubes. Turn the cubes about in the butter for 2 to 3 minutes, or until golden brown on all sides, then add them to the bowl of dumplings. Toss the croutons and dumplings together lightly with a spoon, sprinkle with parsley, and serve at once.

Spiced Plums

Wash the plums under cold running water, drain well, and prick each fruit deeply in three or four places with the point of a small, thin skewer. Place the plums in a heatproof glass or ceramic bowl.

Combine the wine, water, lemon juice, mace and cloves in a small enameled or stainless-steel pan and bring to a boil over high heat. Pour the hot liquid over the fruit, turn the plums about with a spoon and let them soak at room temperature for an hour. Drain the liquid back into the pan and repeat the boiling and soaking procedure two more times.

Transfer the plums to a serving dish with a slotted spoon, moisten them with a few spoonfuls of the spiced liquid and serve at once, as an accompaniment to roast meats and game. Or cover the bowl with plastic wrap and refrigerate the plums in the spiced liquid until ready to serve.

To serve 6 to 8

2 pounds medium-sized firm ripe
  red plums (about 12)
3 cups dry white wine
2 cups water
1 tablespoon strained fresh lemon
  juice
½ teaspoon ground mace
6 whole cloves

VI

Echoes of an Ethnic Legacy

Northwestern cooking is spiced with paradox. On the one hand, it is delightfully American—as American as steak, sweet corn, apple pie and vanilla ice cream. On the other, it is deliciously European. For the cooking of a comparatively new region, it is in many respects surprisingly old, and some of its best recipes are heirlooms, handed down for generations from mother to daughter and constantly enriched in the process by love, nostalgia and American ingredients.

Everywhere, ethnic flavors come through strongly. The state of Washington has concentrations of Norwegians, Swedes, Finns and Japanese. The Canadian provinces of Manitoba, Alberta and Saskatchewan have long been home to Ukrainians, Russian Mennonites and Icelanders, while British Columbia has seen an influx of Germans and Dutch. Even Idaho shows a European influence on its cooking. In that cowboy country, I never expected to find such exotic dishes as *lohimuhennos* (salmon chowder or stew), *bara brith* (a raisin and currant bread), and *makalo eta pipermin* (codfish and peppers), yet find them I did, the respective culinary legacies of Finns, Welsh and Basques who settled in Idaho as miners and sheepherders.

But the best place of all to taste the cooking of many nations intermingled with typical American touches is within the six states of Wisconsin, Minnesota, Nebraska, Iowa and the Dakotas. This immense and rich agricultural domain, the subject of the present chapter, was an American frontier through the latter part of the 19th Century and the first decade of the 20th—and it was a European frontier as well, for im-

In Idaho, where sheep raising is a major industry, many sheepherders are Basque immigrants from the Spanish Pyrenees. The sheep shown here have been brought down from mountain pastures to spend the winter in the lower valley areas. Basques constitute one of Idaho's most colorful ethnic groups, and their food is enjoyed throughout the state. In Payette, for example, one meat packer turns out their *chorizo,* a spicy sausage now eaten in Idaho by Basques and non-Basques alike.

migrants who flocked into the region by the hundreds of thousands to settle on free or cheap land.

Their contribution was enormous. Equipped with little more than the will to succeed, they broke the stubborn sod and planted their crops. Working alongside native-born Americans, they turned their chosen haven into one of the world's greatest food-producing areas. Norwegians helped sow the Dakotas to wheat, while Swiss, Germans and Danes helped to found the dairy industry of Wisconsin. In that state there were enough Germans alone at the start of the Civil War to form no fewer than three Union regiments and enough Norwegians and Swedes to make up a fourth, in which 90 per cent of the men were named Ole. As early as 1860 immigrants constituted a majority of the population in some Minnesota counties. As late as 1910 over a quarter of the inhabitants of North Dakota were of European birth.

To the immigrants, the food they raised themselves on their own fertile acres must have seemed the sweetest of rewards. Perhaps this is one reason that even today eating seems almost a way of life in the land east of the Rockies. People here don't just appreciate good eating—they celebrate it. This is a realm of picnics, fairs and festivals, where everything from American watermelon to German sauerkraut has its special day. It is also a land of abundance—of milk, cream and butter, wheat, corn, hogs and cattle. Its rolling fields, its flat plains and prairies, even the skylines of some of its towns and cities, are dominated by giant canisters of plenty—the grain elevator and the silo.

Paul Engle, the Iowa poet, has noted that the presence of so much food induces a different attitude toward it. "Instead of just possessing it," he writes, "we are possessed by it." This does not mean that the people are gluttons—far from it—but they do care about what they eat. One of the things they care most about, whatever their ethnic background, is sweet corn. It must be fresh, and the fresher the better. Some insist that no more than 10 minutes should elapse between the time the corn is picked and the time it is dropped into the pot. If that seems a bit extreme, consider the trouble Iowa farm wives go to in preparing the delicacy known as corn cream. They slit open each row of kernels and gently press out the milk and flesh. Once they have enough to give everyone a generous portion, they add pepper and salt and a little heavy cream. Then they cook this essence at low heat, lifting the lid of the pot from time to time to make sure that the contents neither boil nor burn. When the corn cream is done, they spoon it into saucers and serve it with such dishes as crisp fried chicken, mashed potatoes and gravy, and a salad made up of sliced tomatoes, cucumbers and onions that comes to the table fresh from the vegetable patch.

When corn is not eaten right out of the garden, it is consumed in other ways, seen and unseen; it is the dominant food of the region, what the olive is to the Mediterranean and lamb to the Middle East. There is, of course, cornbread, the johnnycake of old, slightly sweetened and baked thin and crisp in a large pan. (Some people treat it as a superpancake and spread it with butter and syrup or molasses.) There are corn muffins, corn sticks and corncob jelly, golden and transparent, with a slight taste of apple. There is corn oil, used in salad dressings, and corn syrup; this, boiled with sugar and sweet cream and rich with chopped black walnuts, produces a divinity fudge that is accurately named. But in the end, it is corn transformed into meat that gives the cooking of the area its richness. The Thanksgiving turkey, as Engle has said, gets stuffed on corn long before it is stuffed with dressing; the hog grows fat on corn, and the corn-fed steer puts on a coat of fat that spreads into the red flesh in the creamiest of marblings.

Surrounded by plenty, the cooks of the six states have come to be generous with their food. The best, they believe, is always better when there is more of it, and the Nebraska or Iowa farmhouse table expresses that attitude with heaping platters and bowls of meat, potatoes, vegetables and rolls, relishes and salads, and pitchers of ice-cold milk and cream. But tastes remain uncomplicated, reflecting the simplicity of the European peasants and Yankee farmers, the men and women of the soil, who settled the region. There is another reason for this simplicity: the food has great flavor to begin with. There has never been much logic in trying to improve on meat and vegetables that are wonderful in themselves. Accordingly, more down-to-earth kitchen classics survive here on a daily basis than perhaps anywhere else in North America, everything from roast pork with applesauce to chocolate cake three layers high and frosted all over with fudgy icing. Refreshingly, women still take the trouble to

A tiered Norwegian cake called a *kransekake*, made with rings of almond paste and egg white, rises in a stately tower from a silver tray on the terrace of Mrs. Solveig Ivarsson's residence in Seattle. Born and raised in Norway, Mrs. Ivarsson follows many of the traditions of her native country, adapted to American patterns of entertaining. In Norway, a *kransekake* might be served at weddings or at confirmations; in America, Mrs. Ivarsson presents it as the spectacular finale to a dinner party.

make such a cake from scratch, and they never seem to tire of turning out fresh fruit pies—apple, cherry, plum, gooseberry and rhubarb. Some housewives bottle their own preserves and relishes, and a few traditionalists even let the sun cook their strawberry jam, an age-old method as direct as nature itself. They boil the berries briefly with sugar, spread them in a pan covered with cheesecloth to keep the flies away, and leave the pan under the open sky for a day or two. The heat of the sun melts the fruit into a thick, juicy pulp.

Ethnic cooking is so much a part of this scene that people sometimes forget it once was called "furrin" by native-born settlers. Consider the Bohemian *koláč,* for example. This delicious three-inch circle of pastry, topped with a large button of apricot jam, sour cherries, prune butter, nutmeats or poppy seeds, is now known to everyone in the region as the kolach. In Cedar Rapids, Iowa, one department store sells kolaches for 10 cents apiece, coffee free; and many Iowa and Nebraska women of Yankee descent are as nimble at baking them as they are at oatmeal cookies and brownies. Similarly, the Czech poppy-seed cake crops up in many non-Czech homes and is consumed with as much enthusiasm as kolaches are, especially when there is a large pot of strong coffee on hand. A sugar-dusted cookie called the rosette, made by dipping a special flower- or butterfly-shaped iron into batter and then plunging it into hot fat, has been taken over by so many home bakers that no one seems able to say whether it was Swedish, German or Swiss in origin. Even some esoteric foods, like the lye-cured cod called *lutefisk* or *lutfisk* by Norwegians and Swedes (the spelling depends on one's ancestry), have spilled over into the community at large. In Minneapolis, *lutefisk* is often listed on the winter menus of non-Scandinavian restaurants and eaten by people without a drop of Scandinavian blood in their veins.

The assimilation of ethnic foods is strongest where various groups settled side by side, in states like Wisconsin. Among the first foreigners there were Cornish miners, who arrived as early as 1830 to work the lead mines. Their impact was such that to this day such Cornish specialties as pasties (pocket-sized meat-and-vegetable pies) and saffron cakes are kitchen favorites in Cornish-American localities. The Swiss, also early arrivals, turned Green County into a little Switzerland and spread the fame of their Swiss cheese. The sausages, sauerkraut, rye bread and beer of the Germans, Poles, Czechs and Slovaks in and around Milwaukee have long since become so commonplace that they are now practically divorced from their ethnic associations. From the Swedes, who are plentiful in the north-central part of the state, many non-Swedish households have taken over a number of smorgasbord dishes, including flat, crisp rye breads, tiny meatballs *(Recipe Index),* pickled herring, and beet salad. In Racine, the *kringle,* a butter-rich filled sweet bread sprinkled with sugar, is well loved by many people other than the Danes who introduced it, and in the north, around Lake Superior, the Finns have popularized their *piirakka* (rice-filled pasties) and dark bread.

Both in Wisconsin and in the other five states the two immigrant groups that have had the most effect are the Germans and the Scandinavians. Not only did they come early, but they came in large numbers. The map

148

is dotted with such place names as New Ulm, New Munich, New Holstein, New Upsala, Oslo—all symbols of the settlers' determination to have the best of both their worlds.

The Germans entered the area by way of Wisconsin, whose climate, soil and vegetation were pleasantly similar to those of their homeland. Milwaukee was a magnet for many; it was soon being called Deutsch-Athen, German Athens, because of the Germanic culture that took root and flourished there. As early as 1841, a man from Württemberg founded the city's first lager brewery, launching an industry closely associated with German names ever since. Not until the influx of other Central Europeans at the start of the 20th Century did Milwaukee begin to lose some of its Teutonic character.

Those German immigrants who went out into the countryside and into neighboring states to till the soil lived up to their traditional reputation for industriousness. They introduced a more intensive kind of farming, using fertilizers and diversifying their crops. Many bought partially cleared farms from Irish and American farmers pushing west, and uprooted and burned the remaining stumps to make farms to be proud of. They took a disapproving view of anyone who regarded the soil as expendable, nor did they look kindly on the man who sat whittling by the fire instead of mending his fences, or who hunted while his pigs ran rampant through his cornfields.

Because of their relative isolation, these farming Germans retained more of the old-country customs than the city Germans. Their resistance to change was reinforced by their strong Lutheran or Catholic faith. In German Catholic sections of Minnesota today, wakes go on for two whole days, with rosaries said more or less in tandem, interrupted by meals of sausages, home-smoked hams, coleslaw, fresh-baked breads, beer and coffee. At weddings it is still the custom to pass around the bride's slipper, into which guests slip money, and the feasting is hearty. Whatever the occasion, the rich specialties of the past are the favorite foods—such dishes as hasenpfeffer, rabbit cooked in a spiced, vinegar-tart gravy *(Recipe Index)*; pheasant in a sour sauce; egg dumplings; and *Kuchen*, circles and rectangles of sweet dough covered with cherries, apples, or prunes and cottage cheese. On a few farms, the butchering of hogs and steers is done as of old, yielding a supply of sausages and other *Delikatessen*. The meat of the skull, chopped up, goes into headcheese, the blood into *Blutwurst*, the liver and bits of leftover pork into *Braunschweiger*. Nothing is wasted. This frugality, the mark of the country German, also extends to the Christmas goose. Its grease is saved to spread on bread (it used to be rubbed on chests and throats as a cold remedy), and its bones are boiled for soup and then given to the dogs or ground up for fertilizer.

The Germans who chose to remain in the cities and towns tended to be a more relaxed and sophisticated lot. They enjoyed good eating, especially fine pastries baked with butter, covered with whipped cream, and eaten with hot chocolate or coffee topped by more cream. They liked their Sunday picnics, their beer gardens; in Milwaukee, boys delivering buckets of suds to office workers used to be a regular part of the local scene. The passion for beer, in fact, raised eyebrows among some ab-

Overleaf: A 248-acre livestock and dairy farm in Rock County, Wisconsin, reflects the peace and prosperity of the area. Two brothers, Arthur and Merwin Abrahamson, own and run the farm jointly. They maintain 80 head of dairy cattle, 20 beef steers and 400 hogs. The Abrahamsons are kept busy tending their stock and growing corn, alfalfa and oats for feed, and rarely find time to take their 14-foot powerboat, parked under the trees in the foreground, for rides on nearby Lake Geneva.

stemious Yankees, and the Women's Christian Temperance Union actually attempted—and utterly failed—to get the Germans to mend their ways. On several occasions, the Germans reacted to such meddling by noisily interrupting temperance meetings. Once they were so audacious as to celebrate a Fourth of July that fell on a Sunday, whereupon 1,400 angry Milwaukeeans urged the municipal government to suppress "Sunday orgies and excesses." The Swedish writer Fredrika Bremer, who visited Milwaukee in the 1850s, noted that the Germans' capacity for fun set them apart "from the Anglo-American people, who particularly in the West, have no other pleasure than 'business.' "

Other non-Germans, however, were amused by the German jollities, and those who attended the picnics or dropped by the beer gardens were soon infected by the same spirit. Even teetotaler Horace Greeley, the editor of the *New York Tribune,* found himself responsive to the frothy atmosphere of a German *Pfingstfest,* or Whitsuntide celebration; he later stiffly conceded that "our native citizens would find pleasure in participating in the festivities."

Many native citizens did indeed come to share in such revels and to relish the foods served at them—the plump dark loaves of pumpernickel, the oblong loaves of rye, the plump *Bratwurst,* the spicy wieners. To this day these foods are associated in the American mind with a good time. And there was something else the Germans transmitted to the Americans: their joy in Christmas. The New England Puritans had not celebrated the holiday, and later, in other parts of the country, it was sometimes little more than an occasion for getting drunk. From the Germans came both the idea of making the day one of happy religious observance and the custom of setting up a Christmas tree.

As a group, the Scandinavian immigrants were even more numerous than the Germans. Back home, a succession of bad harvests, combined with unemployment, low wages and short money supply, had driven many of them to the point of desperation. They needed little encouragement from the steamship companies and emigrant agents to pack up and leave, and, like the Germans, they found the region much to their liking. Fredrika Bremer was hard put to contain her joy when she visited Minnesota. "What a glorious new Scandinavia might not Minnesota become!" she wrote home. "Here the Swede would find again his clear, romantic lakes, the plains of Skåne rich in corn, and the valleys of Norrland; here the Norwegian would find his rapid rivers, his lofty mountains, for I include the Rocky Mountains and Oregon in the new kingdom; and both nations, their hunting-fields and their fisheries."

At home the cooking of the Scandinavians had been plain. Porridge was a staple, eaten with a little fresh, salted or smoked fish, or perhaps some cured meat. Another standby was bread, either dark sourish rye or one of the flat dry types that had evolved out of the need to store food for the long, dark northern winter. People used to such a diet had little trouble adapting to the rough fare of the American frontier. While some complained that pork was far too frequent a dish, others could not get enough of it. One man happened upon a dessert he had not had before, and he found it so delicious that he wrote home about it. "Pai" he spelled it, not

Opposite: Two great American desserts are shown together: a rich marble cake *(Recipe Index)* and some even richer peach ice cream. The brown swirls in the cake are not chocolate but a spicy batter flavored with cinnamon, cloves, nutmeg, molasses and brown sugar. A white batter was folded into the dark one just before baking.

152

revealing what kind of pie it was, but commenting, "it glides easily down your throat." Soon Scandinavian housewives were baking apple and pumpkin pies as good as any their American neighbors could turn out, and they began to excel at "American" cakes—chocolate, layer, angel and the rest. In Norway the woman who wove beautifully won fame, but in America honors went to the one who baked the best cakes.

The diary and letters of young Mrs. Elisabeth Koren, a minister's wife who emigrated from Norway to northeastern Iowa in 1853, chronicle one woman's changing attitude toward American foods. Her response must have been fairly typical of a great many European wives. At first she did not mind the relentless servings of pork, "which, curiously enough, tastes just as good to me every time I eat it." But later the monotony began to pall: "The dishes vary from boiled pork to fried pork, rare to well done, with coffee in addition (milk when we can get it), good bread and butter. To this are added now and then potatoes . . . fried onions, once in a while; and above all, the glass jar of pickles. That is our meal, morning, noon and evening. But our appetites seldom fail."

In time Elisabeth developed a yearning for the foods of home. One day she prepared Norwegian barley soup for her husband, Vilhelm, and searched in vain for ground dried barley; in the end, she dried whole barley and ground it in her coffee mill. "Then I had to find something to mix with it; the only solution was to cook some dried apples and use the juice from them—one has to do the best one can." The hunger for familiar foods continued to gnaw at her. "Oh, that I had some new potatoes and a little mackerel from home! It is really boring, this constant puzzling over tiresome food." About the only Norwegian dish she seemed able to make with any regularity was an extremely simple one, *tykmelk,* or clabbered milk, which she probably sprinkled, as do her countrymen today, with bread crumbs and sugar. Once she whipped up an all-milk meal, consisting of *tykmelk* and *rømmegrøt,* a sour-cream porridge still popular in some Norwegian-American homes. By her own admission it was a peculiar repast, but she and Vilhelm enjoyed it, and they topped it off with a glass of port.

In one entry, Elisabeth tells what it was like to dine in a cabin on the prairie. "Here is our dinner. . . . It consists of *tykmelksuppe* [thick milk soup], boiled potatoes, and ham. Here we sit then, we two at Vilhelm's little table . . . with a napkin for a tablecloth, a tin dish for a soup tureen, and bowls instead of soup plates. . . . When the soup is warm, we dish a little at a time into our bowls, each with his own tablespoon, very cozily. We have good appetites, even though my spouse at times hums very softly, 'Milk pottage they gave me, though porridge I asked for.' "

Gradually, Elisabeth began to discover some American foods she really liked. "Do you know the watermelon!" she wrote to her father in Norway. "It is extremely juicy and refreshing—bright red inside. . . . You should see how people here eat one big melon after another." She also acquired a passion for the wild strawberries that grew all over the prairies. On her way to the springhouse she would put down whatever she was carrying and stoop to pick them, even if only one or two nodded at her from the grass. By 1855, less than two years after her arrival, Mrs. Koren was raving about a delicious breakfast "consisting of hot biscuits, corn on the cob, and excellent *knaost* [a Norwegian cheese made from soured skim milk]." She had become a Scandinavian-American.

I have spent much time in Germany and Scandinavia, and have enjoyed each country's cooking at its best. And so I was all the more curious to see what had happened to German and Scandinavian food in Mid-America, and not long ago I set out to taste it for myself. I went first to Iowa, on the theory that ethnic dishes still eaten in that utterly American state would have survived the test of time only if they were very good or deeply treasured. From Cedar Rapids, I drove out to the Amana Colonies, 20 minutes from the city. I had heard about these seven villages and the devout Germans, Alsatians and Swiss, called True Inspirationists, who had founded them in the 1850s and 1860s. The members lived under a form of religious communism as recently as 1932, when they organized a joint stock company. They have prospered ever since, turning a tidy profit on their various business enterprises, including farming, meat-processing, baking and weaving. If more than a century of life in America had not changed them, I thought, then becoming capitalists probably had.

But it was a delightful surprise to find so much of the past surviving in the Amana Colonies, unmolested by the present. German is still taught in the schools and spoken by many of the 1,500 residents. The women wear black caps and black aprons to the weekly church services, which are conducted in both English and German. Most of the houses are built of brick or sandstone, strong, handsome structures, some with trellises for grapes and roses running halfway up the walls. Enormous barns cluster at one end of each village; grouped with the sheds and granaries, they form bold geometric patterns against the blue Iowa sky.

Even more interesting was the persistence of the old German foods. The Inspirationists were a hard-working, hungry people, who raised almost everything they ate. They took their meals in "kitchen-houses," where the dishes were wholesome and plenteous, with such German classics as liver dumplings, *Sauerbraten,* and *Streuselkuchen.* The menus followed a strict pattern: the Tuesday main meal always included *Mehlspeisen,* or plain desserts, such as flour and farina puddings. Wednesday was the day for boiled beef, and Thursday the time for a special dessert, such as a custard or lemon pie. The pies reflected American influence, but there were also such unusual varieties as grape pie, for which the pulp is separated from the skins, cooked and sieved, and then combined with the reserved skins, sugar, salt and lemon. The result is a filling that startles the palate with its combination of sweet and tart flavors.

On my visit to the colonies I ate a hearty old-style Amana meal. It started with "pickled ham," which is simply good boiled ham cut in small chunks and steeped in vinegar, onions and pickling spices. That set the juices flowing; while waiting for the second course, I found myself nibbling at the crisp coleslaw and sampling the cottage cheese, which was thick and creamy, with big tangy curds. Next came an entire parade of dishes: more ham, sliced and lightly fried; fat grilled sausages, with the spicy bits of meat enclosed loosely in the casing; fried chicken, its smooth giblet dressing flavored with a dash of nutmeg; mashed potatoes and

On the Max Larsen farm at Thayne, Wyoming, Mary Williams, a summer visitor, holds a block of Swiss cheese from the Starr Valley Dairy Farms. Unlike Wisconsin Swiss, which is made largely by people of Swiss descent, this cheese is produced by Mormons whose families settled in the valley before 1900 and formed a cheese-making cooperative. Its 264 members graze 5,000 Holstein cows and make four million pounds of cheese a year.

Continued on page 158

Mrs. Henry Loven carefully rolls out a sheet of dough for potato *lefse* as her neighbor, Mrs. Alex Dahlen, watches.

In the Kitchen of an Iowa Farmhouse an Old Norwegian Bread Takes Shape

A taste for the cooking of the Old Country runs deep among the present-day descendants of immigrants in the Northwest, and some of the foods they like best turn out to be the traditional dishes. In the pictures on these pages Mrs. Henry Loven and Mrs. Alex Dahlen, two ladies of Norwegian descent who live on farms near Decorah, Iowa, are shown making potato *lefse,* a venerable Norwegian flat bread baked on a griddle. Both women are third-generation Americans, but they are as adept as their ancestors were at rolling the *lefse* dough paper thin. Mrs. Loven and Mrs. Dahlen delivered the finished bread to a local Lutheran church where a dinner was to be held. Featured on the menu along with the *lefse* was *lutefisk,* or lye-cured cod, served with melted-butter sauce—another well-loved, simple food from the Scandinavian past.

Lefse dough, a blend of riced boiled potatoes, flour, salt, sugar, butter and cream, is shaped into balls *(above)*, then rolled out into a circle with a grooved rolling pin. The dough is thin enough for the light to shine through *(right)*.

Transferred to an electric griddle with a long, flat stick *(left)*, the rolled-out dough is browned slightly on both sides. It should still be moist and pliable after baking.

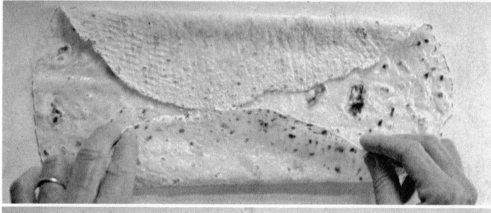

A "loaf" of *lefse* is too flat and far too large to be sliced and eaten like ordinary bread; instead, it is buttered and rolled up somewhat like a crêpe, then sliced on the diagonal for serving. Some people eat the *lefse* plain as part of a meal; others sprinkle granulated sugar over it and eat it with coffee.

157

steamed kernels of fresh corn. The dessert was a rhubarb-custard pie *(Recipe Index)*, the tartness of the fruit contrasting with the bland sweetness of the egg and cream that made up the rest of the filling.

After this pleasant meal I attended a winetasting. I had not expected to find a local wine in Iowa, and it turned out to be a unique one, called Piestengel, made from the juice of strawberry rhubarb and aged in oak casks. My hostess, Alma Ehrle, who runs one of the five wineries in the colonies, poured some into my glass in a golden stream. The wine was sweet, without any discernible rhubarb flavor, and I drained the glass. "Now you must have an 'Amana Martini'—Piestengel and grape wine, a combination we like," said Alma in her charmingly accented voice, and she mixed the two, half and half, in a second glass. The blend was agreeable, though a bit fruity. "Finish that, and have some *old* wine—a real vintage Piestengel," Alma insisted, and reached for another bottle and filled a third glass. The wine was drier and stronger than the first; I began to feel its effect and wondered whether this had been the source of some of the True Inspirationists' inspiration. Alma told me that her people not only drink Piestengel but use it in cooking. For example, she herself takes a steak, pounds seasoned flour into it with the edge of a thick plate, then simmers the meat with onions in rhubarb wine. "Is it ever tender!" Seeing that my glass was empty, she was about to fill it again. I put my hand over the top, explaining that I had another appointment to keep, and floated over to the Amana Meat Shop.

There Carl Oehl, one of the managers, showed me how Amana hams are cured according to the unhurried methods of the past. He led the way to large vats where rotund hams lay submerged in brine. They were delicately pink, with a layer of creamy white fat running around them. "We soak them 28 days," Carl said. "Then we take them to the smokehouse. We burn hickory—and we let them mellow in the smoke, a slow, lazy, moving smoke." Some of the hams are then partially cooked and packaged, while others are shifted to the garret for further aging. "Come see," Carl said, and as we climbed the ladder leading to the garret, the rich odor of hickory smoke and pepper became tantalizingly strong. Dangling from the rafters were a hundred or so Westphalian-style hams, a rich honey brown, dusted all over with finely ground black pepper. Carl took one down and patted its plump side as though it were a pet. "These we age another eight or ten weeks," he said with pride.

I bought one of the precooked hams, and at Carl's urging, a jar of Amana horseradish jelly as well, to use as a glaze. Some weeks later, at home, my wife scored the fat and studded the ham with cloves, then spread the jelly over it. When the ham emerged from the oven it had a sticky, slightly crunchy crust. I did the carving; the pink slices flared away from the ivory bone in limp, tender slices. The meat was juicy and wonderfully textured; it had a soft, smoky taste, set off by the sweet yet fiery horseradish glaze.

From the Amana Colonies I drove north to Decorah, the home of a great many Norwegian-Americans, for I wanted to compare the close-knit Amana folk with a more assimilated group. Decorah, with its snug white houses and tree-lined streets, seemed the very prototype of an American town. Nothing on the surface gave away its Norwegian associations —except perhaps the blond good looks of the people. But I was taken behind the scenes by Dr. Marion Nelson, the director of Decorah's Norwegian-American Museum. It proved a fascinating place, crammed on both its floors with mementoes of Scandinavian immigrants. Among the reminders of spirited living in the old country were beautifully ornamented drinking bowls and tankards.

As Dr. Nelson and I strolled down one of Decorah's streets, I spotted a hand-lettered sign in a shopwindow advertising a *lutefisk* and *lefse* supper to be given by the brotherhood of the Glenwood church. *Lutefisk,* as noted earlier, is lye-cured cod; *lefse* is a kind of flat bread made with mashed potatoes *(Recipe Index).* The two appear often, along with other Scandinavian dishes, on the menus of Norwegian Lutheran church dinners, and such dinners attract large crowds. I suspect that the people who partake of them do so almost ritualistically, as a way of keeping in touch with the past. I asked Dr. Nelson whether we could visit some of the people involved in the preparation of the Glenwood dinner, and, after telephoning around, he told me that two of the women responsible for the *lefse* would be happy to see us if we hurried right on out. They were together at the home of Mrs. Henry Loven, several miles outside town, and they were about to begin work.

We approached the Loven farm over a dirt road that rose and fell with the contours of the smooth hills. The house sat at the foot of one of the hills, a large, white house with a red barn and grazing sheep behind it —and off to one side a grove of tall spruces, planted perhaps to remind some homesick soul of Norway.

Mrs. Loven and her friend, Mrs. Alex Dahlen, welcomed us with shy country smiles and ushered us into the kitchen. The morning light streamed through the windows, lighting up the oilcloth on which they had placed their dough, a mixture of boiled mashed potatoes, flour, a little butter, cream and salt. Mrs. Loven fashioned the dough into a loaf and cut off pieces that she and Mrs. Dahlen shaped into balls with their palms. She then floured a board and rolled one of the balls out in an ever-widening circle with a grooved rolling pin. By the time she was done, the dough was as thin as cardboard. She lifted it up with a long, flat stick —her treasured *lefse* stick—and transferred the pancakelike round of dough to a hot griddle. Almost at once the *lefse* began to blister and the edges to curl up, whereupon Mrs. Loven turned it and let it sit a few moments more until it was done on the other side. Removing the bread with her stick, she spread it out on the table. Mrs. Dahlen buttered it, folded one side and then the other toward the middle, then folded both over again, forming a sort of giant crêpe. She sliced this on the diagonal, and offered me a piece. It was moist and tender, with a slightly sour, potatolike flavor—agreeable, old-fashioned Norwegian peasant food.

While the ladies went on with their *lefse* baking, I wandered through the other rooms. There was something familiar about the house—the living room with its overstuffed furniture, the television set with the framed photographs of the children and grandchildren crowded on its top, the picture of Jesus on the wall, the tick of a clock. I had seen similar farm-

Baking cookies like these is a cherished Christmas tradition among the ladies of Minneapolis' American Swedish Institute. Scandinavian classics shown here include buttery spritz rings *(on the tray)* decorated to look like wreaths; sugar-dusted *fattigmannbakkels (bowl at left);* and ginger-flavored *pepparkakor* and fluted *sandbakkels (bowls at mantelpiece).* The sheaf-shaped cookies on the tray were baked from the *sandbakkel* batter.

houses all over America. Yet here were two women, with the indelible sound of the old country on their tongues, making *lefse* in the kitchen. When they had finished they invited us to have coffee with them. The generous hospitality of the Norwegian pioneer home was still alive in this house. Out came the coffee cups, placed directly on the table without saucers, then the big pot itself. And set down in the middle of the table were three plates, one bearing the buttered *lefse,* another with slices of American-style walnut poundcake, and the third heaped with even-more-American butterscotch brownies.

As I continued my travels, a pattern emerged. In almost every instance the ethnic dishes that survived were the ones that had the longest associations with the past; and most of them had some connection with a holiday, festival or event. I was lucky enough to be traveling in the weeks before Christmas, when all the traditional Old World specialties were beginning to appear or, at least, to be thought about. In St. Paul I talked to a bachelor cook who was getting ready to make Swedish potato sausage. He would not, he told me, consider Christmas complete without it. He grinds 10 pounds of peeled potatoes coarsely and mixes them with a pound of ground pork, three pounds of ground beef, two ground onions, salt and pepper, and stuffs this mixture into 18-inch casings. He then cooks the sausages in water seasoned with salt, pepper and onion *(for another version, see the Recipe Index).* After setting aside enough for

160

himself, he distributes the remainder among friends who share his taste for the flavors of the past. The very prospect of Christmas seemed to evoke a stream of memories for him. He spoke with special fondness of the ceremony of *dopperedan,* or "dipping day," at his grandparents' house, when the family stood around the stove and dunked pieces of home-baked rye bread into a rich meat broth made by boiling equal amounts of beef, pork and veal in salted water.

A Minneapolis woman I interviewed described the trouble she goes to each year to make blood sausage, another Swedish Christmas dish. "I used to be able to get pork blood from a packing plant here in the city, but that's no longer legal, so I depend upon my cousin, who has a farm, to give me some." She thickens the cooked blood with flour, adds chopped suet and onions, and seasons the mixture with nutmeg, sugar and salt. Then, after filling the casings, she bakes the sausages in a pan of water. On Christmas morning she slices them, fries the pieces in butter "until yummy soft," and serves them with fried potatoes and cranberries or lingonberries. This has been her family's Christmas breakfast for as long as she or anyone else can remember. But the tradition seems in some danger of dying out: "My son can't *stand* blood sausages!"

Not all the old Christmas specialties are so rustically plain. In Northern Europe, Christmas was the time to bring out the best foods and to use up the hoarded butter, sugar and eggs. Fortunately, this tradition of cooking with a lavish hand remains strong among people with an awareness of their culinary heritage. In Minneapolis, I came upon the women members of The American Swedish Institute turning out cookies and yeast breads for sale at their annual Christmas fair. The old, sober mansion in which The Institute is housed was redolent with the odors floating from its kitchen, one predominating—the rich scent of butter.

In Grand Forks, North Dakota, I visited two families—one of Norwegian descent, the other of Icelandic—for whom Christmas is the high point of the year, a warm spot in a very cold winter. Dr. and Mrs. Maurice Hoghaug served me Norwegian Christmas cookies while Mrs. Hoghaug described the lengths to which she goes to see that the holiday is celebrated in style (it takes her four days just to put up the decorations). First I tried the *krumkaker,* brittle tubes baked flat on a patterned iron and then rolled; and they dissolved in my mouth *(Recipe Index).* Next I sampled the *fattigmannbakkels.* The name means "poor man's pastry," but there was nothing poor about them. They had been made with an egg-rich batter that had been flavored with brandy, cut in diamond shapes and cooked in hot fat. And finally I had some of the *sandbakkels,* delicate little cups with fluted edges, bearing the imprint of the special tins in which they had been baked.

Mrs. Hoghaug has about 20 guests for her Christmas Eve dinner (the eve, rather than the day, is the time for the big feast in Scandinavia), and she serves them *lutefisk, torsk* (fresh cod), *ribbe* (spareribs), tiny meatballs in thick gravy, *rullepølse* (rolled spiced beef, served cold), *spekekjøtt* (smoked dried lamb), *sylte* (headcheese), *søtsuppe* (sweet fruit soup), *lefse, risgrøt* (rice pudding) and *rømmegrøt* (sour-cream porridge). About the only American touch is the homemade chokecherry wine her son Andy provides. Since the Christmas feasting is an ongoing affair for Scandinavians, she roasts a goose or a turkey on the day itself, and everyone sits down to table again.

Filled with the proper Christmas spirit by Mrs. Hoghaug, I went on to visit the cozy home of Mr. and Mrs. Skuli Stefanson. Both grew up in northeastern North Dakota, and both learned to speak Icelandic as children. These warm, gracious people put me right at ease. "I'll have the coffee on in a minute, and then we'll eat," said Mrs. Stefanson. She is a working woman without a great deal of time to spare, and she had already done the major part of her Christmas baking.

While we were waiting for the coffee to perk, I asked the Stefansons about Icelandic food. I knew that Iceland is beautiful but bleak, and I had read that toward the end of the 19th Century life was so hard there that a third of the population left, mostly for the United States and Canada. I assumed that Icelandic food would be as bleak as the island, and I wanted to know whether any of it had survived in America.

"Well, one thing we ate a lot of," Mrs. Stefanson said, "was *skyr*." I had heard about this milk dish, which was once popular throughout Scandinavia, and whose history can be traced back to the Vikings. Mrs. Stefanson described her mother's method of making it. She would bring sweet milk to a boil, let it cool, and stir in a thickener of egg, sugar and sour cream. Then she would set the milk in a warm place to thicken and sour. Later she would drain off the whey and whip the curds with cream until they were smooth. She would blend in a little sugar and spoon the tart, refreshing *skyr* into bowls, sometimes with blueberries or other fresh fruit as a topping. "Is *skyr* still made?" I asked. "I make it," Mrs. Stefanson said, "but not from my mother's recipe. I use a simpler, modern one that calls for either cultured buttermilk or powdered milk and rennet. If we lived in Winnipeg, we'd be able to buy *skyr*. It's sold there as a ready-made dairy product."

The coffee was ready, and Mrs. Stefanson led me to the table. Resting importantly on a large plate was a cake like none I had ever seen before. It had seven thin layers, each about a quarter of an inch thick, with a filling between them. Mrs. Stefanson cut me a healthy wedge. "Now this is one Icelandic specialty that *has* survived," she said. "It's called a *vinarterta*. See whether you like it." The first bite told me that I liked it very much. The filling was a blend of sweetened puréed apricots and prunes, flavored with vanilla and cardamom; the crisp layers bore a trace of the same flavorings.

At Mrs. Stefanson's urging I helped myself to several of her cookies. One was butter blond and about a quarter of an inch thick. "I make that kind with a pound of butter," said my hostess casually, "a cup of cornstarch, three cups of flour and a cup and a half of powdered sugar. When my sister and I were girls, we used to go off to bed at night with a couple of them in our hands. We'd lie in the dark and just let them melt in our mouths." Mrs. Stefanson's other cookies were as meltingly good, and then and there I revised my notions about the bleak foods of Iceland.

So far, on my journey through the six-state region, ethnic cooking seemed to be in excellent fettle. To make a final test of its viability, I ended my trip with a visit to Milwaukee. Here was a city proud of its ethnic variety. Would its cooking be multifaceted as well? I expected the German culinary influence to prevail, and to some extent I was right. I would guess that more sausages, or *Würste,* are made and eaten in Milwaukee than anywhere else in the United States. No fewer than 50 sausage makers are listed in the city's telephone directory, and the list reveals a preponderance of German names.

One of the oldest and best of the sausage makers is Usinger's, and I repaired to the company's retail store as soon as I could. I pushed open the big front door, stepped inside and was at once enveloped in the rich odor of smoked spiced meat. Even as I write about it, I get hungry. There, in glass cases set atop solid marble bases, were some of the products that have made Usinger's famous since 1880. Laid out in inviting rows were rolls of creamy *Braunschweiger,* encased in white lard; chewy summer sausages; thick, bulging *mortadella;* gleaming blocks of headcheese, the bits of meat embedded in a translucent natural jelly; *Blutwurst* with tongue; plum-red knackwurst; and pale pork-and-veal *Bratwurst.* When the time came to taste them, I was relieved to find that not one smacked of MSG; the fine meat spoke for itself, and so did the garlic, paprika, marjoram and a host of other seasonings.

My last Milwaukee experience was of a very different sort, proving beyond a doubt that widespread fondness for ethnic foods other than German. With 50,000 other people, I attended the three-day Holiday Folk Fair that is held in the Milwaukee Arena-Auditorium every winter. Some 30 different groups participated, and each sold examples of its cuisine at decorated tables and stands. The food was homemade and much of it was very good—as good as it can be when women work under the watchful gaze of other women, using their own time-tested recipes. Some had been busy for a week or more, and when I arrived at the Folk Fair some were still busy behind the scenes, baking and boiling and frying.

Attics, trunks and closets had been ransacked for native costumes and the auditorium, glowing with the bright, true colors of peasant embroidery, looked like a flower-filled meadow. Visitors moved from booth to booth with paper plates in hand, buying foods; some sat at tables, relishing Czech roast pork and dumplings, Hungarian goulash, Polish cheese *pierogi* and countless other specialties. The beer flowed freely, and the atmosphere was that of a big happy picnic. As I went from booth to booth, I could have had any of a hundred dishes—Armenian shish kebab, Latvian roast goose, Greek oregano chicken, Danish liver paste and smoked eel, Bavarian potato pancakes and applesauce, Russian *borshch.* The desserts were even more numerous than the entrees. There were a dozen different strudels, filled with nuts, poppy seeds, cherries, apples and cheese; assorted tortes and *Kuchen;* piles of cookies and small cakes, all with that home-baked, homemade look, the little touches and flourishes and even the endearing ineptitudes that no commercial bakery can ever duplicate. As I tried to make my choices I saw one lean and hungry young man standing in front of a Coke machine. He was balancing a slice of pizza in one hand and a frankfurter and a roll in the other, and he had the blissful look of someone who had found heaven.

A Feast of All Nations
at the Milwaukee Folk Fair

Milwaukee is a mosaic of people of various national origins, and every autumn the county's International Institute sponsors a folk fair in their honor. More than 40 different ethnic groups, ranging from Germans, Czechs and Poles to Japanese and Indonesians, participate in the fair. About 35 of these groups sell examples of their national cuisines at gaily decorated booths, and for a three-day period Milwaukee's Arena-Auditorium, where the fair is held, becomes one of the world's busiest restaurants. At one recent fair this "restaurant" dispensed 120,000 pieces of pastry, 2,635 pounds of sausage and 7,000 pounds of other meats, 120 roast Latvian geese and 250 chickens cooked the Greek way—and 50,000 glasses of beer were drunk by thirsty fairgoers.

High on the list of perennial favorites at the folk fair are homemade baked goods, and this array is only a sampling of the cakes, cookies and breads that are available at the booths. The ones shown here include, among others:

1 Greek bread
2 Ukrainian rum torte
3 Irish soda bread
4 Swedish coffee bread
5 French cherry torte
6 Pastry fritters
   (Czech and Italian)
7 Danish *kringle*
8 Lebanese bread
9 Slovak poppy-seed rolls
10 Norwegian *sandbakkels*
11 Polish *pączki*
12 German gingerbread cookies
13 Italian *cannoli*
14 Norwegian *pepparkakor*
15 Czech *koláč*
16 Dutch *oliebollen*
17 Baltic *Aleksander torte*
18 Rosettes
   (Armenian, Swiss and Swedish)
19 Greek wreath cookies

Bustling Slovak women in national costumes cook sausages for sale at their booth *(above)*. The costumes are often treasured heirlooms, donned once a year for the fair, then cleaned and carefully packed away. *Below:* At the Czech booth, Mrs. Anna Schindler and Mrs. Hilda Urban enjoy a dish of beets, dumplings and pork roast served with three gravies. *At left:* A participant momentarily forgoes all ethnic pleasures —and settles for an American soft drink.

To serve 4

6 medium-sized boiling potatoes,
   peeled
6 slices bacon
½ cup finely chopped onions
4 eggs
1 teaspoon salt
¼ teaspoon freshly ground black
   pepper

Basque Potatoes

Drop the potatoes into enough lightly salted boiling water to cover them by at least 1 inch, and boil briskly until they are almost tender and show only slight resistance when pierced deeply with the point of a small skewer or sharp knife. Drain off the water, return the pan to low heat, and slide it back and forth for a minute or so to dry the potatoes completely. Cut the potatoes crosswise into ⅛-inch-thick slices and set aside.

In a heavy 12-inch skillet, preferably one with a nonstick cooking surface, fry the bacon over moderate heat, turning the slices frequently until they are crisp and brown and have rendered all their fat. Transfer the slices to paper towels to drain, then crumble them into bits.

Pour all but about 4 tablespoons of the bacon fat into a heatproof cup or bowl; set aside. Add the onions to the fat remaining in the skillet and, stirring frequently, cook over moderate heat for about 5 minutes, until they are soft and translucent but not brown. Carefully add the potatoes and mix them with the onions, using a wooden spoon. Slide the pan back and forth until the potato slices lie flat. Then cook over moderate heat until the bottom side of the potatoes is golden brown.

Slide the spatula around the edges of the skillet and as far under the potatoes as you can without crumbling them. Place an inverted plate over the pan and, grasping plate and skillet together firmly, turn them over. Slide the potatoes back into the skillet, browned side up, first adding a few spoonfuls of the reserved fat to the pan if it is not the nonstick type.

Cook over moderate heat for 2 or 3 minutes to brown the bottom, then reduce the heat to low. Meanwhile beat the eggs, salt and pepper with a wire whisk or rotary beater until they are well combined. Pour the eggs over the potatoes and sprinkle the reserved bacon bits on top. Cover the skillet and cook for 5 or 6 minutes, or until the eggs are set and firm to the touch. Serve at once, directly from the skillet.

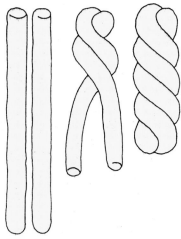

To make one 16-inch twist

DOUGH
¼ cup lukewarm water (110° to
   115°)
1 package active dry yeast
1 teaspoon plus ⅓ cup sugar
¾ cup lukewarm milk (110° to
   115°)
6 tablespoons unsalted butter,
   softened
1 teapoon salt
1 egg, lightly beaten
3 to 3½ cups flour

Swedish Cherry Twist

DOUGH: Pour the water into a small bowl and sprinkle the yeast and 1 teaspoon of the sugar over it. Let stand for 2 or 3 minutes, then stir well. Set in a warm, draft-free place (such as an unlighted oven) for about 10 minutes, or until the yeast bubbles up and the mixture almost doubles in volume. Meanwhile, combine the milk and 4 tablespoons of the butter and, stirring occasionally, cook over moderate heat until the butter has melted and bubbles begin to form around the edges of the pan. Then pour the mixture into a deep bowl and set aside to cool to lukewarm.

Add the yeast mixture, the salt, the remaining ⅓ cup of sugar and the lightly beaten egg and, with a wooden spoon, stir until all the ingredients are well blended. Then add 3 cups of the flour, 1 cup at a time, and continue to stir until the dough can be gathered into a medium-soft ball.

Place the ball on a lightly floured surface and knead, pushing the dough down with the heels of your hands, pressing it forward and folding it back on itself. As you knead, incorporate as much of the remaining

The dish known as Basque potatoes, popular in Idaho, contains the state's famous potatoes, topped with bacon bits.

½ cup of flour as is required to make a smooth, fairly dry dough. When the dough is shiny and elastic, reshape it into a ball. With a pastry brush, coat the inside of another large bowl with 1 tablespoon of the softened butter. Drop in the dough and turn it about to coat the entire ball with butter. Then drape the bowl with a towel and put it into the draft-free place for about 45 minutes, or until the dough doubles in volume. Meanwhile, brush a baking sheet with the remaining tablespoon of butter.

Punch the dough down with a single blow of your fist and place it on a lightly floured surface.

SHAPING AND TOPPING: Cut the dough in half and with your hands shape each half into a cylinder about 18 inches long and 1½ inches wide. Place the cylinders side by side on the baking sheet and pinch the tops together so that the cylinders form a narrow "V." Following the diagram opposite, shape the dough into a twist about 14 inches long. Set the twist aside to rise for 45 minutes, or until it doubles in bulk.

Preheat the oven to 375°. With a pastry brush, coat the twist with the combined egg yolk and milk, then mix the almonds, sugar and cinnamon, and sprinkle them over the top. Set the candied cherry halves in two rows along the length of the twist. Bake in the center of the oven for about 25 minutes, or until golden brown. Turn the cherry twist out on a wire rack to cool. Serve it warm or at room temperature.

TOPPING
1 egg yolk, lightly beaten and combined with 1 teaspoon milk
¼ cup blanched almonds, coarsely chopped
¼ cup sugar
1 teaspoon ground cinnamon
4 candied cherries, halved

167

To serve 6 to 8

3 pounds medium-sized boiling
  potatoes (about 9), scrubbed and
  unpeeled
½ pound bacon, cut into ½-inch
  dice (about 1½ cups)
½ cup finely chopped onions
¼ cup white wine or cider vinegar
¼ cup water
½ teaspoon salt
¼ teaspoon freshly ground black
  pepper
1 teaspoon dry mustard
2 tablespoons finely cut fresh chives

To serve 4

2 strips of spareribs, each about 10
  inches long, trimmed of excess
  fat (about 3 to 3½ pounds in all)
3 teaspoons salt
Freshly ground black pepper
1 pound pitted dried prunes, halved
  (about 2 cups)
4 large firm apples, preferably green
  cooking apples, peeled, cored and
  cut into ½-inch-thick slices
¼ cup light-brown sugar
1 tablespoon ground cinnamon

To make about 15

3 large baking potatoes, peeled and
  quartered
2 tablespoons butter, softened and
  cut into ½-inch bits
¼ cup heavy cream
½ teaspoon sugar
1 teaspoon salt
1 cup flour

Potato Salad with Bacon Bits

Drop the potatoes into enough lightly salted boiling water to cover them completely, and boil briskly, uncovered, until they show only slight resistance when pierced with the point of a sharp knife. Do not overcook. Drain the potatoes in a colander, peel and cut them into ¼-inch-thick slices. Set aside in a large bowl and cover tightly with foil.

In a heavy 8-inch skillet, fry the bacon over moderate heat until brown and crisp. With a slotted spoon, transfer the dice to paper towels to drain. Add the onions to the fat remaining in the pan and stir over moderate heat until they are soft and golden. Add the vinegar, water, salt, pepper and mustard and bring the sauce to a boil. Pour the hot sauce over the potatoes, turning the slices with a rubber spatula to coat them evenly. Stir in the bacon and chives and taste for seasoning. Serve at once.

Stuffed Spareribs

Preheat the oven to 350°. Sprinkle the meaty sides of the spareribs with 2 teaspoons of the salt and a few grindings of pepper. Place one strip of ribs meat side down and spread it evenly with all the prunes and apples. Sprinkle with the brown sugar, the remaining salt and the cinnamon, and cover with the other strip of spareribs, meat side up. Tie the two together, crosswise and lengthwise, securely enclosing the stuffing. Place the ribs on a rack set in a shallow roasting pan and bake in the middle of the oven for 1½ hours, or until the ribs show no resistance when pierced with the tip of a knife. Cut away the strings and serve the spareribs.

Lefse
FLAT POTATO BREADS

Drop the potatoes into enough boiling water to cover them completely and boil briskly, uncovered, until they are soft and can be easily pierced with the point of a sharp knife. Drain thoroughly and force them through a ricer or mash them in a bowl with a fork. (You should have about 2 cups of potatoes.) Add the butter, cream, sugar and salt and beat until the mixture is smooth. Cover and refrigerate for at least 8 hours.

Gather the potato mixture into a ball, place it on a heavily floured surface, and sprinkle with about ½ cup of the flour. Knead the mixture —by pressing it down with the heels of your hands, pushing it forward, and folding it back on itself—for about 10 minutes. Incorporate the remaining flour gradually as you proceed. Divide the dough into 15 small balls. With a grooved Swedish *lefse* pin or a plain rolling pin, roll one of the balls into a paper-thin round about 6 inches in diameter. Heat a large griddle or skillet until very hot, drape one round of dough on the rolling pin, and unroll it onto the hot surface. Cook only a moment or two, until bubbles appear on the surface of the dough and the bottom of the *lefse* browns lightly. With a metal spatula, turn it over and brown the other side. Transfer to a large plate and cover with a damp towel while you proceed to roll out and cook the remaining rounds of dough.

To serve, butter the *lefse*, roll loosely, and cut it into diagonal slices. Or sprinkle the buttered *lefse* with sugar and top with honey or jam.

Spareribs stuffed with apples and prunes, served with potato salad and beer, are a German contribution to Northwestern fare.

Spritz Cookies

Preheat the oven to 350°. In a deep bowl, cream the butter and sugar together by beating and mashing them against the sides of the bowl with the back of a large spoon until they are light and fluffy. Beat in the egg yolks and, when they are well incorporated, add the almond extract. Sift the flour into the mixture about ½ cup at a time, beating the dough well after each addition.

Place the dough in a pastry bag or cookie press fitted with a medium-sized star tip. Pipe the dough out onto ungreased baking sheets, forming rings about 1½ inches in diameter or "S" shapes or crescents about 2 inches long, spaced about 1 inch apart.

Bake in the middle of the oven for about 10 minutes, or until the cookies are firm and delicately browned. With a wide metal spatula, transfer them immediately to wire racks to cool. The cookies can be stored for several weeks in tightly sealed jars or tins.

To make about 4 dozen pressed
  cookies

1 cup butter, softened
1 cup sugar
2 egg yolks
1 teaspoon almond extract
2½ cups flour

The *krumkake,* a light, crisp Norwegian cookie, is traditionally made from thin batter pressed flat on an ornately decorative heated iron. The iron shown above is decorated with a traditional Old World pattern.

After being cooked on the iron, each cookie is rolled around a cylindrical shaft, such as a piece of broomstick *(above).* In a few minutes the *krumkaker* harden and can be decoratively assembled in a sugar-filled bowl *(below).*

Krumkaker

PASTRY CONES FILLED WITH CANDIED WHIPPED CREAM

A special krumkaker iron somewhat similar to a waffle iron, and heated on top of the stove, and its accompanying cone-shaped tube are recommended for the preparation of these pastry cones. These implements can be purchased at specialized cookware shops.

In a large bowl, beat the eggs and superfine sugar together with a wire whisk or a rotary or electric beater and continue to beat until the mixture has thickened and almost tripled in volume. Stir in the flour, a tablespoon at a time, and mix until the batter is smooth.

Lightly butter the cone-shaped tube and heat the *krumkaker* iron over moderate heat. When it is very hot, use a pastry brush to coat both its surfaces lightly with the melted butter. Drop 1 tablespoon of the batter into the center of the iron, close it, and cook for about 30 seconds. Turn the iron over and cook for another 30 seconds, then turn again and remove from the heat. Open the iron and peel off the golden pastry. Immediately wrap the cookie around the tube; as soon as it hardens, slip it off and set aside. Repeat with the remaining batter, buttering the iron and tube for each cone you make.

The pastry cones can be baked several days in advance and kept crisp in airtight containers. Just before you are ready to serve the cones, whip the chilled cream with a whisk or a rotary or electric beater in a large, chilled bowl until it thickens. Add the tablespoon of sugar and the vanilla, and continue to beat until the cream is stiff enough to form unwavering peaks on the beater when it is lifted from the bowl. Fold in the candy with a rubber spatula, and spoon the cream into a pastry bag fitted with a plain or decorative tip. Pipe the cream into the pastry cones and serve at once. Once filled, the pastry cones cannot be refrigerated or they will lose their crispness.

Dreams

Preheat the oven to 350°. With a pastry brush, spread 2 tablespoons of the softened butter evenly over two large baking sheets. Combine the flour, baking soda and cardamom, and sift them together onto a plate or a piece of wax paper. Set aside.

In a deep bowl, cream the remaining 8 tablespoons of butter and the sugar together, beating and mashing them against the side of the bowl with the back of a spoon until the mixture is light and fluffy. Beat in the egg and, when it is thoroughly incorporated, add the flour mixture about ½ cup at a time, beating well after each addition.

To shape each dream, scoop up about 1 tablespoon of the dough, then pat and roll it into a ball about 1 inch in diameter. Arrange the cookies 2 inches apart on the buttered baking sheets and press a whole filbert gently but firmly into the center of each one. Bake in the middle of the oven for about 10 minutes, or until the cookies are firm to the touch and a delicate golden-brown color.

Immediately transfer the cookies to wire cake racks with a metal spatula to cool to room temperature. The dreams can be kept safely in tightly covered jars or tins for several weeks.

To make 16

PASTRY
2 eggs
⅓ cup superfine sugar
3 tablespoons flour
2 tablespoons unsalted butter, melted

CANDIED WHIPPED CREAM
1½ cups heavy cream, chilled
1 tablespoon sugar
¾ teaspoon vanilla extract
3 ounces peppermint candy, pulverized in a blender or wrapped in a towel and crushed with a rolling pin (⅓ cup)

To make about thirty 1½-inch round drop cookies

10 tablespoons butter, softened
1⅓ cups flour
½ teaspoon baking soda
⅛ teaspoon ground cardamom
½ cup sugar
1 egg
¼ cup whole filberts, shelled

VII

The Lure of the Wild

The true, fresh taste of wild berries lends a special touch to otherwise conventional pies. Here salmonberries, relatives of the wild raspberry, have been used to stud the whipped-cream topping of a "no-bake pie" made with a rich graham-cracker crust *(see raspberry pie, Recipe Index)*. Beneath the sweet, creamy topping, crushed salmonberries are held fast in a filling of raspberry-flavored gelatin.

Some of the best foods in life are still free. Hunting or fishing may require licenses and expensive equipment, but it costs nothing or next to nothing, even today, to gather berries, mushrooms and other wild plants from field and forest. And that is where the flavor is, where nature's richness is concentrated.

For many an American, berrying is one of the fondest memories of childhood. I myself grew up in New York City, and down the street from us some blackberry bushes survived as if by magic in a vacant lot. There was never more than a handful of berries, but I can still conjure up their taste and the trickle of their warm juice. In another lot stood a black-walnut tree. I would run to grab its windfall before the other kids arrived, and would stuff the nuts into my jacket. No odor has ever seemed quite so healthy as the lemony smell of their green pebbly rinds.

There is, in fact, a kind of therapy in gathering wild foods. All men were hunter-gatherers once, and it may be that performing an act as old as mankind helps bring out something basic inside ourselves. The goal is never just to fill a bucket: we want the experience of taking food from a bush or a plant that exists almost in spite of us. In a wood or at the edge of a field, where the brambles are often thickest and the berries fattest, we can reach out, touch nature and feel at one with it.

In preparing this book, I traveled through some of the best berry and mushroom territory in North America. Sections of Wisconsin, Idaho and Washington astonished me with their range of edible fungi, and all of the Pacific Northwest turned out to be a berrypicker's Eden. Indeed, the state flower of Oregon, the Oregon grape, is actually a berry—a barberry with hollylike leaves, small yellow flowers in season, and blue berries that make a tart jelly. Elsewhere—in the Dakotas, Montana, Nebraska and the western Canadian provinces—wild plums, wild grapes, choke-cherries, pincherries, serviceberries (pronounced "sarvisberries") and other fruits hang heavy on trees, shrubs and vines in late summer and early fall. As my journey progressed, I tasted all sorts of berries in all sorts of forms—as jams and jellies, as juices and wines, as syrups for pancakes and waffles, in pies, puddings, cakes, muffins and breads. But they were never so good as when they were eaten out of hand, with a little dust or dew on them.

Some experiences stand out from others with a vividness that turns the winter in which I write into summer. There was the day, for instance, when Liet, the girls and I arrived in Prince Rupert, British Columbia. No sooner had we eaten our lunch than we were out berrying. My wife's brother Ernie remembered my enthusiasm for the sport, and thought that we should take immediate advantage of the sunshine and the huckleberries, then at their peak. We pulled on rubber boots, seized our berry pails—which were simply coffee cans with ropes for handles—and drove off in the direction of the Skeena River. We had not gone far when we found what we were looking for: a logged-over area, exactly the kind of place where berries usually thrive. It was a windy day; the sky was piled high with clouds above clouds—boiling, exploding, their shadows speeding across the dark forests and disappearing over distant mountains. Absorbed by the sky and the scenery, Liet and I had a hard time getting down to the business at hand, but Elisabeth and her cousins promptly set off into the brush. They came back seconds later, shouting, "Berries! Berries!"—and we followed in after them.

They had come upon a patch of red huckleberries. (I had not even known until then that there *was* a red huckleberry.) The bushes stood quite tall and Elisabeth, with the perfect illogic of childhood, began picking from the top down, so that she had to stand on her toes to get at them. The berries she picked were about a quarter of an inch across, soft and cool to the touch, and they fell with a muffled kerplunk into the can she was carrying. For every three huckleberries she and her cousin Janie yanked from a bush, they popped at least one into their mouths.

When we had gathered all the berries in sight we burrowed through the brush in search of others. We tripped over brittle silver branches, washed of their bark by rain and snow, and sloshed over a cushion of moss. Parting boughs of cedar, we entered a clearing and saw an abandoned cabin. A plank path led across the soggy ground toward more woods, and we followed it. Frogs and toads, green, brown and black, some not much bigger than a pinkie nail, hopped away in every direction, to the children's enormous delight. At the forest edge we encountered a wall of black huckleberries, and there we stayed for the greater part of the afternoon, happily filling our pails to the brim.

Home again, Liet and our sister-in-law Mollie put aside enough berries for a pie and reserved the rest for a jam that would be spiced with cinnamon and cloves. In preparing the pie, Mollie dispensed with a bottom

Elisabeth Brown, the author's three-year-old daughter, reaches high for red huckleberries, while her cousin, Janie Halewijn of Prince Rupert, British Columbia, takes an easier course on a low-growing branch. The tart red huckleberries, which are found only along the northern Pacific Coast, make a superior jelly.

crust, "which gets soggy anyway," and piled the berries into a deep dish. When the pie came from the oven, the flaky crust floated on the berries. She scooped big, oozing portions of the hot pie onto our plates and passed around thick cream to pour over the top. Our afternoon's labor, we felt, had been amply rewarded.

That experience primed us. During the rest of our trip through the Northwest we kept a constant eye out for berries of all sorts. We looked for the exotic—the saskatoons of Saskatchewan, the nagoonberries, or wineberries, of Alaska—but we did not pass up the familiar. In Oregon, we saw roadsides thick with blackberry bushes, some four to five feet tall. These so-called Himalayas are scorned by some of our Oregon friends. They prefer the earlier-growing variety known as the Western trailing blackberry, or dewberry, which ripens in midsummer and trails along the ground. The dewberries, they claimed, were the *real* pie berries. Nevertheless, I walked slowly along the clustered bushes and reached into them to take the Himalayas, some so ripe they fell right into my hand. Their sun-warmed flavor might have been paler than that of the dewberries, as my friends insisted, but I found them wonderfully sweet, and full of juice.

At Salishan, a serenely beautiful resort on the Oregon coast, we first tasted salal, an aromatic purplish-black berry with red stems, which we

175

had previously known only as a decorative green that our florist in New York sometimes used to fill out his bouquets. Salal, we now discovered, makes a marvelous jelly, and a few salal berries tossed into applesauce turn it into an exciting new dish.

But for all their many berries Oregon and Washington suffer in comparison with Alaska, the true berry kingdom of the United States. In Alaska, most of the berries of more southerly latitudes grow not only bigger, but better. Take the salmonberry, a species of wild raspberry. In Washington it grows to about the size of a cultivated raspberry, but in southern Alaska, near the town of Seldovia, I saw salmonberries larger than my thumb, and incredibly colored—yellow, bright red, dark red. With the sun sparkling on them, they looked like jewels.

Liet and I once stood picking and eating salmonberries, trying to find words to describe their somewhat caramellike flavor, when two elderly men came down the dirt road behind us. They, too, had been berrypicking, and they proudly displayed the fruits of their labors. These included salmonberries in three colors, with bright bits of green fern enhancing their fresh look, and blueberries by the hundreds. Frank and Herb—as we were soon calling them—invited us down to their place to watch them clean the blueberries. They had a technique, they said, much used in Seldovia to make an arduous chore easy.

Frank and Herb lived in a trailer home, disguised by fish nets, floats and a porch that overlooked both the harbor and a small Russian church painted white and pale blue. In the far distance was Mount Iliamna, one of Alaska's active volcanoes. As soon as we got to the trailer, Frank propped a piece of wallboard against two sawhorses. ("The secret," he said, "is to get a good tilt.") He set two two-by-fours on the sloping board, forming a channel wide at the top and narrow at the bottom, covered the board and two-by-fours with canvas and smoothed the canvas out. Then he spread a couple of dampened paper towels near the head of the channel and placed a cardboard box at the bottom. Herb, who had been standing by with a can of blueberries, sprinkled some of them on the wet towels. As if by magic, bright, clean berries rolled into the box; the leaves and other debris remained behind, stuck to the wet towels. Herb repeated the process until the box was filled with the cleaned blueberries. "Talk about pie," he said, grabbing the box, "these make the best pie in the world!"

Across Kachemak Bay from Seldovia is the small town of Homer, and there we came upon an unusual enterprise called Alaska Wild Berry Products. It was founded in the mid 1940s when Hazel Heath set out to make use of the berries growing on the hills around the town, and few companies can ever have started more modestly. Mrs. Heath simply ran ads in the local newspaper telling the townsfolk when her kitchen would be open and how much she would pay for each type of berry. People soon began to show up at her door, and she cooked the berries they brought her into jams and jellies. Her preserves caught on. The business has since changed hands, but the current owners still run the old ads: "Cloudberry—50¢ a pound; Rose Hip, w/blossom end off—35¢; Rose Hip, w/blossom end on—25¢. . . ."

The morning we were there we watched the pickers come and go. The first to arrive were two distinctly Russian-looking types—a boy with a furred, flapped hat and a man with a long blond beard—carrying between them a bucket of blueberries covered with a faded, red polka-dot scarf. The boy, whose name was Ivan, had been born of Russian parents in China, and had only recently moved with his family from Oregon to a Russian-speaking community a few miles outside Homer. His blueberries weighed 16¼ pounds, and he was delighted to be paid $6.50 for them. I asked him what his mother did with the blueberries. He searched for the word. "Say the Russian word," I urged him. "She make *kissel*," he said. *Kissel*, I knew, is a thickened fruit dessert that is one of the glories of the Russian cuisine.

Soon after the Russians left, a car pulled up and out stepped the local rural mail carrier, Mrs. Beth Templeton. She marched forward with a tin basin full of the most delicious-looking wild strawberries I have ever seen. Relatively large, the berries were bright red, with gleaming, snowy-white flesh inside; and when I tasted them I found them to be sweet and tart at the same time—strawberries as strawberries should be. When they weighed out at 22½ pounds, bringing Mrs. Templeton $8.90, she exclaimed, "Oh, *so* much money!"

At Alaska Wild Berry Products the fruit is never washed; Alaska is still so clean, so unpolluted, that there would be no point in washing away any of the fresh flavor. Instead, the berries are simply sorted over by hand and cooked in four- or five-cup batches, a method of cooking that assures a quality product. We were shown some of the berries that had been brought in during the course of the summer and kept in a freezer for display. There were both high-bush and low-bush cranberries; watermelon berries, the fruit of the wild cucumber, each a red oval with a clear, sticky juice inside; large orange rose hips with soft flesh; wild gooseberries; black crowberries that grow on low, trailing evergreen shrubs; and a host of others. I was especially delighted to find nagoon-berries, or wineberries. I remembered having seen such berries in Finland, where they are made into an exquisite liqueur called *mesimarja*. I wished I could tell my Finnish friends that nagoons are still abundant in Alaska, for in Finland they have become quite rare.

Our search for wild Alaskan foods did not end with this treasury of berries. While at Homer, I noticed an item in the local newspaper announcing that Mrs. Yule Kilcher, wife of a former state senator, was giving guided mushroom tours with "a short workshop in edible and inedible specimens and a short lecture on how to identify them." I called her, and she agreed to take us on a tour that very day, and to show us at least 20 different species. We drove at once to a rendezvous several miles from Homer where Mrs. Kilcher—Ruth—was waiting for us with her pretty 11-year-old daughter Catkin.

Ruth turned out to be an interesting woman in her own right. She had come to Alaska from Switzerland just before World War II to join Yule, an idealistic Swiss-American who wanted "to create something out of the wilderness." Other Swiss artists and craftsmen were to follow them, but the war broke out and the colony they hoped to found never came into ex-

Continued on page 180

Wild Nuggets of Sweetness, from Huckleberries to Nagoonberries

Some of the world's juiciest wild berries and fruits grow in America's Northwest—and these wild nuggets of sweetness are treasured by the people who live there. Most of the berries shown opposite have been put to use since the days of the settlers. For example, Oregon grapes (actually a variety of the barberry) and red and blue elders can yield jelly and wine. Rose hips and cloudberries are a source of vitamin C in the Far North. Blackberries and blueberries are used for desserts and preserves, and the salmonberry, shown above in its huge Alaskan variety, is the basis of an exquisite jelly. Berrypickers like Kris Kirby *(left),* a student from San Rafael, California, who came north for the summer, can earn some extra money gathering salmonberries at the edge of the woods. A company called Alaska Wild Berry Products pays Kris 40 cents a pound for the berries.

ROSE HIPS

SALAL

RED HUCKLEBERRIES

BLUEBERRIES

BLUE ELDER

RED ELDER

HIGH-BUSH CRANBERRY

LOW-BUSH CRANBERRY

WILD RED CURRANT

CLOUDBERRY

WILD CUCUMBER

NAGOONBERRY

WESTERN DEWBERRY

HIMALAYA BLACKBERRY

OREGON GRAPE

LONG-LEAVED OREGON GRAPE

A strawberry pie like this one *(Recipe Index)* can be made in either of two ways: with cultivated berries as shown here or with the somewhat smaller wild variety. To make a wild-strawberry pie, several layers of the smaller wild berries would probably be necessary.

istence. The Kilchers stayed on and had eight children, two boys and six girls. After the war, they homesteaded, and built a 160-acre farm out of the wilderness.

Following behind Ruth's car, a gray Volkswagen bearing a green mushroom decal on its back, we bumped along a dirt road into a deep, dark forest until she signaled us to stop. I had wondered as I drove whether she would indeed be able to show us 20 species of mushrooms. The weather had been dry, and we knew that mushrooms need moisture; but we also knew, by then, that in more than 20 years of homesteading Ruth had gone over almost every square inch of the woods. If mushrooms were there, she would find them.

We walked into the gray-green quiet of the forest and crunched softly over the thick padding of moss. In a few minutes we came upon an orange mushroom a couple of inches across, and Ruth knelt and gently cut it from the forest floor with a sharp knife. Her approach was reverent. She cut it, she said, rather than pulling it up with her hands, because she wanted "to preserve the delicate balance of things here." A mushroom is not itself a plant, but the fruit of a plant that lives below the ground, spreading out a network of filaments so thin they can be seen by the naked eye only when they twist around each other or cluster. It was these filaments that Ruth was trying to protect.

Ruth identified that first mushroom as an orange delicious, and cut it open to reveal the orange flesh and the orange-red milk that oozed in droplets from the flesh. Describing it as a good mushroom to fry or pickle, she placed it at the bottom of the bucket and walked deeper into the forest. In a thick grove of spruce we encountered the first of the many chicken mushrooms we would gather that morning. These were choice, Ruth told us, because of their chickenlike flavor. She plunged her fingers deep into the moss to expose the buried stem, cut a mushroom about three inches long with a plump, dome-shaped cap, and laid it beside the orange de-

180

licious. We had not gone another 20 feet when we found a third species, to which Ruth gave its German name—*Schneckling,* or little snail. Its nearly white flesh, she said, could be used in a stew or casserole, or as a filler—"like potatoes"—in other mushroom dishes. Close by, half hidden under fern fronds, stood a so-called inky cap, a fungus so ephemeral that it begins to dissolve into a puddle of its own black juices soon after being picked. Since an inky cap cannot be dried and must be eaten fresh or not at all, it is truly the mushroom hunter's mushroom. We added it to our fast-growing collection.

After finding a half dozen more chicken mushrooms, we returned to our cars and drove to another spot several hundred feet down the road. "This is our enchanted forest, isn't it, Catkin?" said Ruth, smiling at her blond daughter. And indeed it seemed enchanted. There were dense stands of spruce through which we could barely pass, large birches from which the bark was peeling, mounds of moss and little holes in the ground where an elf could live, and scattered on the floor was a slippery carpet of dry pine needles. In a glade thick with grass and ferns, Catkin began to pick "crackleberries," trailing raspberries that cling to the ground, and among them she found three nagoonberries, which she offered me as a special treat. Her interest in the forest was almost a proprietary one. When we happened upon one unusual variety of mushroom—three of them growing close together—she insisted that Ruth leave one to reproduce and cut the other two carefully, "because, Mother, I want to see them again next year."

Less than two hours had gone by, and our bucket was full. We had gathered more than 10 pounds of fresh mushrooms in 16 different species —four short of our goal, but who cared? Among them were several puffballs and four or five different kinds of boletus, meaty fungi with bulbous stems and spongy pores under their thick brown caps. The best of these prizes were three *Boletus edulis,* famous in France as the *cèpe* and in Germany as the *Steinpilz*—a mushroom, Ruth remarked, for connoisseurs, and one she had often gathered as a girl in Switzerland. The oddest of our finds was an "owl" mushroom—a flat disk with flared edges and shaggy, overlapping brown and gray markings that looked somewhat like feathers. "This is a man's mushroom," Ruth said, "a virile one." She considers it too strong to eat by itself, so she dries it and crumbles it into her dishes as a kind of spice.

I was about to thank Ruth for a great morning when she invited us to come home with her and sample some of the mushrooms from the bucket we had picked. We drove to a clearing that held several weathered log buildings reminiscent of chalets in appearance. The main house was a warm, pleasant place, with small rooms and low ceilings. At a table spread with newspapers, Ruth began to clean the mushrooms, carefully brushing off pine needles and bits of moss and dusting away the black, powder-soft loam of the forest. She made a selection of the cleaned mushrooms to sauté, choosing several for body, some for flavor and one or two for tang, and sliced them thin.

Through the open door came her husband Yule, a brisk man with a booming voice, accompanied by his older son Otto. They had been haying, and they went to the pump to wash up after their morning's work. Others began to assemble for dinner: a married daughter and the Kilchers' one-year-old granddaughter, then another daughter and a friend of hers from Anchorage. Yule went outside with the empty mushroom bucket and came back still carrying it. "Catkin," he called, "come and see what a strange mushroom you left here." Catkin ran over to take a look. "Oh, father!" she stammered—and Yule and Otto roared with laughter. Inside was a field mouse they had found while haying.

Soon the table was ready and the food was set before us in large bowls. It was a meal marked by the good strong taste of wild things. There was a moose stew, with a thick, dark gravy, served with new potatoes, a salad of fresh green lettuce and small sweet onions in a tart vinaigrette dressing. There were thin dark-red slices of air-dried moose, cured as the Swiss cure the beef they call *Bündnerfleisch*. But best of all and most exciting to eat were the mushrooms. Ruth had sautéed them on her wood-burning range, and she scooped them onto our plates from the black iron frying pan in which they had taken on a buttery glitter (the butter was home-churned from the cream of the Kilchers' cows). I ate the mushrooms slice by slice, comparing their distinctive flavors. Noticing the pleasure I took in them, Ruth opened a jar of pickled wild mushrooms for me to taste. She had preserved them in vinegar and oil and added hot chilies for fire, and they tingled on the tongue. We ate hungrily, pausing only for deep draughts of a chilled alelike home brew made from honey and hop-flavored malt.

My own experience in gathering wild mushrooms, however limited, made me perk up my ears whenever other people talked about theirs. Their eyes would take on a faraway look and their fingers would all but twitch. "It's a treasure hunt," a Washington woman said to me. "I found one two years ago that *nobody* had ever seen before." A young housewife in Winnipeg, Manitoba, went into ecstasies describing mushrooms she and her brother had picked on their parents' farm. "I've seen a whole wash-tub filled with them," she said. But when I asked for their names she could give them to me only as she knew them—in Ukrainian.

In Wisconsin, I listened to an enthusiast who told how each spring, "around the time when the apple trees blossom and the first trillium appears," he always went out in search of morels—crinkly-capped mushrooms that look like nothing so much as little brown sponges. Even a mere handful of morels, he told me, is like gold to him, and some years ago he found half a bushel of them; but he can never be sure that he is going to find any at all, for their season is short and they hide themselves away among last year's leaves. "You walk right past the spot where you've found morels before and see nothing. Then suddenly you turn around and there they are." Ranking among the finest of the world's 2,000-plus edible fungi, morels have a delicate flavor and an aroma that is redolent of the woodlands; they can be eaten sautéed, herbed and buttered, or floating in cream, or stuffed with minced chicken. In Europe they have been prized by cooks for centuries. A Swiss chef whom I met at Salishan, Oregon, sends all the way to France for dried morels, and pays $17 a pound for them. I found myself wondering whether the same mushrooms could not

182

have been picked fresh in the mountain forests behind his restaurant.

For many people within driving distance of the forests of Washington's Olympic Peninsula, picking mushrooms has become high sport. At least six excellent types thrive here: the chanterelle, the boletus, the morel, the milky cap, the shaggy-mane and the chicken-of-the-woods. Tom Robbins, an enthusiastic amateur mycologist, has valiantly attempted to describe them all. The chanterelle, he wrote in an article for *Seattle Magazine,* "looks like a ruffled yellow trumpet, smells like apricots, has the consistency of chicken and tastes like eggs scrambled in wood smoke and wine." The boletus "has a top of rich brown kidskin and a creamy, porous underside like a queen's bath sponge. It smells a bit like antique silk and its taste, while suggestive of raw chestnuts, would take the combined verbal arsenals of a boxcar full of Romantic poets." Tom compares the famous morel to "mealy sweetbreads, buttery eggplant or country-style steak." He likens the milky cap—the same orange delicious that was Ruth Kilcher's first find on our walk in the forest—to "lamb kidney done up in crumbs." Faced by the shaggy-mane, which happens to be his own favorite, Tom throws up his hands and quotes someone else; it has, says his informant, "a slightly meaty taste combined with something like the perfume of burning leaves." (Tom himself adds that if he were really pressed for a description, he would say that it resembles "roast suckling unicorn.") As for the chicken-of-the-woods—well, it simply "tastes like chicken," just as the oyster mushroom tastes like oysters and the garlic mushroom like garlic.

In the mountains and along the coast of the Pacific Northwest, under evergreens or in thickets of rhododendron or black huckleberry, grows one species of mushroom that Japanese-Americans, in particular, love above all others. Known as the *matsutake* or pine mushroom and famous for its size (a mature specimen may be as much as 10 inches across), it is an essential ingredient in sukiyaki. *Matsutake* heave their broad shoulders up through the forest floor in the fall—but their aficionados are loath to reveal where they grow. One man told me that he once spotted a car full of Japanese-American mushroom hunters at a gas station and followed them in hopes of learning their secret hunting ground. After driving for half an hour or more, he suddenly realized that he was back at the same gas station. The occupants of the car he had been trailing pulled up and parked, smirked and went inside the station for a Coke.

Many mushroom hunters share this unwillingness to divulge their special preserves. Angelo Pellegrini, who teaches English literature at the University of Washington and writes passionately about food and drink, describes the characteristic in his book *Wine and the Good Life.* "Strange creature, the mushroom hunter . . . the apotheosis of suspicion. For even when he is absolutely alone in the forest, and he comes upon a mushroom, he behaves as if he were surrounded by spies. He creeps up on it, looking warily this way and that, plucks it and whisks it into his sack, ghost-like in stealth and silence; then, as the golfer replaces the divot, so does he smooth over the ground and otherwise camouflage the spot whence he took his prize." Pellegrini himself admits to the malady. He once served wild mushrooms at a Pacific Northwest dinner of his own de-

Continued on page 189

Mrs. Ruth Kilcher stands at the door of a log cabin built by her husband Yule from trees he cut on their homestead.

A Wealth of Mushrooms from an Alaskan Homestead

No one who has feasted on wild mushrooms needs to be told how good they are or fails to appreciate the pungent woodland flavor that sets them apart from the pale, bland cultivated varieties. Mrs. Ruth Kilcher *(above)* of Homer, Alaska, is one of many Northwesterners who gather wild mushrooms and cook with them. But she is more fortunate than most mushroom hunters: she and her husband Yule, a former Alaska state senator, have their own mushroom preserve, a virgin forest within the boundaries of their 160-acre farm. On a foray one morning with the author of this book *(opposite, top)*, Mrs. Kilcher found 16 different species in about two hours—10 pounds of mushrooms to sauté, pickle and dry, or to serve as an ideal accompaniment to the game shot by her husband. At such meals she also often serves a dessert of wild berries, picked in her private forest along with the mushrooms.

A study in concentration, Mrs. Kilcher and author Dale Brown scrutinize the forest floor in their hunt for wild mushrooms.

Moist, warm and still partially coated with the moss and loam in which they grew, three mushrooms of the *Cortinarius* genus are among the hunters' first finds. Mrs. Kilcher fries rather than pickles this example of the genus, because of its distinctive taste and firm texture.

Poisonous Mushrooms: A Word of Caution

Though poisonous mushrooms are comparatively rare, they may outnumber edible fungi in some places and no one should ever eat a wild mushroom that has not first been positively identified. Here are some good rules to follow: get a study guide to the mushrooms of your area; learn which local varieties are dangerous; and until you acquire expertise gather only the one or two kinds you absolutely know to be edible.

PUFFBALLS

"OWL MUSHROOM"

BOLETUS

Mushroom hunting is not a sport to engage in lightly *(box, opposite)*. Mrs. Kilcher has spent years learning to recognize the different fungi that pop up in her forest. She picked the specimens shown below and on the opposite page without trepidation—several had already been nibbled by forest creatures —but she also came across a few unfamiliar fungi and took them home for her husband to identify *(right)*. Experience has taught her how best to cook the mushrooms she gathers. For example, she considers the *Sarcodon imbractum (bottom left, opposite)* too strong-flavored to cook whole; instead, she dries it and crumbles bits of it into her dishes as she would an herb.

vising, and announced that he had driven 90 miles into the Cascade Mountains to get them. His guests found them delicious and wanted to know, "Where in the Cascades?" "North of Mount Rainier and south of Mount Baker," was Pellegrini's answer. The two mountains are about 140 miles apart as the crow flies.

Mushrooms and berries lead the list of wild plant foods that lend excitement to eating in Northwestern America, but there are others that are less well known. The lacy flowers of elder, for example, are dipped in an egg batter flavored with brandy and then deep-fried. Served hot and crunchy with a sprinkling of sugar, they make an unusual and delicious dessert. The tender young shoots of cattail are steamed and served as a green, and a cake can be made of the pollen. The boiled stems of dock are also good; early settlers used to call this plant wild rhubarb. And an imaginative cook in an experimental frame of mind should be willing to try such delicacies as cow parsnip, fireweed, horsetail, miner's lettuce, nettles and peppergrass.

Many of the edible plants of the Northwest were first utilized by the Indians. Both the camas and the wapatoo, or arrowhead, for example, were important items in their diet. The camas, which grows in the rich, dark soil of the prairies, has a starchy bulb that Indian women cooked, pounded and made into a sort of sun-dried or smoked bread. The wapatoo, a water plant, has a round red tuber with a chestnutlike flavor and a mealy texture. Squaws would wade through ponds or marshes and dislodge the tubers with their toes. They steamed the wapatoo in pits covered with grass, mats and soil, and ate it dried in winter. More than 20 other kinds of roots were dug and eaten by the Indians, including fern, sunflower, skunk cabbage, giant dogtooth violet, Venus's-looking-glass (which tastes like salsify), and blue lupine (which resembles sweet potato). The seeds of the yellow pond lily (called wokas by the Indians), sunflower, balsam root, vetch, pea, rush, wild broom corn, tar weed, portulaca—all these and others were dried and ground. Shoots and stalks of salmonberry, sweet coltsfoot, fern milkweed and wild celery were used as greens. And acorns, chinquapins (wild chestnuts), hazelnuts (wild filberts) and pine nuts were enjoyed not only as readily available foods, but as foods that could be conveniently stored.

Most of these plants go unnoticed today, and there is little likelihood that any of them will ever achieve the status and current esteem of another Indian staple, wild rice. The Indians knew wild rice under its Chippewa name, *manonim,* or "good berry," and valued it so highly that in Minnesota, before it became a state, they waged wars for control of the lakes in which the rice grew. In late August they would tie the stalks into bunches, then cover the bunches with bark shields to keep hungry birds away. When the rice began ripening, they harvested it by knocking it into their canoes with thin sticks. Among the earliest Europeans to encounter it were French voyageurs, who called it *folle avoine*—"fool oats." A trader who spent time among the Indians recorded that, "When it is Cleaned fit for youse Thay Boile it as we Due Rise and Eat it with Bairs greas and Sugar." Actually, the Indians seem to have employed wild rice in their cooking much as housewives do today; they even stuffed turkeys with it.

Opposite: A favorite way of preparing wild mushrooms at the Kilchers' homestead is simply to sauté them in freshly churned butter. Mrs. Kilcher mixes varieties, choosing some mushrooms for body, others for flavor, and still others for their contrasts of texture.

On a lake in northern Minnesota, a Chippewa Indian couple gather wild rice—which is actually not rice at all, but the kernel of an aquatic grass. In an age-old method of harvesting, the man poles the canoe through the shallow water, while the woman bends the stalks over the canoe's sides with one cedar flail and with another taps the ripened kernels into the bottom of the boat.

Mrs. William T. Boutwell, a Minnesota missionary's wife, was perhaps the first white woman to serve it to her guests, who pronounced it very good indeed and noted its slightly smoky taste. In modern times wild rice has steadily grown in popularity and today the supply cannot keep up with the demand.

Notwithstanding its name, wild rice is actually an aquatic grass that grows best in lake water usually less than three feet deep. It occurs in greatest concentrations in Minnesota, Wisconsin, Manitoba and Ontario (Minnesota produces about 60 per cent of the wild rice now sold). In spring the plant begins to sprout, and by the beginning of August, the stalks stand three to five feet out of the water. The heads of rice ripen from the top downward. Many more grains drop off and fall into the water than ever get harvested, but those that are lost serve a useful purpose, as food for waterfowl and as the seeds from which next year's rice will grow. Because the grains do not ripen all at once, each plant must be harvested several times.

For the most part, harvesting is still carried out much as it was in Indian days; in Minnesota, in fact, the law requires that on public waters it must be gathered by hand from a canoe or skiff. The harvester uses wooden flails to knock the loose grains into the boat, and at the end of the day usually bags them and sells them to a buyer at once, for the harvested rice is perishable, and must be processed immediately. The Indians used to heat it on a scaffold over a fire, then place it in a hole, cover it with a deerskin, and prance on top to remove the hulls. Today the rice is spread on cement slabs and turned frequently to dry it. Then it is fed into heated revolving drums for hulling and parching. The grains turn black as they

roast, and must be polished to remove some of the dark coating. The costs of processing and—even more important—of harvesting have kept the price of wild rice high; in a year when the harvest is small, it may cost the consumer $8 to $10 a pound.

Numerous attempts have been made to grow wild rice by more modern methods. In recent years, for example, some Minnesota farmers have cleared patches of flat land, built eight-foot-high dikes around them, tilled the soil, flooded the enclosed areas and seeded them with wild rice. Just before the grain starts to ripen, the farmers drain the water off; later, they go into the dried-up paddies with huge mechanical harvesters. Rice grown in this way produces heavier stands and higher yields; although it still "shatters"—that is, drops its grains because of the progressive ripening of the heads—much less of the potential crop is wasted with this more efficient method of harvesting. The development of nonshattering strains, now an object of intensive research, gives promise that wild rice will become more widely available—and cheaper.

Even so, it is likely that wild rice will always be a delicacy. Its nutty taste will always be a natural complement to the taste of wild meat and fowl, as, for example, in quail stuffed with wild rice and served with a cream-and-morel sauce *(Recipe Index)*. A far less elegant dish of wild rice and mushrooms *(Recipe Index)* still appeals to refined tastes in spite of—or perhaps because of—its basic simplicity. Just as wild rice represents a historical link between the Indian past and the present day, it links the simplest of cuisines with the most sophisticated. It seems fitting that this many-faceted wild food should be a product of the American Northwest, where cooks see little need to improve upon nature's flavors.

A harvester rolls through a cultivated paddy of wild rice near Deer River, Minnesota. With the modern method of raising and harvesting a crop, more plants can be grown in a cultivated and flooded field and, once the water is drained off, the yield is far greater—from 200 to 400 pounds an acre, compared with 40 to 80 pounds by the old method shown opposite.

191

Marinated Mushrooms

Make the marinated mushrooms at least 2 days before you intend to serve them. Wipe the mushroom caps with a dampened kitchen towel and drop them into a deep bowl. Pour in the wine and turn the mushrooms about with a spoon to coat them evenly. Cover with foil or plastic wrap and marinate in the refrigerator for about 1 hour.

With a small, sharp knife, score the lemon by cutting V-shaped grooves, about ⅛ inch wide and ⅛ inch deep, from one end of the lemon to the other and spaced about ½ inch apart. Then slice the lemon crosswise into ¼-inch-thick rounds.

In a mixing bowl, beat the olive oil, Tabasco sauce, salt and pepper together with a wire whisk. Add the onions and garlic and stir well, then drop in the lemon slices, cloves and bay leaf. Drain the wine from the mushroom caps and in its place add the oil mixture. Turn the caps about gently with a spoon until they are evenly coated.

Transfer the entire contents of the bowl to a wide-mouthed 1-quart jar or crock equipped with a tight-fitting lid. Cover and refrigerate for at least 2 days. Sprinkle with parsley before serving. The mushrooms can safely be kept in the refrigerator for 2 to 3 weeks.

To serve 6 as a first course

1 pound firm fresh mushroom caps, each about 1 inch in diameter
1 cup dry white wine
1 lemon
1⅔ cups olive oil
1 teaspoon Tabasco sauce
2 teaspoons salt
⅛ teapoon freshly ground black pepper
3 tablespoons finely chopped onions
1 tablespoon very finely chopped garlic
3 whole cloves
1 medium-sized bay leaf
3 tablespoons finely chopped fresh parsley

Fresh Strawberry Pie

Pick over the berries carefully, removing the stems and hulls and discarding any fruit that is badly bruised or shows signs of mold. Wash in a sieve or colander under cold running water, then spread on paper towels to drain. Pat the berries completely dry. Place half of them in the cooled baked pie shell and set aside.

Chop the remaining berries fine and combine them with the sugar in a 2- to 3-quart enameled or stainless-steel saucepan. Stirring from time to time, bring the berries to a simmer over moderate heat. In a small bowl, mix the cornstarch, cold water and lemon juice together to make a smooth paste. Then, stirring constantly, pour the paste into the berry mixture and continue to cook for 2 or 3 minutes, until the mixture thickens enough to hold its shape lightly in the spoon. Purée through a fine sieve set over a bowl, pressing down hard on the berries before discarding the seeds. Taste and add more sugar or lemon juice if desired. Pour the purée over the berries in the pie shell, spreading it evenly with a rubber spatula. Drape the pie lightly with aluminum foil or wax paper and refrigerate for at least 2 hours.

Just before serving, whip the cream in a chilled bowl with a wire whisk or a rotary or electric beater. When it is stiff enough to stand in unwavering peaks on the beater, scoop it over the pie and spread it out with a spatula. Make decorative swirls in the cream with the tip of the spatula and serve at once. Alternatively, you may serve the cream separately, permitting each diner to add as much as he wants to his portion.

To make one 9-inch pie

6 cups (1½ quarts) firm ripe strawberries, preferably wild strawberries
A 9-inch short-crust pastry pie shell, baked and cooled (*Recipe Index*)
½ cup sugar
3 tablespoons cornstarch
2 tablespoons cold water
1 tablespoon strained fresh lemon juice
1 cup heavy cream, chilled

Either wild or cultivated mushroom caps can be used for the tangy appetizer shown at left. After soaking in a wine marinade, the caps are steeped two days in olive oil flavored with herbs and sharp seasonings.

To make one 9-inch pie

GRAHAM-CRACKER CRUST

1½ cups fresh crumbs made from
graham crackers pulverized in a
blender or wrapped in wax paper
and finely crushed with a rolling
pin
½ cup walnuts, pulverized in a
blender or with a nut grinder or
mortar and pestle
1 tablespoon sugar
¼ teaspoon ground cinnamon
4 tablespoons butter, softened and
cut into ½-inch bits

RASPBERRY FILLING

1 envelope unflavored gelatin
¼ cup cold water
2½ cups fresh raspberries, or
substitute 2 ten-ounce packages
frozen raspberries, thoroughly
defrosted and drained
1 teaspoon vanilla extract
6 ounces cream cheese, softened
⅓ cup confectioners' sugar
2 tablespoons strained fresh lemon
juice
¾ cup heavy cream, chilled

CREAM TOPPING

1 cup heavy cream, chilled
1 tablespoon sugar
½ cup whole fresh raspberries, or
substitute defrosted drained
frozen raspberries, for garnish
(optional)

To serve 4 to 6

5 tablespoons butter
4 tablespoons finely chopped onions
1 cup wild rice
2 cups chicken stock, fresh or
canned
1 teaspoon salt
¼ cup slivered blanched almonds
½ pound firm fresh mushrooms,
wiped with a dampened towel,
trimmed, and cut lengthwise,
including the stems, into ⅛-
inch-thick slices
Freshly ground black pepper

Raspberry Pie

Preheat the oven to 375°. Combine the graham-cracker crumbs, walnuts, sugar and cinnamon in a deep bowl and mix well. Add the butter bits and, with your fingers, rub the crumb mixture and fat until they resemble moist coarse meal. Press the mixture smoothly and evenly into the bottom and against the sides of a 9-inch pie pan. Then bake in the middle of the oven for 8 to 10 minutes, or until the crust is firm to the touch and delicately browned. Remove the pan from the oven and let the crust cool to room temperature.

Meanwhile, prepare the raspberry filling in the following fashion: Sprinkle the gelatin into a heatproof measuring cup or small bowl containing the ¼ cup cold water. When the gelatin has softened for 2 or 3 minutes, set the cup in a small pan of simmering water and stir over low heat until the gelatin dissolves completely. Remove the pan from the heat but leave the cup in the water to keep the gelatin fluid.

With the back of a large spoon, purée the raspberries through a fine sieve into a small mixing bowl. Stir in the vanilla extract and set aside. In a deep bowl, cream the cream cheese and confectioners' sugar together, beating and mashing them against the sides of the bowl with the back of a spoon until they are light and fluffy.

Add the raspberry purée to the cream-cheese mixture and beat them vigorously together with a rotary or electric beater. Stir in 1 teaspoon of the lemon juice, and the gelatin. Pour in ¾ cup of cream and beat vigorously until the mixture is smooth and no trace of the cream remains. Taste and add more lemon juice if desired. Pour the filling into the cooled crust, spreading it and smoothing the top with the spatula. Cover loosely with foil or plastic wrap and refrigerate for at least 4 hours, or until the filling is firm to the touch.

Just before serving, prepare the topping. Whip 1 cup of heavy cream in a chilled bowl until it forms soft peaks. Sprinkle in the tablespoon of sugar and continue to beat until the cream is stiff enough to stand in unwavering peaks on the beater. Spread the whipped cream evenly over the pie, creating decorative swirls with the tip of the knife or spatula. If you like, arrange whole fresh or defrosted frozen raspberries on top.

Wild Rice with Mushrooms and Almonds

Preheat the oven to 350°. In a heavy 2-quart casserole equipped with a tightly fitting lid, melt 2 tablespoons of the butter over moderate heat. When the foam begins to subside, add 2 tablespoons of the onions and, stirring frequently, cook for about 5 minutes, until they are soft and translucent but not brown.

Add the wild rice and stir until the grains glisten with butter. Then pour in the chicken stock and ½ teaspoon of the salt, and stir until the mixture comes to a boil.

Cover the casserole with a double thickness of aluminum foil and set the lid in place. Bake in the middle of the oven for 1 hour, remove the casserole from the oven, and let the rice rest at room temperature for 15 minutes before removing the lid and foil.

Meanwhile, melt 1 tablespoon of butter in a heavy 10-inch skillet and

194

brown the almonds for a minute or so, stirring constantly so that they color delicately and evenly. With a slotted spoon, transfer the almonds to paper towels to drain.

Add the remaining 2 tablespoons of butter to the skillet and melt over moderate heat. When the foam begins to subside, add the remaining 2 tablespoons of onions and stir for about 5 minutes, until they are soft and translucent but not brown.

Add the mushrooms and, stirring frequently, cook for 10 to 15 minutes, until the moisture they give off has evaporated. Do not let the mushrooms brown. Season with the remaining ½ teaspoon of salt and a few grindings of pepper and set aside.

To serve, combine the wild rice and mushrooms in a heated bowl and toss them together gently but thoroughly. Scatter the almonds on top and serve at once.

Marinated Fiddlehead Ferns

In a 3- to 4-quart enameled or stainless-steel saucepan, combine the water, vinegar, lemon juice, oil, celery, the cheesecloth bag of coriander, fennel and peppercorns, and the salt. Bring to a boil over high heat, then reduce the heat to low. Stir in the fiddleheads and simmer partially covered for 15 to 20 minutes, or until the ferns are tender.

Remove and discard the bag of coriander, fennel and peppercorns. Drain the fiddleheads and celery in a sieve or colander and place them in a serving bowl. Cool to room temperature, cover with plastic wrap and refrigerate for at least 2 hours before serving.

Mushroom-and-Potato Soup

In a heavy 4- to 5-quart enameled or stainless-steel casserole, melt 4 tablespoons of the butter over moderate heat. When the foam begins to subside, add the mushrooms and onions, and stir until they are evenly coated with the butter. Reduce the heat to low, partially cover the casserole, and simmer for 20 minutes.

Stir in the chicken stock, potato slices and salt, and bring the mixture to a boil over high heat. Reduce the heat to low, cover partially, and simmer for about 25 minutes longer, or until the potato slices are tender but still intact.

Meanwhile, melt the remaining 2 tablespoons of butter in a heavy 8- to 10-inch skillet. When the foam begins to subside, add the celery, scallions and parsley and, stirring frequently, cook uncovered over low heat for about 15 minutes, until the celery is tender but not brown.

In a small bowl, combine the sour cream with about ½ cup of the simmering mushroom soup stock and mix well. Stirring constantly, pour the sour-cream mixture into the skillet gradually and bring the mixture to a boil over high heat.

Add the entire contents of the skillet to the mushroom soup and stir together gently but thoroughly. Taste for seasoning. Then pour the soup into a heated tureen or individual soup plates, sprinkle with the dill and a few grindings of pepper, and serve at once.

To serve 10 as a first course or 8 as a salad

3 cups water
5 tablespoons wine vinegar
3 tablespoons strained fresh lemon juice
½ cup vegetable oil
2 medium-sized celery stalks, trimmed of all leaves and finely chopped
1 teaspoon coriander seeds, 1 teaspoon fennel seeds and 6 whole black peppercorns, wrapped together in cheesecloth
1½ teaspoons salt
3 cups fresh fiddlehead ferns, thoroughly washed and trimmed, or substitute two 10-ounce packages frozen fiddlehead ferns, thoroughly defrosted and drained

To serve 8 to 10

6 tablespoons butter
1½ pounds firm fresh mushrooms, wiped with a dampened towel, trimmed, and cut lengthwise, including the stems, into ⅛-inch-thick slices
1 cup finely chopped onions
6 cups chicken stock, fresh or canned
6 small boiling potatoes (about 1½ pounds), peeled and cut into ¼-inch slices
1 teaspoon salt
¼ cup finely chopped celery
¼ cup finely chopped scallions, including the green tops
2 tablespoons finely chopped fresh parsley
1 cup sour cream
1 tablespoon finely cut fresh dill leaves
Freshly ground black pepper

Common Sport Fish of the Northwest

The chart on these pages provides a comprehensive survey of the fish sought by sportsmen from the Great Lakes westward to the Pacific Coast and north to Alaska. For each fish, the most widely used name is given in small capital letters; below this are listed regional or local names, if any.

FISH	HABITAT	DISTINCTIVE FEATURES	WEIGHT
AMERICAN SMELT	Fresh and coastal salt waters, in depths of less than 20 feet	Back green, shading to silver on belly; greenish sides, each with a silver stripe	4 to 5 ounces
ARCTIC GRAYLING	Deep pockets of fresh-water streams and lakes	Back and sides gray, brown or silver, with brassy, silver or purplish sheen; V- or X-shaped markings on the foreparts of the sides; saillike, pink-tinged dorsal fin	1½ to 3 pounds
BLACK CRAPPIE *bachelor perch* *calico fish* *papermouth*	Vegetated areas of quiet, fairly cool fresh waters	Back dark green to black; sides and belly silver; light-colored blotches on body	1 to 2 pounds
BLUEGILL *copperbelly* *blue sunfish* *sunfish* *bream* *sun perch*	Quiet, weedy fresh waters	Body gold to shades of blue; black gill flap; black spot on dorsal fin	½ to 1¼ pounds
BROOK TROUT	Large, cold (under 65° F.) fresh-water lakes and streams; an Eastern fish, introduced to Western waters	Back and sides varying from brown and olive to orange and red, marked with red spots outlined in blue; dark wavy lines on back and dorsal fin	½ to 5 pounds
BROWN BULLHEAD *brown catfish*	Mud- or sand-bottomed fresh waters and sluggish streams	Back yellow brown to chocolate brown, with lighter gradations on sides; belly yellow or white; dark mottlings on back and sides. The bullhead can breathe out of water for many hours	½ to 2 pounds
BROWN TROUT	Large, clear lakes and rivers	Back and sides golden brown, belly dusky yellow; black or brown spots on back, sides and dorsal fin	½ to 10 pounds
CHINOOK SALMON *king salmon*	Salt and fresh waters. The sea-dwelling mature fish migrate to fresh water for spawning	Belly and sides silver, shading to dusky gray or black on back. In maturity, black spots appear on the back and on dorsal and tail fins, while the male grows darker and the female brassier in color	18 to 60 pounds
COHO SALMON *hooknose salmon* *silver salmon*	Salt and fresh waters; a Pacific Coast fish, introduced to the Great Lakes and neighboring waters	Body silver, spotted with black on dorsal and tail fins	6 to 12 pounds; 15 to 20 pounds in some fresh waters
CUTTHROAT TROUT *Colorado trout* *Columbia River trout* *Tahoe trout* *(also numerous other local names)*	Salt waters and deep fresh-water pools near shores, rocks and underwater ledges	Red to greenish blue, with slashlike red markings below lower jaw. Cutthroats often interbreed with other trout, causing wide variations in appearance; the slashlike markings, however, are a stable characteristic	½ to 5 pounds
DOLLY VARDEN *bull trout*	Salt waters, headwaters of streams, and deep lakes near rocks and logs	Salt-water varieties silver; fresh-water varieties silver with red, orange or yellow spots on sides or back	1 to 4 pounds in streams; 10 to 15 pounds in lakes and ocean
LAKE STURGEON	Shallow lakes and streams of central Canada, Wisconsin, Minnesota and Nebraska	Body brownish; snout conical, with a row of four whiskerlike barbels just ahead of the mouth; bony plates (not scales) on the body; skeletal structure cartilaginous rather than bony	2 to 70 pounds, with specimens up to 300 pounds
LAKE TROUT *Mackinaw* *gray trout* *togue*	Deep, clear fresh-water lakes and, occasionally, tributary rivers and streams	Back and sides most frequently steel blue or bronze green; light spots on back, sides and fins	3 to 20 pounds

FISH	HABITAT	DISTINCTIVE FEATURES	WEIGHT
LARGEMOUTH BASS *black bass* *green bass* *green trout* *Oswego bass*	Shallow fresh-water lakes and river backwaters near rooted vegetation	Body black to deep green; black band along the sides from head to tail; broad upper jaw extending behind the eyes	2 to 5 pounds
MUSKELLUNGE *blue pike* *great pike* *jack* *muskie* *(also numerous other local names)*	Quiet, clear lakes and streams at depths of more than 6 feet	Body dark gray to olive brown, with dark spots or stripes; head duckbill-shaped and covered with scales, except for gill flap and lower half of cheeks; 12 to 18 sensory pores in lower jaw	15 to 30 pounds, with specimens up to 60 pounds
NORTHERN PIKE *northern*	Fresh-water lakes near weed beds	Back green; sides lighter green; belly white; light bean-shaped spots on body and fins; head duckbill-shaped; lower half of gill flap scaleless	4 to 15 pounds
PADDLEFISH *shovelnose cat* *spoonbill* *spoonbill cat*	Large rivers and lakes in the Mississippi, Missouri and Ohio river systems	Body blue gray to black; long, flattened snout; large head and mouth; small eyes; cartilaginous skeleton	40 to 90 pounds, with specimens up to 200 pounds
PINK SALMON *humpback salmon*	Pacific Ocean and fresh waters, including waters of the Great Lakes region	Body silver; black oval blotches on tail fin. Mature males have a hooked snout and a large hump on the back	3 to 5 pounds
PUMPKINSEED *sunfish*	Still, soft-bottomed fresh waters near weeds or submerged logs	Back and sides olive, with spots of various colors; aqua-blue lines radiating from snout and eyes; rigid black gill cover with a bright red-orange spot at the tip	½ to 1 pound
RAINBOW TROUT *(see also steelhead trout)*	Clear, fresh-water lakes and streams	Back blue to green; sides and belly silvery; lake dwellers unspotted, stream dwellers heavily spotted. At maturity, the body darkens and a characteristic red stripe appears on the sides	2 to 6 pounds
ROCK BASS *redeye*	Cool, clear mud-bottomed lakes and streams near rocks, logs and lily pads and in deep holes	Back olive green shading to a yellowish-white belly; eye red	½ pound
SMALLMOUTH BASS	Deep areas of clear, rock-bottomed fresh-water lakes and streams	Body brown, with six or seven vertical olive bars on the sides; upper jaw extending to the eye	4 to 5 pounds
SOCKEYE SALMON	Salt waters and fresh-water rivers and lakes	Body reddish in mature males, olive to light red in mature females; minute black spots on back	5 to 7 pounds
STEELHEAD TROUT *(a migratory variety of the rainbow trout)*	Salt waters, migrating to fresh waters for spawning	In the sea, back light blue to green; sides and belly silver. In fresh water the body becomes darker, with spots and red stripes	6 to 20 pounds
WALLEYE *jack* *pickerel* *jackfish* *pike* *walleyed pike*	Large, cool, clear rock- or sand-bottomed bodies of fresh water	Sides and back olive green to brass colored, with dark bands; belly light colored; eyes large, gold colored and glassy	2 to 5 pounds, with specimens up to 20 pounds
WHITE BASS	Large bodies of rock- or gravel-bottomed fresh water with extensive areas more than 10 feet deep	Skin silver tinged with yellow; 10 narrow, dark unbroken lines extending the length of the body on sides and back	1 to 2 pounds
WHITE CRAPPIE *bachelor perch* *papermouth*	Fresh-water lakes and streams with muddy, rocky or sandy bottoms	Back olive; sides and belly silver; eight or nine vertical bands on body	½ to 2 pounds
YELLOW PERCH *coon perch* *ringed perch* *jack perch* *striped perch*	Bodies of cool fresh water with depths over 30 feet	Back olive; sides yellow; belly white; six to eight dark vertical bands. The head is concave just above the eyes, giving the fish a humpbacked appearance	⅓ to 2 pounds

How to Clean and Smoke Fish

Landing an elusive fish is not the last of a sport fisherman's problems. Unless a friendly fishmonger is nearby, the fisherman must clean his catch, a job that often entails boning the fish and may also require skinning it, as shown in the drawings opposite. And when the fish are biting, a sportsman is likely to take more than he can eat. The cleaned surplus can be given to a neighbor or frozen, but a third alternative—perhaps the best way to deal with a large catch —is to smoke the fish. Smoking preserves fish and gives the meat a distinctive taste that is appropriately reminiscent of campfires and forest lakes. The diagrams below illustrate the basic principles of smoking sport fish.

TWO METHODS OF SMOKING FISH

Fresh fish can be successfully smoked at home, with the use of equipment as simple as an oil drum, or as elaborate as a custom-built smokehouse with electric blowers. In hot smoking *(left)*, a fire is built directly beneath the fish, usually at a distance of three or four feet. In cold smoking the heat is comparatively indirect; typically, the fire may be set in a separate pit connected to the smoking chamber by a pipe *(below)*. Hot smoking takes only a few hours, but the finished fish are relatively perishable and must be refrigerated. Cold smoking may take from 24 hours to five days; the longer the smoking, the better the fish will keep.

For more detailed instructions on the construction and use of smokers write for "Fishery Leaflet 18," Division of Public Documents, U.S. Bureau of Commercial Fisheries, 1801 N. Moore St., Arlington, Virginia 22209 (free), or "Smokehouses and the Smoke Curing of Fish," Washington State Dept. of Fisheries, Olympia, Washington 98501 (50 cents).

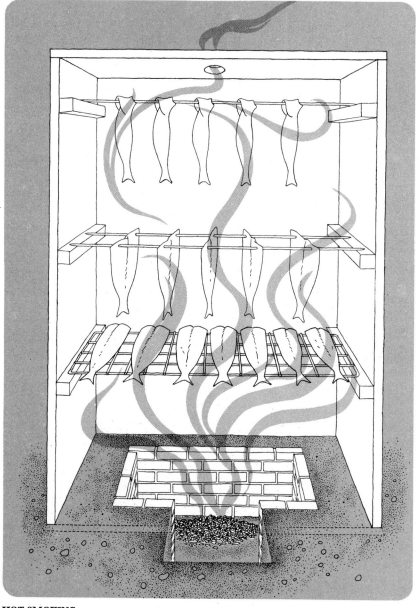

HOT SMOKING

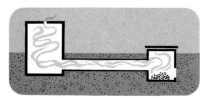

COLD SMOKING

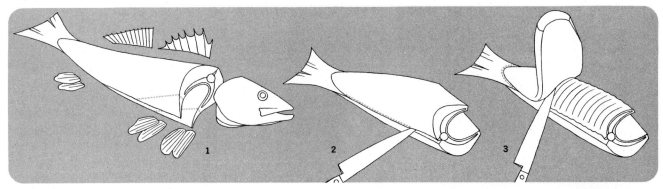

FILLETING AND SKINNING A RAW FISH

Slit the fish open along the belly and gut it. Wash the fish inside and out under cold running water. With a large sharp knife, cut off the fins, head and bony plates below the gills (1). Starting at the head end, cut along the back (2) and free the flesh from the skeleton (3). Turn the fish over and repeat the procedure, starting from the tail. Discard tail and skeleton. Some fish, such as largemouth bass and catfish, must be skinned after being filleted. Insert the knife between the skin and flesh at the tail end (4). Holding the skin with one hand, cut and push the flesh away from it with the edge and side of the knife blade.

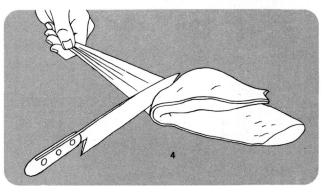

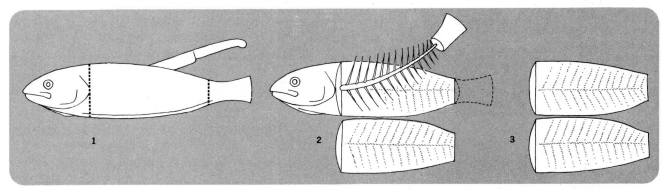

FILLETING A COOKED TROUT

With the trout laid flat on a plate, use a knife to free the top fillet from the rest of the body by cutting through to the skeleton behind the gills, just above the tail and along the back (1). Lift the freed fillet and turn it skin side down (2). Pick up the tail and carefully cut and lift the skeleton and the head away from the bottom fillet. Discard the bones—and enjoy your two fresh fillets of trout (3).

CLEANING AND BONING A RAW SMELT

Slit the smelt open along the belly, gut it and wash it under cold running water. Slit through the skin and meat behind the gills from the belly to the back (1). Holding the edges of the belly in both hands, turn the sides of the fish back to open up the body and spread it flat. With sharp scissors, sever the backbone just behind the head (2) and at the base of the tail. Then, starting at the tail end, pull the entire skeleton up and away from the flesh (3). The result: boneless smelt, ready for cooking (4).

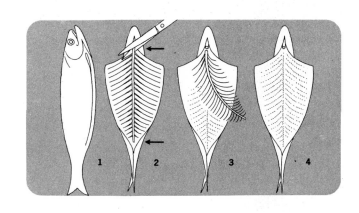

Recipe Index

NOTE: An R preceding a page refers to the Recipe Booklet. Size, weight and material are specified for pans in the recipes because they affect cooking results. A pan should be just large enough to hold its contents comfortably. Heavy pans heat slowly and cook food at a constant rate. Aluminum and cast iron conduct heat well but may discolor foods containing egg yolks, wine, vinegar or lemon. Enamelware is a fairly poor conductor of heat. Many recipes therefore recommend stainless steel or enameled cast iron, which do not have these faults.

General Index
Numerals in italics indicate a photograph or drawing of the subject mentioned.

Madison County, Iowa, 76
Makalo eta pipermin (codfish and peppers), Basque, 145
Mallard ducks, *131;* stuffed with goose pâté and rice, 121
Manitoba, *map 6,* 7, 135, 145, 182, 190
Marble cake, 152, *153*
Matanuska Valley, Alaska, *map 6,* 41, 43, 45, 50
Mayonnaise, 69, 74, 75
McLoughlin, Dr. John, 79
Meats: jerky, 10, 11, 17, 22, 120; meatballs in thick gravy, 161; *Sauerbraten,* 155; steak with onions and rhubarb wine, 158. *See also* names of meats; Game; names of game
Medford, Oregon, *map 6,* 78
Meek, William, 79, 80
Meeker, Ezra, 11
Mehlspeisen (plain desserts), 155
Mennonites, Russian, in Canada, 145
Mignonette sauce, *110*
Miller, Mrs. Floyd, *12*
Miller, William, 121
Milwaukee, Wisconsin, *map 6,* 148, 149, 152, 163, 164, 165; first lager brewery established, 149
Milwaukie, Oregon, 79
Minneapolis, Minnesota, *map 6,* 145, 148, 160, 161
Minnesota, *map 6,* 7, 132, 133, 134, 138, 145, 146, 149, 152, 189, 190, 191
Mississippi River, *map 6,* 8, 18
Missouri Republican, 8
Missouri River, *map 6,* 8, 127, 129, 130
Molasses, 22
Montana, *map 6,* 7, 19, 24, 61, *118,* 119, 121, *122-123,* 124, *125,* 132, 174
Moose, 48; air-dried *(Bündnerfleisch),* 182; marinated in red wine and soy sauce, 50, 51; roast, 121; stew, 182; in wild-mushroom Stroganov, 50
Morels, 10, 182, 183
Mormons in Wyoming, 155
Mortadella (sausage), 163
Mount Baker, Washington, 70, 189
Mount Hood, Oregon, *60, 61*

Mount Iliamna, Alaska, 176
Mount McKinley, Alaska, *map 6,* 41, 44, 46, 49, 51, *52, 55*
Mount Rainier, Washington, *map 6,* 61, 70, 189
Mountain goat, roast, 121
Mulled wine, 126
Mushrooms, 68, *186, 187;* boletus, 181, 183, *186; cèpe (Boletus edulis),* 181; chanterelle, 183; chicken, 180, 181; chicken-of-the-woods, 183; *Cortinarius, 185;* garlic, 183; hunting, 181-185; identification of, 186; inky cap, 181; little snail *(Schneckling),* 181; marinated, 192; milky cap, 183; morels, 10, 182, 183; orange delicious, 180, 183; owl, 181, *186;* oyster, 183; pickled, 182, *192, 193;* pine *(matsutake),* 183; poison-ous, identification of, 186; puff-balls, 66, 181, 186; *Sarcodon imbractum, 187;* sautéed in butter, 182, *188,* 189; shaggy-mane, 183; *Steinpilz* (or *cèpe),* 181; with wild rice, 191
Muskellunge, 132-133

Nagoonberries (wineberries), 175, 177, *179,* 181
Nampa, Idaho, 81
Nebraska, *map 6,* 7, 19, *22,* 145, 147, 148, 174
Nectarberries, 68
Nelson, Dr. Marion, 159
New York Tribune, 8, 152
Nisqualli Indian, 90
North Dakota, *map 6,* 7, 146, 161, 162
North Slope, Alaska, discovery of oil, 41
Northern Pacific Railroad, 80
Northwest, *map 6;* ethnic groups, 145; first emigrants, 8; psychology of frontier, 7. *See also* names of states; Pacific Northwest
Norwegian-American Museum, Decorah, 159
Norwegians: Christmas cookies, 161, *164;* in Dakotas, 146; in Iowa, 148, 154, 158, 159; in Washington, 145; in Wisconsin, 146
Nuts: gathered on prairies, 21; used by Indians, 189

Oahe Reservoir, South Dakota, 132
Ocean Shores, Washington, *92-93*
Oehl, Carl, 158
Old Yukon, James Wickersham, 40
Oliebollen, Dutch, *164*
Olympia oysters, 11, 78, 91, 95, *110*
Olympic Peninsula, Washington, 66, 96, 99, 102; mushroom species, 183
O'Malley, Robert, 49
Onions: in Idaho, 80-81; pickled, *31;* sweet red, salad, 86, 87
Ontario, 190
Oregon, *map 6,* 7, 8, 10, 11, 25, *60, 61,* 62, 63, 73, 76, 77, 78, 80, *88,* 89, 90, 92, 95, 97, 101, *106,* 107, 127, 152, 175, 176, 177, 182; pears, *61,* 77, 78
"Oregon country," 8, 17
Oregon grape, 174, 178, *179*
Oregon Trail, *map 6,* 7
Otter Rock, Oregon, 89
Otter Trawl Commission, Oregon, 101
Overnight pack trip, Glacier National Park, *118,* 119, *122-123, 125*
Oxtails, braised, with onions and carrots, 16, 17
Oysters: marinated, *114;* Olympia, 11, 78, 91, 95; Pacific, 95, *110,* 111

Pacific Northwest, *map 6, 60,* 61-81, *88,* 89-117; apple production, 77; eating outdoors, 74, *75;* fishing industry, 102; influence of Orient, 63; logging, 68; pear production, 73, 77, 79; regional specialties, 78, 79; vegetables, 86, 87; wild berries, 173-177, *178, 179;* wild mushrooms, 173, 177, 180-184, *185, 186, 187,* 189
Pacific Ocean perch (rockfish), 102
Pacific oysters, 95, *110,* 111
Pack trip into wilderness, Montana, *118, 122-123,* 125
Paczki, Polish, *164*
Paddlefish, 132
Palmer, Joel, 10
Pancakes, 7; sourdough, 40, 41 *46-47,* 48, 49

Pasties, 148
Pastry fritters, Czech and Italian, *164*
Payette, Idaho, 146
Peach ice cream, *153*
Pears: Anjou, 78, *80;* Bartlett, 78, *80;* Bosc, 78, *80;* Comice *(Doyenne du Comice),* 77, *80;* dried, 73; Eldorado, *81;* Forelle, *80;* poached in ginger sauce, *79;* production, Oregon, 61, 77, 78; production, Pacific Northwest, 73, 77, 79; Red Bartlett, *80;* seckel, *81;* trees, Oregon, *60;* varieties, 80-81
Peas with mushrooms and water chestnuts, 63
Pellegrini, Angelo, 183, 189; *Wine and the Good Life,* 183
Pemmican (pounded jerky with fruits), 11
Pepparkakor (ginger-flavored cookies), Swedish, *160, 164*
Peppermint, 81
Petrale sole with hazelnuts, 102
Pfingstfest (Whitsuntide celebration), 152
Pheasant: breasts with mushrooms in white-wine sauce, 121, *131;* in chicken stock with apples, 140, *141;* in sour sauce, 149; tidbits in sauerkraut, 126, *131;* with wild rice and mushrooms, roast, 121
Pickles and relishes, *30-31;* carrots, pickled, *31;* corn relish, *31;* giant kelp, pickled, 64, *65,* 66, 89; lingonberry relish, 44; mushroom caps, pickled, *192, 193;* onions, pickled, *31;* relishes and chutneys, 73; wild mushrooms pickled with chilies, 182
Pierogi, cheese, Polish, 163
Pierre, South Dakota, *map 6,* 24, 26, 121, 129
Pies: baked by Scandinavians, 154; blackberry, *25;* boysenberry, 69, 74, *75;* dried-apple, 11, *15;* grape, 155; green-tomato, for mock mincemeat, 23; huckleberry, 175; molasses, 23; New England tradition carried to West, 23; potato, for mock apple, 23; pumpkin and wild grape, for mock mincemeat, 23;

Credits and Acknowledgments

Sources for illustrations in this book are shown below. Credits for the pictures from left to right are separated by commas, from top to bottom by dashes.

Photographs by Richard Meek—Cover, pages 9, 16, 29, 30, 31, 34, 56, 83, 87, 94, 95, 103, 110, 113, 114, 116, 117, 137, 141, 143, 144, 153, 160, 167, 169, 180, 192. Photographs by Joseph S. Rychetnik top left page 4, 41, 42, 43, 44, 46, 47, 49, 53, 54, 96, 97, 99, 100, 172, 178, 184, 185, 186, bottom 187, 188. Photographs by Robert W. Kelley pages 25, 64, 65, 66, 67, 69, 70, 71, 72, 74, 75, 76, 78, 79, 84, 88, 92, 93, 102, 106, 108, 148. Photographs by Fred Schnell pages 12, 13, 14, 15, 26, 27, 128, 129, 131, 138, 156, 157, 164, 165 except bottom right, 170. Other photographs page 4—top right Salvatore Fragliossi for SPORTS ILLUSTRATED—Richard Henry, Walter Daran. 6—Map by Gloria du Bouchet and Lothar Roth. 19, 20, 21—State Historical Society of Wisconsin. 22—S. D. Butcher Collection Courtesy Nebraska State Historical Society. 37—University of Washington Library Special Collections, Seattle. 38, 39—Wayne Miller from Magnum. 52—Dale Brown. 60—Ray Atkeson. 80, 81—Don Condit Studio. 104, 105—Dale Brown. 118 through 125—Steven C. Wilson. 132—Dale Brown. 134, 135—Rosa Tusa. 146—Harold West. 150, 151—Mark Kauffman. 155—Richard L. Williams. 165—Bottom right Rosa Tusa. 166—Drawing by Gloria du Bouchet. 175—Dale Brown. 179—Dale Brown (3), Joseph S. Rychetnik—Dale Brown (3), Joseph S. Rychetnik—Joseph S. Rychetnik (2), Dale Brown, Joseph S. Rychetnik—Dale Brown (4). 187—top Dale Brown. 190, 191—Richard H. Hofstrand. 198, 199—Drawings by Matt Greene.

For their help and advice in the production of this book, the author, editors and staff wish to thank the following people: *in Alaska:* Mr. and Mrs. Phil Brandl, Spenard; Mr. and Mrs. James Branson, Kodiak; Mr. and Mrs. Harry Brundage, Alaska Wild Berry Products, Homer; Mr. and Mrs. John Bush, Palmer; Ruth and Yule Kilcher, Homer; Miss Virginia L. Peri, Anchorage; Mr. and Mrs. Sherman Powell, Talkeetna; Harry L. Rietze, U.S. Bureau of Commercial Fisheries, Juneau; Don Sheldon, Talkeetna; Mr. and Mrs. Thomas C. Sweeney, Kodiak; U.S. Bureau of Commercial Fisheries, Gibson Cove Facilities, Kodiak; Wakefield Seafoods, Seldovia, Dick Pace, Gordon Sutor; Mr. and Mrs. Milstead C. Zahn, Kodiak; *in California:* Johnny Kan, San Francisco; Miss Shirley Sarvis, San Francisco; *in Connecticut:* Fleischmann Laboratory, Stamford; Albert Stockli, Stonehenge Inn, Ridgefield; *in Idaho:* Peter Cenarrusa, Idaho Secretary of State, Boise; Harold West, Idaho Wheat Commission, Boise; *in Iowa:* W. L. Crookham, Caldwell; Mrs. Alex Dahlen, Decorah; Mrs. Alma Ehrle, Ehrle Bros. Winery, Homestead; Bud and Margaret Jensen, Cedar Rapids; Mrs. Henry Loven, Decorah; Dr. Marion Nelson, Norwegian-American Museum, Decorah; Charles Nicolay, Oelwein; Carl Oehl, Amana Society Meat Department, Amana; Mr. and Mrs. Walter Seifert, Homestead; Miss Jean Strong, Cedar Rapids; *in Kansas:* Mr. and Mrs. Frank Hefner, Quinter; *in Maryland:* U.S. Bureau of Commercial Fisheries, College Point; *in Minnesota:* Nils William Olsson, Director, The American Swedish Institute, and Mrs. Christine Carlson, President, The Women's Association of The American Swedish Institute, Minneapolis; John Dobie, Minnesota Department of Conservation, St. Paul; George L. Herter, Waseca; Mrs. Norbert Johanneck, Wabasso; Miss Eleanor Ostman, Food Editor, St. Paul *Dispatch-Pioneer Press*, St. Paul; Mrs. Wesley Scott, Minneapolis; Mr. and Mrs. S. G. Turbes, St. Paul; *in Missouri:* Dr. Eugene Garbee, Springfield; *in Montana:* Mrs. John Christian, Big Fork; *in New York:* Dr. Paul Buck, Cornell University, Ithaca; Mrs. Ellen Bates, New York; John M. Harrison, Canadian Government Travel Bureau, New York; Mrs. Charles Samuels, New York; *in North Dakota:* Dr. and Mrs. Maurice Hoghaug, Grand Forks; Mr. and Mrs. Skuli Stefanson, Grand Forks; Mrs. Theodore Thompson, Grand Forks; *in Oregon:* Bear Creek Orchards, Medford; Mr. and Mrs. Dunbar Carpenter, Medford; Robinson Collins, Jacksonville; Mrs. John Cotton, Ashland; Matthew Cullen, Portland; Beale Dixon, Tillamook County Creamery Association, Tillamook; Carl Gohs, Portland; Miss Mary Hamblet, Portland; Misses Martha and Mary Hanley, Medford; Dr. Edward Harvey, Otter Trawl Commission of Oregon, Astoria; Don Holm, *The Oregonian*, Portland; Wally Huntington, Portland; Mr. and Mrs. Alan Knudtson, Roseburg; Charles Miles, Cannon Beach; Mr. and Mrs. Roy Nisja, Ontario; Edwin L. Niska, Oregon Fish Commission, Astoria; Oregon-Washington-California Pear Bureau, Portland, Richard Glaspey, R. A. Patterson; Pooley Fruit Company, Hood River; Salishan Lodge, Gleneden Beach, Franz E. Herrmann, Alex Murphy; "Buckskin" Schaefer, Coffee Creek; *in South Dakota:* Kings Inn, Pierre, William Miller, Bryce McDonnell; Triple-U Enterprises, Pierre, Roy Houck, Mr. and Mrs. Jerry Houck; *in Washington:* Mr. and Mrs. A. Stewart Ballinger, Seattle; Peter Bunzel, *Seattle Magazine;* Mr. and Mrs. John A. Conway, Seattle; Robert Cunningham, I.T.T.-Rayonier, Northwest Timber Division, Sappho; Richard Desimon, Seattle; Mr. and Mrs. Maurice Dunn, Seattle; Mr. and Mrs. William Dwyer, Seattle; Boyd Graves, Snoqualmie Falls Lodge, Snoqualmie; Mrs. Laurie Howe, Seattle; Mrs. Solveig Ivarsson, Seattle; Cedric E. Lindsay, Olympia; Miss Dee McGregor, Pacific Kitchens, Seattle; Edgar Olson, Washington State University Creamery, Pullman; Captain Torger Skolmen, Seattle; Victor Steinbrueck, Friends of the Market, Seattle; Mr. and Mrs. Bill Youlden, Sekiu; U.S. Bureau of Commercial Fisheries, Seattle, Donald Johnson, Roy C. Stevens; Washington State Apple Commission, Wenatchee, Joseph Brownlow, Ron Hughes; Washington State Department of Fisheries, Olympia; Western International Hotels, Seattle; Richard White, Seattle; *in Wisconsin:* Roland C. Behle, Wisconsin Cheese Foundation, Madison; Miss Gladys Fossum, Madison; The International Institute of Milwaukee County, Milwaukee; Stanley Kmiotek, Wisconsin Department of Natural Resources, Madison; Miss Nellie McCannon, Madison; Mr. and Mrs. Karl Ratszch, Milwaukee; Daniel Smith, Port Washington; Miss Rosa Tusa, Food Editor, Milwaukee *Sentinel*, Milwaukee; Fred Usinger, Fred Usinger, Inc., Milwaukee; *in Wyoming:* Frank Brog, Thayne; *in British Columbia:* Mr. and Mrs. Ernest Halewijn, Prince Rupert; Mr. and Mrs. Alan Harris, Coquitlam; Ken Harris, Prince Rupert; Miss Elaine Johnston, British Columbia Government Travel Bureau, Victoria; John G. Lindenlaub, Vancouver; Lloyd Manuel, British Hotel Association, Vancouver; Mrs. Jean Nichols, Prince Rupert; Prince Rupert Fishermen's Co-operative Association, Prince Rupert; *in Manitoba:* Mrs. Edward Langevin, Winnipeg; Miss Gwen Leslie, Canadian Department of Fisheries and Forestry, Winnipeg; W. E. Organ, Manitoba Department of Tourism and Recreation, Winnipeg; *in Ontario:* Canadian Department of Fisheries and Forestry, Ottawa; *in the Yukon Territory:* W. J. M. Gibson, Yukon Department of Travel and Publicity.

The following shops and individuals supplied antiques, tableware and other objects that were used in the studio photography for this book: *in New York City:* Amber Springs Antiques; James A. Beard; Bonniers, Inc.; Frances Broughton Antiques; Encore Studio; Hammacher Schlemmer; Jean's Silversmiths, Inc.; Grace Manney; Rebecca Morris; The Peaceable Kingdom, Ltd.; RMH International, Inc.; Lyn Stallworth; *in Anchorage, Alaska:* Nerlands Home Furnishings.

Sources consulted in the production of this book include: *Delights and Prejudices* and *James Beard's Fish Cookery*, James A. Beard; *The Centennial Food Guide*, Pierre and Janet Berton; *Westward Expansion*, Ray Allen Billington; *The Gentle Tamers*, Dee Brown; *The Complete Book of Outdoor Cookery*, Helen Evans Brown and James A. Beard; *West Coast Cook Book*, Helen Evans Brown; *Sunset All-Western Cook Book*, Genevieve A. Callahan; *The Hunter's Encyclopedia*, Raymond R. Camp, ed.; *Across the Wide Missouri*, Bernard DeVoto; *The Journals of Lewis and Clark*, Bernard DeVoto, ed.; *The Sod-House Frontier*, Everett Dick; *Northern Cookbook*, Eleanor A. Ellis, ed.; *Sourdough Sagas*, Herbert L. Heller, ed.; *Cooked to Taste*, Junior League of Portland, Oregon; *Mary Cullen's Northwest Cook Book*, Cathrine C. Laughton; *Westward Vision: The Story of the Oregon Trail*, David Lavender; *McClane's Standard Fishing Encyclopedia*, A. J. McClane, ed.; *One Man's Gold Rush*, Murray Morgan; *The Wake of the Prairie Schooner*, Irene D. Paden; *Crab & Abalone: West Coast Ways with Fish & Shellfish*, Shirley Sarvis; *Market Sketchbook*, Victor Steinbrueck; *Sunset Seafood Cook Book; Pioneer Cook Book*, Volunteers of the Norwegian-American Museum, Decorah, Iowa.